MORE STRAIGHT TALK ON INVESTING

LESSONS FOR A LIFETIME

JACK BRENNAN

with John Woerth

WILEY

Published by John Wiley & Sons, Inc., Hoboken, New Jersey.

Published simultaneously in Canada.

For general information on our other products and services or for technical support, please contact our Customer Care Department within the United States at (800) 762-2974, outside the United States at (317) 572-3993 or fax (317) 572-4002.

Wiley also publishes its books in a variety of electronic formats. Some content that appears in print may not be available in electronic formats. For more information about Wiley products, visit our web site at www.wiley.com.

Library of Congress Cataloging-in-Publication Data is Available:

ISBN 9781119817338 (Hardcover)
ISBN 9781119817352 (ePDF)
ISBN 9781119817345 (ePub)

Cover Design: C. Wallace
Cover Image: Paper Speech Bubble © iStock.com/Aquir

SKY10025689_032221

To my growing and loving family. Once we were 5 and now we are 11, with another on the way!

and

To the millions of Vanguard investors, thousands of crew members, and hundreds of investment professionals who have inspired me and taught me for four decades.

Contents

PART III
MANAGE YOUR INVESTMENTS WITH FOCUS AND DISCIPLINE

Once you assemble a well-constructed portfolio, you don't have to spend every waking moment of your life tending to it. In fact, you'll be better off if you don't.

PART IV
STAY ON COURSE

A look at the things that can cause investors to come unglued.

Preface

In July 2002, I began the preface for the first edition of *Straight Talk on Investing* by observing that the previous "five years have been extraordinary in the history of investing. A record bull market swelled into one of the largest speculative bubbles in history. Then we saw the bursting of that bubble and the onset of a prolonged bear market, the worst one that the U.S. stock market has experienced since World War II. If many investors seem shaken and unsure of what to do, no wonder. Within half of a decade, we have been presented with a lifetime's worth of lessons about investing."

It is with a dose of cruel irony as I sit down to write the preface for the second edition in late 2020. The world at large is struggling with the coronavirus pandemic, which initially brought on a swift and severe drop in the global stock markets. While the markets quickly recovered, this marked the third shock experienced by investors in the first 20 years of the twenty-first century. Given this backdrop, it is no wonder investing can appear to be so daunting.

Albert Einstein once said, "The only source of knowledge is experience." Maintaining a long-term perspective and controlling one's emotions are valuable lessons that investors can glean from trying times. However, the impetus for updating this book with a second edition goes beyond the teachings of these distinct market events. While the financial planning and investing principles covered in these pages are timeless, a considerable amount has changed in the nearly 20 years since the first edition. I've learned a bit more along the way, including framing investing as a series of trade-offs—a theme that I will weave into this latest version.

At the outset, a new generation of investors has come of age and could benefit from understanding that sensible investing is an effective way to achieve financial security. I will note, too, studies indicate that members of the Millennial Generation—one of the audiences for the initial book—are far more wary of the stock market than Baby Boomers. Their wariness is understandable, having seen their parents withstand the bear market of 2000–2002, or experiencing 2008–2009 and 2020 themselves. But participating in the market is a must for long-term financial security, and for this generation now in the prime of their investing years, as well as for Generations Z and Y, a primer may be helpful.

I also underscore the concept of thinking of yourself as a *financial entrepreneur*—managing your financial life as an owner manages his or her business. And it is your financial life and no one else's, which is saying that financial planning and investing are highly, highly personal. While your age and goals may be similar to those of a friend, colleague, or neighbor, your investment program may be vastly different based on your ability to withstand risk, your means, and your time horizon, among many other factors.

The investing landscape has also changed considerably, and changed for the better in terms of choice, cost, and convenience. I genuinely believe that there has been no better time to be an investor.

Perhaps most obviously, the costs of investing have declined dramatically. Commissions or front-end loads, once as high as 8-1/2% on mutual fund purchases, have virtually disappeared. The average asset-weighted expense ratio of stock funds has dropped nearly by half, from 0.99% in 2000 to 0.52% in 2019—roughly $100 on a $10,000 investment to around $50, according to the Investment Company Institute. Costs, risk, and reward are the three critical factors when considering any investment. But only cost is actually known in advance and, all things equal, lower costs will result in higher returns for investors. As you can see from the cost figures cited here, investors today have a strong relative tailwind compared to only a short two decades ago.

Products such as exchanged-traded funds (ETFs) and target-date funds, which were nascent in 2002, have become core investment tools today and offer low-cost, diversified exposure to the global stock and bond markets. Today, the growing number of environmental, social, and governance funds offer an opportunity to align your investing with your values. There are newly popular options, too, for using your money for charitable purposes, such as donor-advised funds.

We have also seen the advent of robo-advisors and other digital money management services. A growing number of start-ups, banks, and asset management firms offer apps featuring asset allocation guidance, investment recommendations, and saving rate suggestions. These digitally delivered services have made financial advice more accessible and affordable.

However, I believe that most investors in the accumulation stage (i.e., saving for retirement or college) can—with some *knowledge, confidence,* and *discipline*—manage their investments on their own and not incur the extra costs of obtaining professional advice. Let's consider these three traits for investing success, and I will come back to them again and again. For those near or in retirement, obtaining professional help at a reasonable price is a valuable option for navigating the complexities of maintaining and drawing upon their nest eggs. The options available to obtain that advice at attractive prices—digital, in-person, or virtual—are now more plentiful and convenient.

Regulatory and legislative developments have improved investor protections and disclosures; brought forth new savings options, such as the Roth IRA; and enhanced the inner workings of the financial markets. 529 plans, in their infancy two decades ago, have emerged as the funding and investment vehicle of choice for college savings. There will be additional developments that impact the financial services industry in the years ahead, some of which will benefit individual investors and, unfortunately, some that may not. This is why it is important to stay abreast of things that could impact your investments, as well as changes in your own personal circumstances, that may require changes to your investment program.

What has not changed is the overabundance of information on investing. Entire TV networks are devoted to covering the markets' minute-by-minute movements, accompanied by provocative commentary by personalities and colorful graphics. You don't need a financial SportsCenter to manage your money effectively. In fact, it's more likely to hurt than help you perform that task. Further, the internet and social media abound with advice from self-professed financial experts. Some are legitimate and offer practical guidance. Most do not and actually are a hazard to your financial well-being.

I will share some insights from the mistakes and missteps of professional investors—Wall Street financiers, hedge funds, and university endowments. A short-term mentality, a lack of diversification, and an underappreciation of liquidity, among other things, have tripped up the "smart money" time and time again.

The goals of this book have also not changed. First, this is the type of book that parents give their children when they strike out on their own. Like many of my contemporaries, I wish I had had such a book. In my case, I am looking forward to giving this second edition to my grandchildren.

Second, I want this book to serve as a useful refresher about the basics of sound financial planning and prudent investing. No matter what one's age, sophistication, or experience, a back-to-basics course is always helpful—particularly during difficult times, when conflicting advice typically abounds. On a personal basis, I consider working on this book my own back-to-basics course and a very helpful one at that.

Finally, this book is aimed at helping people to think about their serious money—the dollars that they set aside for long-term goals, such as retirement or the education of their children. Frankly, this book won't do much good for those who are seeking guidance about finding "hot stocks" or tips on how to "play the market." That is why I will focus on mutual funds and ETFs as your primary investment vehicles.

The simple approach to investing that I present here is not derived from my years in the university classroom, but from the wisdom of many smart minds that I've had the privilege to meet and learn from during my nearly four decades in the investment industry. These include former and present colleagues at Vanguard, the world-class advisors we hire to oversee the Vanguard funds, and other investment professionals, including the managers of college endowments and non-profit organizations with whom I have had the privilege to be associated over the years.

I've also picked up a great deal from friends, family members, and Vanguard retail clients—"Main Street" investors who've navigated the markets and achieved financial success over the long term. There is simply nothing that I enjoy more than being stopped in the grocery store by someone who says "I just want to say 'thank you' for what you and your colleagues have done to provide me with a comfortable, secure retirement." If this book helps you with your financial future, I look forward to running into you at the market!

Jack Brennan
Valley Forge, Pennsylvania
December 2020

Author's Note

In this book, I cite several Vanguard funds to buttress specific investing lessons. These citations should not be construed as endorsements or recommendations. I use Vanguard funds simply because I am more knowledgeable about them than other funds. One of the lessons I hope to impart is that you should never make investment decisions based on incomplete information. If you become interested in one of the funds mentioned here (or any fund or exchange-traded fund, for that matter), consult its prospectus before taking any action.

Note that in the writing of this book, I sought to avoid investment jargon to the extent possible. In the appendix, you will find definitions of investment terms to help you along the way. When warranted, I employ call-out boxes titled **Baseline Basics** to make clear terms and concepts that will add to your foundational knowledge. You'll also come across **Portfolio Pitfall** sidebars, which offer caveats about common investor mistakes and cautions about questionable industry practices. At the end of each chapter, I wrap it all up with **In a Nutshell**—a bulleted summary of key takeaways.

As you read this book, you'll encounter bolded passages that highlight key, stand-alone investing principles. These principles are condensed and summarized in the **Afterword** at the end of the book and serve as a handy compilation should you need to reference it in the future. In some ways, this compilation represents my off-the-cuff response when someone in a social setting—be it on the sideline at a grandkid's soccer game or at a dinner party—is looking for my high-level thoughts on successful investing. I hope you find these CliffsNotes, if you will, useful and practical, too.

Finally, I use a considerable amount of data—market returns, hypothetical examples, and fund performance—throughout the book to support my points. **(Due to production constraints, most of the data is cited through December 31, 2019. The addition of 2020**

would not substantially alter the long-term data featured in the figures and text.) You need not be facile with advanced calculus, but having some faculty with numbers will help you become a better investor. I also draw on events; some may appear ancient or irrelevant to you. However, the wisdom offered by the past will help make you a sharper and more discerning consumer of investment products and services.

I am pleased to report that all proceeds from the sale of this book will be donated to Vanguard's signature charitable initiative—the Vanguard Strong Start for Kids Program™. Strong Start for Kids invests in tomorrow by supporting the development, learning, and joy of young, especially underserved, children today. The program aims to create partnerships that advance early learning programming in Greater Philadelphia, Phoenix, Charlotte, and London, and focuses on respecting and building upon local strengths to ensure families, programs, and communities have the resources needed to help all children have the best possible start in life.

An investment tenet emphasized in this book is similar to the approach that Vanguard takes to make a difference in the community: Investing early pays off. Research shows that investing in early learning opportunities for young children pays off in lifelong benefits. When children are supported during the first few years of life, they are more prepared to succeed in school, lead healthier lives, and contribute to creating stronger communities. But the reality is that significant barriers exist that disproportionately shut out some children from these meaningful opportunities. Strong Start works to increase access to a rich ecosystem of support so all young children are able to benefit and reach their full potential. Having spent much of my civic time on this endeavor, I can assure you that the return on an investment on high quality early childhood services would make most professional investors jealous!

Acknowledgments

I'm amazed at how many people it takes to move a book like this from concept to reality—even if it's the second time around. And, of course, I'm grateful to all who have been part of that journey. I'll take the risk of naming names, with the full expectation that I will leave someone out, and for that, I apologize in advance.

I want to start by thanking my collaborator, John Woerth. John is a three-decade colleague and, more important, a friend for all that time. It has been a joy to work with him on this book. He's a superb editor, a gifted writer, an astute observer of markets and investor behavior and, fortunately, a brutal taskmaster. I am confident that without that final character trait, *More Straight Talk on Investing* would still be mostly in my head.

As with the prior edition, I want to acknowledge the wonderful, trusting investors at Vanguard, with whom it has been my pleasure to be associated for nearly 40 years. These investors—small and large; sophisticated and new to investing; beginning their careers and enjoying retirement—have demonstrated all the good traits that we try to articulate in this book. They are disciplined, long-term oriented, cost conscious, and continually learning how to be better investors. It's been a remarkable journey together.

A second acknowledgment goes to my colleagues over the years at Vanguard, especially my two predecessors as chairman of our funds, the late Jack Bogle and Walter Morgan, as well as my successor as chairman, Bill McNabb. What a gift it was for me to be colleagues with Jack and Mr. Morgan, to learn from them, and have the honor of succeeding them. And throughout his career, Bill's engagement with investors and his commitment to their success and well-being is legendary. I have learned much from him from his first days as a colleague and continue to do so today as we discuss this topic as friends.

It has been an equal honor to serve with, and learn from, the thousands of Vanguard crew members who believe in Vanguard's mission and relish the chance to serve investors on their way to financial success.

Our first version of this book could not have been published without the wonderful work of my collaborator, Marta McCave, and several members of our team of writers and editors at Vanguard, particularly Mary Lowe Kennedy and Craig Stock. *More Straight Talk on Investing* is built on the chassis that they helped construct, and I hope they'll be as pleased with this version as I was pleased with their work on the first.

Numerous members of the Vanguard crew have provided statistical assistance and counsel, and I mention a few here. David Walker and Dominick Petruso, who did a remarkable job updating and developing the myriad statistics featured in the book. Many of their colleagues also contributed along the way, including Corinne Morrone, Michael Damico, Adam Schickling, Arvind Narayanan, Antonio Picca, Roger Aliaga-Diaz, Don Bennyhoff, Chris Tidmore, Andrew Hon, Jean Young, John Hollyer, James Rowley, Michael Johnson, Doug Grim, Dan Newhall, Jon Cleborne, Bill Oppelt, Ted Dinucci, Inna Zorina, and Hank Lobel. I thank them for their hard work in the background to ensure that we produced a high-quality book that will provide good value to our readers.

I'm particularly grateful to three wonderful Vanguard investment professionals—Maria Bruno, Fran Kinniry, and Rodney Comegys—who took the time to read and comment on our final draft to ensure it met their standards of quality, which are high on all counts. And, finally, a hearty thanks to Tim Buckley, Vanguard's terrific CEO and my good friend, who endorsed and supported this project from the beginning.

We relied on a number of data sources for this book, including Standard & Poor's, FactSet, Dow Jones, Frank Russell Company, Morningstar, Bloomberg, Morgan Stanley Capital International, the Investment Company Institute, the Federal Reserve Bank of St. Louis, and the Center for Research in Security Prices. Our thanks to all of them.

Of course, none of this happens without a great support team. Vickie Leinhauser and Katie Kimmel have been of invaluable assistance to John and me throughout this project. Again, without their help, this project would have gone nowhere.

Two last points. First, I mention here, and often in the body of this book, the value of being a continual learner with respect to investing. I believe that's true whether you are 25 or 75; whether you are just starting out or have years of experience under your belt; whether you're an amateur or a seasoned professional. I love it when someone approaches me (usually starting out by being nice and saying, "Other than *Straight Talk*, which I loved ...") and then asks, "What would you recommend that I read to help me be a successful investor?" I usually mention three books. *Winning the Loser's Game* by Charles Ellis and *A Random Walk Down Wall Street* by Burton Malkiel are investment classics that have been continually updated, a tribute to their enduring value to generations of investors. Each had a significant influence on me before I began my career at Vanguard. The third book is a newer classic, first published in 1996, *The Millionaire Next Door*, by Thomas Stanley and William Danko. It provides real-world examples of people who have found long-term financial success and security through very unglamorous actions—the type of actions that we catalogue for you here.

Finally, our editor at Wiley, Bill Falloon, has been a constant source of guidance and support to us as we marched down the field and carried the book over the goal line. I'm grateful for his efforts.

PART I
MASTER THE BASICS

1

Successful Investing Is Easier Than You Think

Successful investing is not difficult. But it can seem intimidating. Some assume that you have to be rich or possess an advanced degree to accumulate wealth as an investor. They think you have to be able to understand all the topics covered in *The Wall Street Journal*—the ups and downs of the stock markets; the interest-rate decisions of the Federal Reserve Board; corporate earnings announcements and dividend policies; the meaning of economic indicators; and so forth. All of these things have meaning, but you don't have to follow them closely to invest successfully. In reality, investing is easier than most people think.

The purpose of this book is to give you the understanding you need to accomplish your financial goals through investing. Over the past 40 years, I've talked to tens of thousands of successful investors. They come from all backgrounds and all stages of life. Some are young; others are old. Some are sophisticated; others are unsophisticated. Many have elite undergraduate and graduate educations; some never went to college.

Despite their differences, all the successful investors I've met share several traits, beginning with a very important one: **They invest with confidence.** They don't spend their lives searching for a get-rich scheme or investment gimmick that will lead them to a pot of gold, or worrying about what other people are doing with their money. Frankly, they really don't care—nor are they influenced by—how their neighbors, friends, or relatives invest. Confident investors make decisions based on their own personal financial situations, goals, and ability and willingness to take risks.

A Great Time to Be an Investor

This is a great time to be an investor. You have a wide variety of investment vehicles, including thousands of mutual funds and exchange-traded funds (ETFs), from which to assemble an investment program. Educational material has never been more accessible, which means you'll have no trouble finding resources to help become more knowledgeable about the subject. The internet makes it easy to monitor and manage your investments at any time of day, no matter where you are. And thanks to Individual Retirement Accounts (IRAs), 401(k) plans, and other tax-advantaged vehicles, you can secure attractive tax benefits when you put away money for your future. Generally speaking, the financial markets of today work effectively and efficiently. And, very importantly, the costs to invest have never been lower.

Today, millions of people are investing. For instance, 46% of American households own mutual funds and 63% invest via a tax-advantaged savings plan, according to the Investment Company Institute. Still, many segments of our country are not investing. Data from the Center for Household Financial Stability reveals that three in five millennials have no exposure to the stock market. And for those in this generation who invest in stocks, their holdings are low. Meanwhile, Black and Hispanic households are also more likely to lack investment accounts relative to other races. We will never be the country of equal opportunity that we must be if this holds true in the future.

Today's era offers great advantages, but they are only advantages if you participate. You must also steel yourself for two challenges. The first challenge comes from the traditional and social media, as well as those who make a living or a hobby of sharing their "wisdom." Most pay far too much attention to short-term events in the financial markets. In fact, news stories about the markets and investing read like the articles in the sports pages. Who won today? Who are the hot players? Who's going to have the best season? Who's first in the standings? With so much excited and inescapable commentary about every market move, it's no wonder that ordinary people sometimes feel intimidated or overwhelmed.

This is not to say that there is not thoughtful coverage of investing matters. In investing, less is often more in terms of news flow. Without being too nostalgic, my favorite example of that view is a TV show that ran from the early 1970s to the early 2000s. *Wall Street Week with Louis Rukeyser* offered sensible and studied observations of the financial markets. One key attribute was that it aired only once per week, which enabled the host and guests to move away from the minute-to-minute commentary that's now all too frequent. (The program continues today on Bloomberg TV.) Today, of course, there are plenty of reputable websites, radio programs, and podcasts accessible to you that can help you take charge of your financial life and become a better investor. I merely encourage you to be a discriminating consumer of financial media. And don't let it become a competitor of your favorite steaming series, radio program, or podcast for your time.

The second challenge comes from the financial services industry itself. To be clear, it's in the interest of many companies to make you think that investing is difficult and complex. They make money by selling investment products and advice. As you've no doubt noticed, there's no shortage of brokers, investment advisors, and financial planners eager to sign you on as a client and charge you for their services. Recognize that there are some financial professionals who want to make you think you can't make your own investment decisions. Don't believe them.

Your task is to separate the proverbial "wheat from the chaff" (i.e., the useful and actionable information from the noise). The reality is that you can succeed at accumulating wealth without spending time trying to keep up with daily events, incessantly listening to talking heads on TV, or paying someone else hefty sums to invest on your behalf. When you feel intimidated by the so-called experts, remember that they don't necessarily know more than you do. Indeed, every few years, we see headlines about financial hotshots who have lost millions and even billions of dollars through complicated trading schemes or big bets that went awry. What you don't see frequently in the news are the countless stories of individual investors who are quietly and prudently amassing wealth through sensible and disciplined investment programs. These individuals follow the four priorities of confident investing:

1. Be knowledgeable: Do your homework.
2. Be disciplined: Develop good habits.
3. Be skeptical: Avoid fads.
4. Be observant: Keep learning about investing.

The following section covers each priority in greater detail.

Be Knowledgeable: Do Your Homework

Building your confidence as an investor begins with developing some level of knowledge on the subject. Yes, you must be willing to put a little time into understanding the fundamentals of investing. But not much time! I am talking about knowledge at the very basic level.

There's no need to immerse yourself in thick treatises on financial theory. You don't have to subscribe to investment newsletters or attend seminars. You don't need to watch the financial news networks for the latest insights on why the markets did whatever they did today or this week or month, nor do you have to start each day knowing what happened in the Asian markets or in the Chicago futures pits in overnight trading. None of that is essential homework for individual investors concerned with their serious money.

But before you put your dollars in any investment at any firm, you do need some fundamental knowledge. Right now, I'm going to tell you what you need to know at a baseline level, saving the details for later.

First, you need to know a little about three primary types of investments, or asset classes. You've heard of them: They are stocks, bonds, and cash. (Cash means not just cash money, but ready stashes for it, like a bank savings account, certificate of deposit, or a money market mutual fund.) We cover each in our first Baseline Basics call-out box.

Baseline Basics: Understanding the Asset Classes

To be a successful investor, you need to be an informed investor. For starters, you should have a basic understanding about the risks and rewards of three fundamental asset classes—stocks, bonds, and cash instruments. We'll discuss the asset classes in more detail further on in this book, but for now, an introduction is sufficient.

Asset classes

An *asset* is simply something of monetary value. In finance, *asset classes* are types of investments that offer different combinations of risks and rewards.

Stocks

Stocks represent ownership. If you own a share of Google stock, then you are a part-owner of Google. That gives you the right to vote on certain policy issues, and it means that you share in the company's business results. If the company does well, you can benefit in two ways: (1) The value of your stock rises, so you could sell it at a profit if you so desire, and (2) The company passes along profits to you and the other owners in the form of a dividend. On the other hand, if the company does poorly, your stock can fall in value and dividend payouts can be cut or ceased altogether. In the worst case, the company could go bankrupt and leave your stock utterly worthless.

What makes a company do well or poorly? There are many variables. A company with prudent management, a sound business strategy in an attractive industry, and high-quality products or services that steadily sell is likely to do well. But other, external forces will also affect a company's prospects. These forces include interest rates and other economic factors, new technologies, competition, government regulation and legislation, and customer preferences. In addition to all those pragmatic influences, a company's stock can rise or fall due to investor sentiment, which is fickle and more difficult to forecast than the weather. In addition, even the smartest company leaders can make mistakes that affect the stock price. As such, many people view stocks as the riskiest investment among the three asset classes.

Stocks are risky—over the short term. As traders constantly second-guess each other about market trends and analysts make predictions, stock prices jump around from day to day and month to month. However, over long periods, stocks as a group have rewarded investors more than any other investment. Since 1926 through 2019, stocks have provided average annual returns of 10.3% a year.

A final note: Stocks are often called *equities*.

Bonds

A bond is essentially an IOU. When you buy a bond, you are lending your money to the issuer, typically a company, a government agency, or state or local municipality. The issuer is promising to pay you a stated amount of interest on the loan and to return the

(continued)

Baseline Basics: Understanding the Asset Classes   (*Continued*)

money at a certain time (the maturity date). When you buy a typical bond, you know in advance how much money you are going to
receive in interest and when it is going to come; that's why bonds
are called *fixed income* investments. (You'll often hear a bond's interest rate called the *coupon*—a term dating to when investors actually
clipped coupons from paper bonds and presented them to get their
interest.)

Though bond holders are creditors, rather than owners, they care
about the soundness of the company or agency that issued the bond
because that affects their prospects for payment of interest and repay-
ment of principal at maturity. U.S. Treasury bonds are considered the
safest investment in the world because they are backed by the full
faith and credit of the U.S. government. Most established companies
can be counted on to pay the interest on their bonds and repay the
principal at maturity, no matter how their stock prices are faring.

Retirees who need a steady source of income tend to favor
bond investments because of the periodic interest payments they
provide. But you don't have to be a retiree to appreciate the stabiliz-
ing force that bonds can provide in an investment portfolio. As I'll
explain later, many stock investors also hold bonds to help smooth
out the inevitable fluctuations in the value of their overall investment portfolios.

But bonds have risks. The worst-case scenario is default: The
bond issuer runs into trouble and can't pay you the promised interest or return your principal. Fortunately, defaults are relatively
uncommon. A much more immediate risk involves bond prices.
Existing bonds are constantly being traded on the market, and their
value changes along with market interest rates. That's no problem
for you if you don't need to sell your bond before its maturity date,
but for those who do need to sell, the changing prices can result
in losses. Also, if you invest in a bond mutual fund, your share price
and the income payments you receive will fluctuate based on the
ups and downs of the underlying bonds and as the fund buys and
sells its holdings.

Finally, there is the invisible risk of inflation. There have been
periods when the interest paid on bonds did not keep up with rising prices, so that bond investors were steadily losing purchasing
power. At one point in the 1970s, bonds were facetiously known as
certificates of confiscation.

Cash

You may think of cash as the bills in your wallet, your Venmo balance, or change in your car's cup holder, but it's something a little different in investing. Cash investments are very short-term IOUs issued by governments, corporations, banks, or other financial institutions. Bank deposit accounts and money market mutual funds are among the most popular forms of cash investments. Cash investments have been the least volatile of the three major asset classes historically, which means they are a safer choice than stocks or bonds if your biggest priority is not losing money. But they have also provided the lowest returns. Cash investments are said to have good liquidity because it's generally possible to withdraw your cash immediately and without penalty, but their disadvantage is that they will provide a return that keeps you just about in line or maybe slightly above inflation. While cash investments are a useful vehicle for emergency funds or money that will be needed just around the corner, they don't belong in your long-term investment account.

As you can see, there are trade-offs with each of the asset classes, so you'll need to set your objectives before deciding how to invest. If you want to reach for the greater potential returns that are offered by stocks, you must be willing to also accept their increased risk. If you want to opt for the greater safety of cash instruments, you must be willing to accept lower returns.

You need to know a little about some of the places to invest, including banks, mutual fund providers, financial advisors, and brokerage firms. You'll need to understand the benefits of tax-advantaged accounts, such as IRAs and 401(k) plans. In this book, I'll explain why mutual funds and exchange-traded funds (ETFs) are the best long-term investment vehicles for the bulk of your serious money. Chapter 8 is devoted to a full explanation of funds and ETFs.

You need to know what risk means. And here's a case where many people assume they already know all about it. But as we'll see, in investing, the obvious risk isn't always the most dangerous one.

You need to know yourself as an investor. You can make all kinds of wise investments and adhere to a sound long-term strategy, but still find yourself unable to sleep at night for worry when the markets are down. Life is too short for that! There are many ways for you to invest at a level of risk with which you can live, and I'll be discussing them in Chapter 11.

> **Portfolio Pitfall: There Is No Free Lunch**
>
> Avoiding mistakes (many self-inflicted) and behavioral errors is key to successful investing. One pitfall is failing to understand the risk/ reward trade-off.
>
> The single question I've heard most from investors over the years is this one: "What should I invest in if I want to make a lot of money but I don't want to take a lot of risk?" There is no investment that fits that description. I always reply this way: "If you don't want to take risk, put your money in the bank in an insured account. You cannot invest in the markets without taking on risk."
>
> There is a risk/reward trade-off in every investment choice— from publicly traded stocks and private equity to certificates of deposit and money market funds. If you want to reach for bigger returns, you must accept greater risks. Conversely, if you want to minimize your risk, you must accept lower returns. Think of it in terms of the saying, "There is no free lunch." You must give up something to get something. What's important is to understand the risk you're taking on so you won't be surprised.

Be Disciplined: Develop Good Habits

The second key characteristic of successful investors is that they develop good habits. You can start out with the very best investment plan and still end up disappointed if your own behavior undermines your plan. And the first and most important habit to develop is saving money. You simply cannot spend every penny you earn if you hope to accumulate wealth. The sooner you start saving, the better. When people ask me for my best financial advice, I have only one answer: **Live below your means.**

Saving is so important—and for many, so difficult—I am devoting Chapter 4 to the topic. In this chapter, we'll examine the other good habits you'll need for managing your investments. But as you read them, keep in mind that your first priority is a disciplined saving (and, eventually, investing) program. There is nothing that will put you on a sounder footing for success.

Baseline Basics: Saving, Savings, and Investing

In this book, when I refer to *saving*, I mean the activity of putting away money. Some consider savings as the remainder of one's money after meeting spending commitments. I want to teach you to be more deliberate in your saving approach. *Savings*, generally speaking for our purposes, refers to money earmarked to a bank account, CD, or money market fund. *Investing* means committing money to the financial markets.

In managing your investments, what matters most is how much buying and selling you do. The choice is pretty simple: Either you are a buy-and-hold investor or you are a trader. If you are a buy-and-hold investor, then once you have done your homework and set up an investment program, you just live your life. Yes, you'll want to monitor your investments on a regular basis, but you won't be inclined to make meaningful changes unless something major happens to alter your circumstances, such as a job loss, birth of child, or retirement. Or, there is a legislative or regulatory change that could be beneficial or detrimental. The introduction of the Roth IRA in 1997 is a good example.

Traders—even those who think they're being cautious—are risk-takers. They believe they can turn quick profits or avoid big losses by pouncing on fleeting opportunities in the markets. Traders spend an inordinate amount of time deciding when to get into some investment and when to get out. They aim to invest when they expect stock or bond prices to go on a run, and they sell out when they think prices are about to fall. This approach is known as *market timing*.

What makes the odds for market-timers so long is something that few seem to think much about: You have to be right at least twice. You need to know the right time to get in and the right time to get out. Some people may succeed at it in the short run, but it's extremely rare to hear of anyone winning at it over a period of years. It brings to mind the old Wall Street joke: "If you want to make a small fortune, start with a large one and trade a lot."

Another consideration is taxes. You have to pay taxes on any profit you make from the sale of securities held in a taxable account. Even if you are smart enough to beat the market through trading activity, taxes are likely to put a big dent in your gains over time. Indeed, taxes can confiscate 10% to 37% of any gain, depending on your tax bracket.

Many academic studies have shown that holding investments for the long term works far better than trying to time the market. I'm a buy-, buy-, buy-and-hold investor, and so are all of the successful investors I know. I firmly believe in committing money on a regular basis to an aggressive portfolio heavily weighted in stocks and holding pat no matter how the markets are performing in the short term. It has worked for me and millions of people like me. If you follow this simple formula— tailored to your personal situation—you'll be successful over the long term, too.

I'll come back to this topic later, but I want to be clear about my convictions up front. Trading is really all about speculating, not investing. If you are a trader, this book isn't for you. Sell it to someone else—or better yet, set it aside. One day you will be ready to read it when you've found out for yourself that frequent trading doesn't work. Traders spend considerable amounts of time and effort on investments but get back less than the buy-and-hold investors who choose to spend their hours on other pursuits—a hobby, exercise, reading, or time with family.

Another habit to cultivate is to resist keeping score too frequently. We're all susceptible to the temptation to check how our investments are doing at frequent intervals, or when the market posts a healthy gain and dramatic decline. Compulsive monitoring isn't worth the effort. It doesn't matter how your portfolio is doing from day to day or from week to week or, really, from year to year. Look at your balance every quarter if you must, but you shouldn't check more frequently. The danger in looking at your portfolio too frequently is that the short-term fluctuations will make you think that you have to take action, when, in fact, your best course is to sit tight. Think about how nervous, novice drivers always oversteer a car because they think they "have to do something" as a driver. With experience, and perhaps an accident or two, we all learn that less is more with respect to activity behind the wheel. I think the instincts are the same.

We'll discuss other good investment habits later in this book, but these are the most important ones:

1. Live below your means (i.e., spend less than you earn).
2. Be a buy-and-hold investor and rebalance periodically.
3. Don't keep score too often.

Be Skeptical: Avoid Fads

Many financial services firms have an interest in selling you something. If you are susceptible to the cold call from a broker or financial advisor with a hot tip, pitches about the latest tax shelter, or hype over last quarter's high-performing stock market sector, you can do a great deal of damage to your financial health.

I can't overemphasize the importance of avoiding fads. I've known many investors who have gone to great lengths to do their homework and learn what they need to do to be successful. And I've seen a few of those who did all the right things turn around and make one major mistake. Fads can lead you into great errors, the kind that can wipe out gains achieved through years of patient investing. Successful investors understand that doing the right things is not the only key to success—you also have to avoid big mistakes.

My own investment experience was shaped by a trend in the late 1960s and early 1970s when there was considerable hoopla over the so-called Nifty Fifty—"one-decision stocks" that you could supposedly buy and hold forever. At the time, the 10 largest publicly traded U.S. companies were IBM, AT&T, General Motors, Eastman Kodak, Esso, Sears, Texaco, Xerox, General Electric, and Gulf. They were seen as one-decision stocks because they were world leaders with sustainable business advantages and seemingly would always dominate the market. I remember my parents, who had very little experience with investing, giving me a single share of Eastman Kodak stock for my 16th birthday in 1970 and assuring me I would be able to hold it forever and reap the rewards.

The Nifty Fifty craze lasted until the 1973–1974 bear market dragged the one-decision stocks down with all the rest. As of December 2020, none of those former market titans rank among the 20 largest-capitalization stocks in the United States; three are among the 50 largest. Six of these companies experienced bankruptcy or a merger. Only two outperformed the broad market over the 51-year period.

As for Kodak, it posted a 10.8% loss per year from 1970 to 2020. (Kodak filed for bankruptcy in 2012, and since relisting in 2013, it has lost 76% of its value.) The Standard & Poor's (S&P) 500 Index's return for that period was 10.7%.

To put it in dollar terms, the $60 gift of Kodak stock was worth 18 cents at the end of 2020. The same investment in the S&P 500 Index was worth nearly $10,250 (assuming the reinvestment of all dividends and no taxes assessed).

In addition to a warning of fads, this case study highlights the great risk of holding single stocks. It may appear easy to select the future winner, but as we'll see, it is anything but.

Be Observant: Keep Learning About Investing

As common sense might dictate, successful investors need to keep absorbing new information. In any endeavor, whether it's parenting, a profession, or athletics, you must keep learning to stay up to speed.

Your efforts don't need to be time-consuming. Devote a little bit of regular attention (or a regular bit of a little attention) to the markets and to your own investments. Read, on occasion, reputable websites or publications that cover business and investing news. I say periodic attention because it's misleading—and downright hazardous to your wealth—to slavishly follow the movements of the markets or the fortunes of particular segments or companies on a daily, weekly, monthly, or even annual basis.

What you want to accomplish is threefold:

1. To deepen your understanding of what happens to your investments.
2. To protect yourself in case of developments that threaten your investments.
3. To keep abreast of new opportunities.

New investment opportunities will surface from time to time. You can distinguish the significant ones from the ephemeral ones by taking a close look at the trade-offs. Should you be willing—as some investors were in the 1990s—to give up the diversification of a broadly based mutual fund in order to seek a higher return by sinking all of your money into one hot-performing technology stock? No way, and I'll explain why in Chapter 6. Should you be willing to give up the safety of a passbook savings account at the bank for a higher-yielding money market fund that invests in high-quality, short-term commercial debt, as millions of investors have done in the last few decades? Sure.

Missing valuable new investment opportunities can hurt you—sometimes a little, sometimes a lot. The rise of money market funds in the late 1970s is a perfect case in point. In retrospect, money market funds revolutionized the financial industry because they offered market interest rates on very liquid, high-quality securities. Investors who continued to keep their short-term savings in non-interest-bearing checking accounts after money market funds became available missed an important opportunity to create more wealth for themselves.

With any new, innovative financial product, however, there's no need to rush in until it is determined that the solution is truly enduring. As my good friend Burt Malkiel once said: "Never buy anything from someone who is out of breath." As I mentioned in the Acknowledgments, if you wish to become a student of investing, I suggest you read Malkiel's *A Random Walk Down Wall Street*. This classic popularized the theory that stock prices take a random and unpredictable path, and thus predicting future, short-term price movements is futile. In his book, Malkiel says "a blindfolded monkey throwing darts at a newspaper's financial pages could select a portfolio that would do just as well as one carefully selected by experts." (I had the pleasure of serving on Vanguard's Board of Directors with Burt for nearly 18 years. He is a great investment mind and was a valued Trustee during his 28-year tenure.)

Malkiel's random walk theory is an important underpinning of another important innovation: Index mutual funds, which were largely an institutional investment strategy until the mid-to-late 1990s. Indexing is an investment strategy in which a fund seeks to match the performance of a market index (e.g., the S&P 500 Index) by holding all the securities in the index or a carefully chosen sample of them. That may sound less than exciting until you realize that index funds have a tremendous cost advantage that can mean greater returns for their investors. The trade-off is that with an index fund, you will never "beat the market." It took decades for the merits of index funds to gain traction, but by now millions of investors have realized that the certainty of keeping up with the market is a very worthwhile trade-off for the possibility of beating it. Investors who have forgone investing in index funds have done so to their detriment. I'll discuss the index funds and actively managed funds later in this book.

So, there you have it. I've introduced you to the four priorities of confident investors. In the next chapter, I'll cover another important factor: trust.

In a Nutshell

You can invest successfully and confidently if you establish four priorities:

- **Do your homework.** Develop an understanding of investment basics, such as the concept of the risk/reward trade-off.
- **Develop good habits.** Become a disciplined saver. Be a buy-and-hold investor. Resist the temptation to keep score too often.
- **Avoid fads.** Refrain from abandoning good habits in order to embrace the latest investment sensations. You can wipe out the gains of many years of patient investing by falling for a scheme or "sure thing."
- **Keep learning about investing.** Stay abreast of new opportunities and protect yourself from developments that threaten your investments.

2

You Gotta Have Trust

I t all starts with trust. To succeed as an investor, you first must trust yourself to make sound decisions. Second, you must trust the world's economies and the financial markets to be your allies in building wealth over the long term. Third, you must trust in time and the power of compounding—the way that "money makes money." Finally, you must trust in the firms and financial professionals who serve as your partners in your investing journey.

When I was nearly finished with the first edition of this book in the summer of 2002, the broad issue of investor trust and confidence was a staple topic of newspapers and newscasts. Not only had the stock markets taken a proverbial drubbing during the previous few years, startling revelations about misdeeds at companies, including Enron, Tyco, World-Com, Xerox, and Qwest, resulted in huge investor losses and shook the capitalist system to its core. All, or nearly all, of the value of these once-admired companies was wiped away when the market learned that management had misled investors through deceptive or fraudulent financial statements.

While employees, investors, and the general public were injured in the devastation caused by these high-profile breaches of trust, there was a silver lining to these stories: They showed that the system worked. Corporate executives who manipulated their financial statements and violated investor trust were eventually caught and brought to justice. Moreover, these abuses led to improvements in corporate governance and regulatory changes from which today's investors benefit immensely.

You're likely to witness untrustworthy behavior by firms and individuals in your investing lifetime. Some of the high-profile cases in the past 15 years include the Madoff Ponzi scheme (2008), the Theranos fraud (2015), and the Wells Fargo scandal (2016). Because humans are involved and greed is an eternal human failing, the system probably will always be subject to scandals and schemes, but I am confident it remains fundamentally sound. The reality is that most companies and most company leaders behave ethically and with integrity. The reality is that the markets ultimately reward honesty and punish untrustworthy behavior. And the reality is that you are left with little choice.

I would be remiss if I didn't mention that the mutual fund industry had its own bout of scandal. In 2003, it came to light that some two dozen mutual funds were illegally allowing trades after market close or permitting trades to favored investors that exceeded the limits stipulated in the fund's prospectus. There were subsequently trials, enforcement actions, hefty fines that gave the industry—and deservedly so—a black eye. In my view, the industry was humbled and, importantly, the Securities & Exchange Commission took actions to beef up fund policies and controls, as well as regulatory reviews to ensure compliance to them.

The act of investing is fundamentally a matter of trust. So, let's now look at the role that trust should play in your approach to investing.

Trust Yourself

Trusting yourself sounds easy, but it's hard for many people to believe they can trust their own judgment about investing. So I'm going to emphasize this point: Investing takes common sense and self-knowledge, and you possess both of those already. Trust yourself to know your current financial situation, your objectives, and your tolerance for risk better than anyone else. You know your own strengths and weaknesses. Is it going to be easy for you to develop disciplined savings habits, or will you need to find ways to motivate yourself to save? Will you be able to maintain a long-term focus, or will you be losing sleep every time the Dow Jones Industrial Average swoons? You'll want to tailor your investment program accordingly. You are the expert about you.

If you trust yourself, you'll be able to develop a baseline level of knowledge about investing and then make sound decisions based on factors that you thoroughly understand. As a result, you'll be less apt to second-guess yourself every time you see or hear something about a particular investment or market movement. You'll be better equipped to tune out misinformation and bad advice. You won't be swayed by ego and emotion. Having faith in yourself doesn't mean you'll never need professional advice. But if you should decide at some point that you do want help, you'll seek out a credible, qualified source instead of being vulnerable to a smooth-talking salesperson who cares little for your interests. Think of it as being the hunter instead of the hunted.

Suppose your brother-in-law brags about the killing he made on some obscure stock. It's human nature to grind your teeth and think, "*Yeesh*—if I were playing the market, I'd be a winner, too." (Sadly, there are online brokerage companies that encourage that mindset in their advertising. I find it incredibly irresponsible.) But if you have faith in your own ability to make investment decisions, the envy will quickly pass. You'll know that your brother-in-law's investment activities are not relevant to your life because you have your own set of objectives and a roadmap for getting to them. Your risk tolerance and time horizon are unlikely to be the same as someone else's. And you may also realize that your brother-in-law is unlikely to tell you about the severe losses he took on his three other "can't miss" stocks.

Having faith in your own ability to manage your financial affairs should make it easier to avoid the pitfalls that you'll encounter as an investor. As mentioned in the previous chapter, I'll be discussing quite a few pitfalls in this book, but here are some obvious ones for starters:

- **Don't pay attention to hot tips.** Whether the tip is from a friend or from a knowledgeable-sounding "insider" in an online forum or community, be very leery. Your friend may know plenty, but who's to say he knows the whole story about that stock or mutual fund? If it's the online insider who has the tip, you have even more reason to be suspicious. There have been many cases in which unscrupulous people used these forums to deceive gullible investors and drive up the price of a worthless stock.
- **Ignore invitations for free financial seminars.** Some financial advisors will seek to drum up new business by inviting you and other members in your community to free seminars, perhaps with dinner and cocktails as extra enticements. Sure, you might learn something, but you might also have to fend off a hard sales pitch on why you need to sign on as a client to the advisor.

- **Disregard sage-sounding aphorisms about the markets.** I mean sayings like "buy on the dips" or "the trend is your friend." Buying during a market dip would be a splendid strategy if you could ever be sure it was really a brief dip and not a deep plunge. As for the friendly trend, the idea is that if you find out about a rising stock or a hot industry, you should jump on the bandwagon. In fact, the trend is not your friend. By the time a market trend is noticeable, chances are that the bandwagon is already overloaded, the early money has jumped out, and you're arriving just in time for the end of the parade.

You're sure to be faced with situations like these as an investor. You won't be susceptible once you know that you can trust your own abilities.

Trust the Financial Markets

The second dimension of trust is having confidence that your investments in the financial markets will grow time over time. An expanding economy generally means more jobs, higher incomes, and increased opportunities for businesses to earn profits. And increased profits will ultimately raise stock prices, producing gains for investors. Personally, I believe that the U.S. economy will continue to grow over the long run, as it has in the past. While any economy will have ups and downs, the U.S. economy is the envy of the world because of its resilience and its ability to adapt and grow over the years. Over the long term, economic growth has averaged 3.1% a year over and above the rate of inflation.

As shown in Figure 2.1, there have been many peaks and valleys in the growth of the global stock markets, but the general direction has been upward, as measured by two common stock market benchmarks: the Standard & Poor's 500 Index (a proxy for U.S. stocks) and the MSCI EAFE Index (a proxy for international stocks). A $1 investment in the S&P 500 Index on December 31, 1969, would have been worth $153.64 as of December 31, 2019, assuming dividends were reinvested. The same $1 investment over the same time period in the MSCI EAFE Index would have a value of $86.45, assuming dividends were reinvested.

People tend to forget that long-term upward trajectory when the market has one of its periodic downturns. Conversely, when the market spends a year or two doing notably better than its historical average, people tend to become euphoric and forget that a downturn is sure to come at some point. That's just human nature.

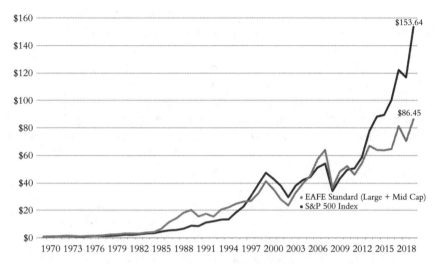

Figure 2.1 Growth of $1 in U.S. and International Stocks (1970–2019)

Sources: Morgan Stanley Capital International (MSCI), Standard & Poor's

This behavior came to the fore shortly after I was named CEO at Vanguard in 1996. The market went on an extraordinary surge (up 166% from December 1995 to September 2000) in a continuation of a bull market that started in the early 1990s. With such a prolonged period of gains, investors become infatuated with the stock market and investing. The ardor dissipated quickly when the market came back to earth with the bursting of the so-called *tech bubble*. Stocks fell 49% and didn't turn around for another two years. It was a painful, but instructive, period.

Despite periodic setbacks, the historical trend suggests that you'll be rewarded if you invest in the stock market. But there is no guarantee, of course. You shouldn't put your money in stocks if you don't share the belief that the economies around the world will continue to grow over the coming decades. Without growth in productivity and innovation in the products and services in our collective economies, there will not be good returns on stocks, and corporate bonds will prove risky. Instead, put your money in the bank and collect a guaranteed return, or buy U.S. Treasury bills, the safest debt instrument in the world. Recognize that you'll have to be content with very modest returns that may not keep ahead of inflation. Remember the trade-off: **Lower-risk investments (i.e., ones that possess price stability) cannot be expected to reward you as well as riskier ones (i.e., ones that possess price volatility).**

Portfolio Pitfall: Keeping Your Emotions in Check

When you follow the market's ups and downs on a regular basis, you allow the market to dictate your mood, so to speak. If you hear on the car radio or read on your daily newsfeed that the Dow Jones Industrial Average plunged 1,200 points, you are naturally inclined to calculate that you've lost money. If the market falls three days in a row and posts considerable losses, you may feel despondent. It might even compel you to check your balance. Don't!

This penchant for "mental math" can also play out over years. Suppose you had a $100,000 balance in your investment account at the end of 1994, as shown in Figure 2.2. Five years later, you are feeling pretty good with a balance of more than $350,000 in 1999. The market suddenly reverses and, at the end of 2002, your balance now stands at $219,000, and you figure that you've lost more than a third of your portfolio!

Only you haven't. These are paper losses. By 2006, your portfolio has recovered. To demonstrate how the market can quickly give and quickly take away in the short term, refer to Figure 2.2. As you can see, the value of your investment account is subject to euphoria-inducing gains and gut-wrenching losses over the short term. But over the long term, you are well rewarded for participating. (This example is for illustrative purposes and is based on $100,000 invested in the S&P 500 Index with dividends reinvested. Your portfolio is likely to include bonds and cash reserves that will offset the short-term losses incurred by stocks.)

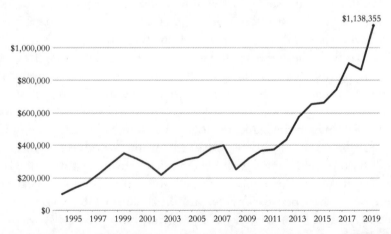

Figure 2.2 Growth of $100,000 Invested in the U.S. Stock Market (1995–2019)

Sources: Vanguard, S&P

Trust in Time

If you believe that the economy will grow over the long term, time will be your greatest ally in accumulating wealth. That's because of the power of compounding. Compounding is what happens when you invest a sum of money and then reinvest the earnings instead of withdrawing them. Your nest egg grows much faster because those prudently reinvested interest payments, dividends, or capital gains in turn generate further earnings. My friend at a competitor firm, Mellody Hobson, aptly observes, "We talk about long-term patient investing, and that idea that slow and steady does win the race, that time can be your best friend when it comes to investing. That's why we have a turtle as a logo at Ariel."

So, think tortoise, not hare. The longer you invest, the effects of compounding are all the more astonishing. Consider the simple example shown in Figure 2.3. Suppose you invest $5,000 in a tax-advantaged account at the start of each year for 10 years and then contribute nothing more. Next, suppose that the account earns 8% a year, after expenses, and that you have all of your earnings reinvested in the account. After 25 years, you would have more than $248,000, of which only $50,000 came from your pocket. And after 40 years, that sum would have grown to more than $787,000. The power of compounding is absolutely amazing.

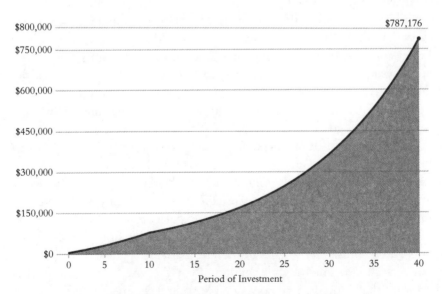

Figure 2.3 The Power of Compounding

Source: Vanguard

Here's a point that requires special emphasis. If you're going to make the most of the power of compounding, you must reinvest all the income and dividends that you earn on your investments instead of taking them in cash. You must also keep your hands off the money in your accounts. If you repeatedly dip into your long-term accounts to pay for living expenses or big splurges, your wealth won't grow as efficiently as it could otherwise. Like a chef who keeps sampling the food while it's cooking, you're apt to end up with a lot less in the pot than you planned.

Trust Your Financial Partner

For your safety and peace of mind, you need to establish a relationship with a financial services provider or two that you can trust. Or, a relationship with a financial advisor whom you can trust. (I will focus largely on firms in this section, although some of the lessons apply to financial advisors, which I cover in more detail in Chapter 12.) A trustworthy firm will serve you with integrity and help you accomplish your financial goals. And it won't push products and services that meet the company's quarterly sales goals but that do little for you, or seek to lure you with bait-and-switch tactics. Fortunately, there are plenty of good investment companies that offer sound products and quality services.

Picking a trustworthy partner is important to your success in more ways than one. If you do business with a firm that you trust, you will be better able to endure the misgivings that come when your portfolio has an off year. Believe me, sooner or later, that will happen. It's one of the facts of investing. If you trust your investment partner, you'll realize that a mutual fund or exchange-traded fund with a strong long-term track record is still a good investment even after it's had a bad year.

How can you be sure you are dealing with a firm that deserves to be trusted? There are several factors to examine, but it's not a bad idea to start by collecting referrals from friends, co-workers, or family members. Word-of-mouth is fine, if you trust the person giving you the recommendation and know that he or she has experience and good judgment. Though I warned earlier about believing stock tips from family members and friends, referrals are a different matter. If your sister, to whom you're willing to entrust your children if you die, says, "I trust this organization," that should carry considerable weight. Even this endorsement deserves scrutiny, however. It is a good idea to trust, but also to verify. I've known several colleagues fall prey to too-good-to-be-true propositions or put their trust in questionable firms or individuals.

The firm's history is an additional consideration. An institution that has been in the business for many years will have a track record and experience serving clients effectively through up and down markets. For example, I've always believed an investment firm's greatest competitive advantage is its demonstrated trustworthiness through good times and bad. And the market agrees—the three largest fund families have roots in the business that go back for 75 years or more. There are plenty of newer firms with talent and ambition, but they must overcome the formidable advantage of tenure and credibility accumulated by established firms. It's very tough to earn marketplace acceptance in the absence of long-standing relationships with business partners and clients, along with a record of good service over the long term.

Experience also counts in the professionals who manage your money. There's a reason that sophisticated institutions look for gray hair (figuratively speaking!) when they hire money managers. Those who have endured feast and famine in the markets have the wisdom of experience. Some lessons simply are better learned by living through them than by reading about them in a textbook. The performance records of tenured money managers are much more meaningful than those of managers with limited experience. A young money manager with a good track record for four or five years isn't necessarily a great stock-picker—he or she may have simply floated up with a rising market. Even in a falling market, a money manager can look better than the competition—for a while—by sitting out the market and holding considerable cash.

For these reasons, I always want to know how a money manager has performed relative to the competition over the full cycle of a bull market and a bear market. An added advantage of experience is that it teaches humility. Investors who have been through up and down cycles tend to avoid overconfidence and are cognizant of risks. Anyone who's been in the financial business for a lengthy period of time has hit some rough patches and does not take lightly the unpredictability of the markets.

So experience is important, but don't let it be the sole factor in your decision. Being the oldest doesn't make a firm the best one, nor should you rule out a young firm purely because of its limited experience. Experience is not a litmus test; it's just a factor to be weighed. Still, if you're thinking of dealing with a small organization that you know little about, it makes sense to seek references from others who have done business with the company.

In any case, you'll also want to request the following information from any provider:

- A complete and candid explanation of the costs of the investments and any additional fees you'll be charged.
- A clear and comprehensive description of the fund's investment strategy and policies.
- A record of the past performance of fund and the background on the managers responsible for producing it.
- An explanation of how the performance of your own investments will be reported to you.

These are the questions that any sophisticated investor will ask before hiring an investment firm for a mutual fund, pension fund, endowment, or foundation. They're the questions we always asked at Vanguard before appointing an investment advisor to one of our funds. Whether you're looking for a mutual fund company, a brokerage firm, a robo-advisor, or a financial planner, these questions are as relevant for you as they are for a sizable company like Vanguard.

Once you've selected a trustworthy provider, stay alert for changes in the ownership or leadership of the firm. Rapid turnover of portfolio managers should also trigger some concern. Regulatory actions and security breaches are another red flag.

An important gauge of any company is communications. How frequent? Are they clear and candid? Are they consistent in good markets and bad? Are they selling or telling? Or, better yet, are they contrarian, giving you a dose of reality in times of market ebullience and perspective in seemingly dire days? If you ever have doubts about whether your company is being forthright with you, it's time to switch. Firms deserve to have your money only as long as they deserve your trust.

Get in the Game

If you trust in yourself, in the markets, in time, and in your investment provider, you still have to do something else to accumulate investment wealth. You must invest. This seems obvious, but believe me, some would-be investors get stuck in the ready . . . aim . . . aim . . . aim . . . mode. They never fire because they are always waiting for the right moment to begin investing. They feel considerable envy of those who have invested successfully. But they never take steps to get in the game themselves.

There's a story about a man who prayed night after night, "Dear God, let me win the lottery." But the man despaired every evening when the winning numbers were announced, and he was not a winner. This went on for many months until one night, as the man was praying for the hundredth time, the heavens opened up and a deep voice boomed: "Meet me halfway. Buy a ticket."

Trust should give you the courage to take the plunge, secure in the knowledge that you are investing with intelligence and discipline.

In a Nutshell

Your success as an investor is dependent on knowing whom to trust (and whom not to trust):

- **Trust yourself to make sound decisions.** Don't trust hot tips and sales pitches.
- **Trust the financial markets to be your partner in accumulating wealth.** Despite the short-term ups and downs of the stock market, the strength and resilience of the U.S. economy suggest that long-term investors will continue to be rewarded.
- **Trust in time.** Start early and put the power of compounding to work for you.
- **Trust a financial provider.** Find a trustworthy provider that will serve you with integrity and help you accomplish your financial goals.

3

A Map to Success: Hmm, Sounds Like a Plan

L egendary baseball catcher Yogi Berra once said, "You got to be very careful if you don't know where you're going, because you might not get there." Although Yogi wasn't likely talking about investing, the quote hits the mitt right on target. Having a plan will help make your financial life less burdensome and more gratifying.

Developing a financial plan need not be complex. It entails looking ahead and assessing where and when your needs for money will occur. Then you decide how you're going to meet those needs. It's essentially a three-step process:

1. Determine how much money you'll need for your goal(s).
2. Determine the mix of investments that should provide you with that targeted amount.
3. Determine how much you need to set aside in order to reach your goals.

If you're like most people, you have more than one investment goal. For nearly all of us, a secure retirement is the largest goal in terms of the amount of money required. It's also the one for which you have the longest time to achieve. But other needs may be more immediately pressing, such as a down payment on a house or a child's college education. In addition to your primary goals, you'll need to have a plan for meeting rainy day needs—the unexpected financial hurdles that life has a way of putting on your path.

In this chapter, I'll share some financial planning tips based on lessons I learned from my own experience and from the thousands of successful investors I've talked to over the years, including the concept of thinking of yourself as a financial entrepreneur.

The Single Most Important Thing to Do

As I noted in Chapter 1, when people ask me how to go about setting up a financial plan, I usually offer them four words of advice: "Live below your means." Simply put, to live below your means, you must not spend more money than you earn.

Living below your means is the ultimate financial strategy. Actually, it's more—it's a way of life. If you want to be able to invest and accumulate wealth to help yourself or others in the future, you simply cannot spend more than you earn. Living beneath your means and becoming a saver are so critical to your financial success that I'll talk about it here and again in the next chapter. And I'll discuss some tools and techniques to help you do it.

Effective saving isn't just tucking away as much money as you possibly can. It's also knowing where to put your money so that it will earn a reasonable rate of return and be there when you need it.

A friend whose firm is one of Vanguard's large corporate clients frames the concept as follows: "When I'm talking to our employees about the importance of saving and investing, I urge them to think of themselves as 'personal financial entrepreneurs.' We're all financial entrepreneurs, running our own financial operations, first in our working years and later in retirement."

As a financial entrepreneur, you'll want to create an *income statement*. In business, that's a summary of how much profit (or loss) a company had during a certain period of time. For you, it's the same thing. Your personal income statement would list your *revenues* (e.g., your pay, plus any investment income or gifts you receive) and your *costs*. The costs would include your fixed expenses (e.g., taxes, mortgage, insurance premiums, student loan payments, car payments, and the like) and your variable expenses (e.g., food, clothing, entertainment, charitable donations, and discretionary items).

When examining your income statement, if there is money left over after expenses are subtracted from revenues, you'll have a *net profit* that is available to invest. If you have no net profit, and in fact are borrowing to maintain your lifestyle, you are operating at a loss.

Living below your means is tough in a materialistic culture in which advertisements constantly play to our egos and the media provides endless images of "the good life." But the unsung benefits of being a saver are priceless. You'll have enviable peace of mind because you won't have to worry about making ends meet. You won't feel wistful about your goals because you'll know you're traveling steadily toward them. And you'll know that, if need be, you're in position to withstand unexpected financial challenges. Let's face it: Unexpected financial needs occur in everyone's lifetime. People get laid off from their jobs, incur extraordinary medical expenses, or need to offer financial assistance to a family member. If you're a saver following a plan, you can weather those challenges far better than people who spend every penny they earn.

But what about the "good life"? Don't savers miss out? No, they don't. They simply gain control. Living the good life isn't just about material possessions—it's also about possessing financial flexibility and broadening your options, and, importantly, about having things to which to look forward. Accumulating capital is the reward if you choose saving in the saving/spending trade-off.

If you have a job and are earning money, the most fundamental financial planning question is this: Are you going to spend it all on current needs and wants, or will you set your living standards below what you can afford so you can save some of what you earn? Even if you can afford many things, the reality is that you cannot afford all of them. Before you decide how you'll spend your paycheck, decide how much you want to be setting aside for saving and investing.

Two additional thoughts on saving:

1. It's never too late to become disciplined about saving, but the sooner you develop the saving habit, the easier it will be to achieve your goals.
2. It's a good idea to reevaluate your savings habits from time to time, particularly when going through major transitions in life.

Think of Your Financial Needs as Imaginary Buckets

One of the most useful concepts in financial planning is to think of your financial needs as "buckets." The idea is to determine how your money needs to be divided among the buckets, and then be very disciplined about filling those buckets. These are typical buckets of most people:

- **Current expenses.** This is what you live on—the money you use for your mortgage or rent payments, food, clothing, car payments, and other essentials.
- **Emergency fund.** Many experts recommend that you have six months' worth of take-home pay available to meet unexpected difficulties, such as a short-term layoff from your job or large expense.
- **College.** The cost of a college education keeps climbing, and though you can take out loans, you'll come out ahead if you can pay for as much of it as possible out of savings.
- **Retirement.** Many Americans today spend a quarter century or more in retirement. You can't count on Social Security payments as your sole support for all those years. Most people will need to draw on their own savings to live comfortably while they continue to pay taxes, medical insurance, and everyday expenses.
- **Other goals.** Add as many buckets as you want for other savings needs, such as replacing your car, buying a first or second home, taking care of elderly parents, giving to charity, or anything else you deem essential.

You'll note that I've included charitable donations to the other goal bucket. At the risk of sounding sanctimonious, my personal view is that giving is important, and I encourage you to build it into your financial plan. Anyone who has accumulated money to invest should be willing to give something back to society. You don't have to be wealthy to give to a house of worship, the local fire department, your alma mater, or national fundraising organizations that serve your community or the broader world. Even small contributions can make a difference when they are combined with those of other givers. And they will make a difference in your own life, too. As my wife and I have increased our giving over the years, we've found it deeply satisfying to be supporting programs to help others, and we're most pleased that our children have adopted this same point of view.

Once you have designated target goals for each of the buckets in your financial plan, you will need to think about where you will keep the money. The idea is to maximize the return for each bucket within the parameters of your time horizon and risk tolerance. As a result of the varying issues in each situation, different buckets will call for different approaches.

Saving for Short-Term Needs

You need immediate access to the money to meet current expenses, so you would eliminate long-term investment vehicles like stock funds and long-term bond funds from consideration. A rule of thumb in investing is that you should not invest money in stock funds that you will need in less than five years. Most people use a checking account for the money that's needed to meet current expenses. That's typically a checking account that pays little or no interest, so the trade-off for the convenience of this account is that you are earning virtually no return.

Your rainy-day fund is a slightly different issue. Since this is money that you don't plan to touch except in an emergency, leaving it sitting in an interest-free bank account makes no sense whatsoever. A better choice would be to invest it in a money market fund, an ultra-short bond fund, or short-term Certificates of Deposit, which offer some return while still being relatively liquid, or readily available should an emergency arise. Such a choice will enable you to make your money work as hard for you as possible. If interest rates are low, you may wonder what the fuss is over a return of 1% or 2%. But ask yourself a simple question: Would you rather have the 1% or 2% in your pocket, or let the financial institution have it? Small amounts of interest eventually add up to impressive sums. Suppose you put $10,000 in a savings account that pays 2% a year, and it sits there untouched for 25 years. It will turn into more than $16,406.

Saving for College

You'll face a different set of considerations with mid-term financial goals. College is one of the most interesting investment planning issues because of the special considerations involved. We can all hope that our children will receive full or partial scholarships, or generous financial aid. But, realistically, most of us need to plan on paying for college either out of savings or with loans. And it makes more financial sense to be able to pay for it out of savings than for either you or your child to take on considerable debt. Start saving early, and time can help you foot the bill. College will be a more manageable expense if you finance it with savings that have compounded over the years (particularly if they compounded in a tax-advantaged account) than if you take on debt and pay off the loans and interest with out-of-pocket money. When you save, compounding works for you. When you borrow, it works for the lender.

Your college savings bucket will require more active monitoring and management than the others for two reasons. First, you can already figure out when you're going to need the money and roughly how much you may need. If your child is 5, it's reasonable to assume that college bills will start arriving in 13 or 14 years. You can look at tuition data now and forecast what your costs could be for a private or public college. Tuition data are available from a number of sources, including the College Board's website (www.collegeboard.org). Given this information, you'll want to keep an eye on your college-savings bucket as time goes by to make sure it is moving you toward your goal. You may have to increase your savings, for instance, if you determine you are falling short.

The second reason for actively monitoring your progress in saving for college is the relatively short time frame. Suppose you begin saving on the day your child is born. You'll probably want to start out with stocks because they are likely to offer more growth. But that growth offered by stocks is accompanied by considerable ups and downs over the short term, and you don't want to have to start using those funds for tuition during a prolonged down period. So, as your child enters her teens and college approaches, it may be prudent to shift into more conservative investments, such as a money market fund and a short-term bond fund, that emphasize preservation of capital while paying some level of income. My colleague Glenn learned this lesson the hard way when one of his children reached college age during the 2008–2009 market drop, and he had failed to adjust the child's college portfolios to a more conservative stance. It pays to pay attention.

Note that many 529 plans, discussed in more detail in the accompanying Baseline Basics, offer age-based or target enrollment portfolios. You simply select the portfolio that matches your child's current age or expected matriculation date. The portfolios are diversified among stock, bond, and cash investments; the allocation then automatically and gradually adjusts over time to a more conservative mix as your child approaches the first day of college.

Baseline Basics: Accounts for Saving for College

There are a variety of ways to save for college, and the investment vehicle that's best for friends or relatives may not be the best one for you. The trade-offs involve costs, taxes, financial control, investment choices, and the impact that the plans have on eligibility for financial aid. Here is a brief look at the three popular ways to save for college.

- **529 College Savings Plans** are a tax-advantaged means of accumulating money to pay for college or graduate school. These plans, named for a section of the tax code, are usually sponsored by states and have emerged as the go-to accounts for many Americans. The earnings of 529 accounts are exempt from federal income and capital gains taxes so long as the money goes for qualified school expenses. You are not relegated to investing with the plan in your home state, and some states offer deductions on contributions. And there are no income limits to be eligible to use the plans. 529 plans may also be used to pay up to $10,000 in student loans. The main drawbacks of 529 plans are the overwhelming number of choices both among state plans and investment options in those plans and, in some cases, high costs of those options. The sponsoring state selects the investment manager and investment options available to you. In addition, some 529 plans layer administrative fees on top of the fees charged by the underlying mutual funds. Before investing, do some comparison shopping. The effect of 529 College Savings Plan assets on eligibility for financial aid depends on who is the named owner on the account. A 529 account held in a parent's name will cut into financial aid eligibility far less than will an account held in the student's name.
- **Education Savings Accounts (ESAs; formerly known as** *Education IRAs***)** are another, but less commonly used, tax-exempt investment vehicle. You can contribute up to $2,000 a year on behalf of a beneficiary under age 18, assuming that you do not exceed income limits. The funds can be withdrawn tax free to pay for qualified educational expenses at primary schools, secondary schools, colleges, and universities. Another plus: You may choose the financial provider and the investments for your ESA, so you'll have a wide array of investment options from which to choose and can seek out low-cost options. With ESAs, the main drawback is the

(continued)

Baseline Basics: Accounts for Saving for College   (*Continued*)

low maximum contribution. An ESA account alone may not enable you to save enough to cover four years of college. In addition, assets in an ESA count heavily against a child's eligibility for financial aid. In financial aid calculations, ESA assets are considered to be the student's property. As a result, financial aid providers will expect that up to 25% (for college aid) or 35% (for federal aid) of the ESA will be spent for college each year.

- **UGMA and UTMA Accounts** are custodial accounts for children established under the Uniform Gifts to Minors Act or Uniform Transfers to Minors Act (hence the acronyms). These accounts have been around for decades. With an UGMA/UTMA, you or another adult custodian opens an account on behalf of a minor at the financial institution of your choosing and invest as much as you like.

  They offer fewer tax benefits than the other savings programs. For children under 14, the first $750 of annual investment income is tax-free; the next $750 is taxed at the child's tax rate; income above $1,500 is taxed at the parents' rate. All income for children 14 or older is taxed at the child's rate. Also, when the beneficiary reaches the age of majority, he or she takes control of the assets—whether to pay for college or buy a sports car. In college financial aid calculations, UGMAs/UTMAs are considered the property of the student, so aid providers will expect up to 25% (for college aid) or 35% (for federal aid) of the assets to be used for college each year.

Saving for Retirement

Personal finance experts have a rough rule of thumb about how much money you'll need in retirement. It states that to live comfortably, you'll need annual income that's at least 70% to 80% of what you were earning before you retired. This money will have to come from a combination of Social Security, pension or other workplace retirement plan, and personal investments.

People often underestimate how much they'll need in retirement savings. The retirement phase of your life will hopefully last decades, and although your investments will continue to produce returns during that period, you are likely to be drawing down your portfolio at the same time. Suppose, for example, that you plan to draw on your retirement savings for 30 years and expect to take a little more out each year so that your spending can keep up with inflation. To be able to ride out periods when the financial markets turn sour or inflation runs high, you probably should not spend more than 4% of your retirement savings in the first year. A little math shows that you'll need an initial nest egg of $500,000 if you want to be able to spend $20,000 in the first year, and to increase that amount by the rate of inflation in the ensuing years.

The 4% withdrawal rate is another common financial rule of thumb. It is grounded in academic research, but it is not foolproof. For example, if you invest too conservatively and have a longer-than-average retirement, you could run out of money. I am admittedly conservative, so, when asked, I always suggest that people consider a more conservative 3% or 3.5% rate of withdrawal to ensure that they don't deplete their savings. (As an aside, any rule of thumb should be taken with a proverbial grain of salt. Your withdrawal rate, for example, should be personalized to your situation and reviewed periodically to account for environmental factors, such as market returns and inflation.)

Fortunately, there are many ways to accumulate a nest egg for retirement. And today's savers have some rewards that their great-grandparents would have envied. Employer-sponsored retirement plans and Individual Retirement Accounts (IRAs) shelter your investment earnings from current taxes, which makes it much easier to accumulate wealth. With a company retirement plan, your employer may even supplement your savings with matching contributions, in effect giving you a pay raise that will grow and compound over time. The most common workplace plans include 401(k) plans, 403(b)(7) plans, and 457 plans, which are named for sections of the tax code that established them. You can also invest for your retirement by setting up an IRA with an investment provider.

Your retirement savings bucket may be the biggest bucket you need to fill, but it also may be the easiest of the buckets to fill as long as you get an early start. If you start in your early 20s, building a retirement nest egg is more a matter of saving than investing. Time and the compounding of your investments will be bigger factors in your success.

Here's a piece of advice: If you have a 401(k) or other retirement plan at work that lets you have savings automatically withheld from your paycheck, go for it. Contribute as much as the plan permits. If you can't make the maximum contribution, at least contribute enough to receive the full matching amount that your employer contributes, assuming that your employer offers a matching contribution. Then make it your goal to make the maximum contribution as quickly as you can.

Portfolio Pitfall: Be Alert to Low Default Rates

Many employers will automatically enroll you in the company 401(k), which is a good thing, since inertia precludes some individuals from signing up on their own. Automatic enrollments get workers in plans and help them begin saving at the outset of employment. However, many employers will automatically set your contribution rate at 3%, which is a bad thing. Nearly 40% of Vanguard plans have a default rate for contributions at 3%, which I believe is too low. You should set your sights on saving 10%–12%. Add to that the typical 3% match from your employer, and you are putting away a healthy 13%–15% of your take-home pay into a tax-advantaged account. If you join a company that features a 401(k) plan, be sure to check the default rate and increase it if necessary—even if the plan offers an auto-escalation feature that increases your savings rate each year.

Here's a strategy I frequently recommend as a very easy way to build a retirement program, and I'll use one of my colleagues, Jane, to demonstrate. When Jane began working at Vanguard, she contributed to the 401(k) plan at a level to receive the company matching contribution. Then, she gradually increased her savings rate by funneling an amount equivalent to half of each annual salary raise into her 401(k) until she reached the maximum allowable contribution. (Jane believed she could do this because her living costs hadn't increased just because she'd received a raise. Most people should take the same point of view.) By continuing to pump money into her retirement plan at that level, Jane accumulated an impressive sum of money over her 30-year career. It takes discipline not to use all of that salary increase for immediate gratification, but in time you won't miss that "extra" money and will be better served in the long run by earmarking it for retirement.

There are three great advantages to saving through an employer plan. First, your contributions will accumulate on a tax-advantaged basis. Second, the process keeps you saving without any effort of your own. You don't have to make yourself transfer money or write any checks, and you won't be tempted to spend the money before "paying yourself" first. Third, you will be investing a regular amount on a regular basis, a prudent and effective strategy known as *dollar-cost averaging*. (I'll discuss this strategy several times throughout the book.)

Plenty of ordinary people are saving an unbelievable amount of money through employer-sponsored retirement plans. In the 401(k) plans managed by Vanguard in 2019, there are more than 62,000 individuals who are millionaires. And thousands of other ordinary people are on the way to amassing extraordinary wealth.

Baseline Basics: Accounts for Retirement Investing

There are numerous retirement-oriented accounts to help achieve your investing goals. Similar to college savings programs, there are pros and cons associated with the various options, along with rules that may limit their use and availability. I will cover the two mainstays—IRAs and 401(k) plans—at a high level. However, you may have other options available to you depending on your employment status. For instance, if you work for a non-profit institution, such as a hospital or university, a 403(b)(7) plan may be an option. If you are self-employed, you'll have your pick of a SEP IRA, Simple IRA, or individual 401(k) plan.

- **Individual Retirement Accounts.** IRAs enable you to invest on a tax-advantaged basis for retirement. With a traditional IRA, you may be able to deduct some or all of your contribution from your current income taxes depending on your income. Once you start taking withdrawals, they are taxed as regular income. Note that you'll be required to take distributions as some point in your early 70s. Roth IRA contributions are not tax deductible, but your withdrawals in retirement will be completely tax-free and you will not face required minimum distributions. Your income, however, may limit your ability to contribute to a Roth IRA.

  You can establish an IRA at a bank, brokerage firm, or mutual fund provider and, therefore, have many investment options from which to choose. You can contribute up to $6,000 a year ($7,000 if over 50 years of age) in 2021 to a traditional IRA, a Roth IRA, or a combination of the two. For most people, though, the Roth IRA is the better bet because of the tax-free withdrawals in retirement.

- **401(k) plans.** If you work for a company, it is likely that a 401(k) will be among the benefits you receive as an employee. Like an IRA, you'll be able to sock away money on a pre-tax basis, which will

  (continued)

Baseline Basics: Accounts for Retirement Investing (*Continued*)

then grow on a tax-advantaged basis. When you start to withdraw the money in retirement, it will be taxed at your then-current rate. With a Roth 401(k), your contributions are made with after-tax dollars and your account grows tax-advantaged. When it comes time to tap your account in retirement, your withdrawals won't be taxed. You can invest up to $19,500 in a 401(k) plan in 2021. You can kick in another $6,500 if over the age of 50.

If you are fortunate, your employer will offer a matching contribution up to a certain level. For instance, you might receive a full match of your contributions up to 4% of your take-home pay. A good 401(k) plan will also offer you a full menu of low-cost funds from which to assemble a portfolio.

Your Debt Plan

So far, I've been discussing how to manage the assets on your personal balance sheet. Now let's think about *liabilities*—the debts you owe in the form of credit card bills, car payments, mortgage payments, and so on. Part of a sound financial plan includes developing a philosophy on debt. My philosophy can be summed up with a simple proverb: "Loans and debts make worry and frets."

I've long had a strong aversion to debt. My wife and I started our life together with sizable loans from graduate school and no tangible assets other than a 10-year-old Volkswagen Rabbit. I loathed writing those loan payment checks every month throughout the early 1980s, especially because of the relatively high interest rates that existed at the time. As a result of that experience, my wife and I resolved to avoid debt whenever possible. Not everyone feels as strongly about debt as I do, but even if you don't, you should give serious consideration to several debt issues.

With debt, I recommend borrowing only for long-lived assets. An education serves you throughout your life, so college loans are okay, or "good debt." A house will last a long time, so mortgage loans are necessary and sensible. You will also be building equity in your home. That said, be cautious about home-equity loans and other second mortgage borrowing. Cars also are relatively long-lived purchases, so car loans at reasonable interest rates make sense if the length of the loan is less than the length of time you expect to own the car. But borrowing for *consumables*—clothes, dining out, entertainment, and travel—is likely to get you into trouble and hinder reaching your investment goals. I would consider a credit card balance with a high interest rate as "bad debt."

Indebtedness is both an economic issue and a peace-of-mind issue, so the following are some other important debt considerations to weigh.

Are You Mortgaged to the Hilt?

For most people, the single biggest debt obligation is a mortgage. The question here is not whether to have a mortgage—few people could buy a house without one—but how to minimize the weight of that debt. Many people view their home as their biggest investment, hoping that it will appreciate in value and help to finance their retirement.

But the debt issues of homeownership sometimes get overlooked. Taking out a big mortgage in order to buy an expensive house could create a debt burden that you'll regret later. What's more, you might become *house poor*, meaning that the expenses associated with homeownership preclude you from spending on other things or, more importantly, saving.

You can measure your mortgage burden by calculating your *loan-to-value ratio*. Think of the loan-to-value ratio as the percentage of your house that belongs to the mortgage company instead of to you. Suppose that at age 30 you buy a home for $250,000. You make a down payment of $25,000 and take out a 30-year mortgage for $225,000. Your loan-to-value ratio is 225/250, or 90%, because you've paid for only 10% of the house's value. As you make payments over the years, you will steadily build up equity in your home, and your loan-to-value ratio will decline. If your home also grows in value over the years, the ratio will shrink faster. Suppose you still own the house when you're 50 and your remaining mortgage is $125,247, but the house is now worth $350,000. Your loan-to-value ratio is just 36%.

Most homeowners don't worry much about their mortgage debt because they count on their house rising in value over time. It doesn't always work that way. The bursting of the housing bubble in 2007 was one of the key catalysts of the Global Financial Crisis and led to a tidal wave of foreclosures. Here's what happened. Housing prices were on the rise. Relaxed lending standards enabled many individuals to purchase a home, and many overextended themselves. When housing prices then declined dramatically, many homeowners found themselves *upside down*, meaning their home was valued less than their mortgage. Some had trouble making the monthly mortgage payments; others became forced sellers in a down housing market.

Returning to our example, consider the home you purchased for $250,000 is now worth $175,000, or 128%! With a mortgage of $225,000, your loan-to-ratio is 225/175. Consider a house a place to live, not an investment. If you are fortunate, it will rise in value over time, but don't bank on it.

If you are in a high-risk profession that is subject to industry downturns and periodic layoffs, it is sensible to avoid a heavy mortgage burden because you don't want the fixed cost of a large monthly mortgage payment if you are out of work for a time. But if you have some reasonable level of job security, you may not be as concerned about the size of your mortgage. The point is that you should think about your personal situation before taking on a mortgage or other major debt.

Are You Carrying Credit Card Debt?

If you have high-interest credit card debt, you should pay it off before you begin investing. Some people think it makes sense to start investing even though they are carrying balances on their credit cards. They hope to come out ahead by earning returns on their investment that exceed the interest they are paying on their debt. But you'll see the danger in this approach if you think about it.

Most credit cards charge interest rates that are 15%–18% or higher. To earn even higher returns as an investor, you'd have to be investing in stocks, and you'd have to be picking investments that beat the long-term average annual gains of 10% that stocks have earned over the long run. The odds aren't very good that your investment will do that in a one-year period.

There's an additional danger in thinking that you can get ahead as an investor in spite of credit card debt. When you do this, you are hoping that the short-term returns on your investment (a big uncertainty) will offset debt payments that are a certainty. No matter what the market does, you will still have to make those credit card payments.

I can think of just one situation where it would make sense to start investing before you have paid off credit card debt. If your employer matches contributions to your 401(k) plan, you should get started in the plan right away, while of course paying down your debts as soon as possible.

Are You Investing with Borrowed Money?

For the same reason that credit card debt and investing don't go well together, it's never wise to invest with borrowed money. It's a certainty that you'll have to repay the money you borrowed. It's never certain that you'll receive the investment returns you're hoping to receive.

In the day-trading frenzy of the 1990s, some investors began buying stocks with borrowed money. The practice, which is called *buying on margin*, is very risky because it magnifies the impact of gains and losses. If the margin investor's holdings suddenly drop in value, he is often forced to sell the stocks that serve as collateral to pay off the loans immediately.

What this means is that debt with an after-tax cost of 4% is not a terrible thing if you are earning a 5% after-tax return on your investments and you can deduct the margin interest. But you're not getting ahead financially if you're earning after-tax returns of 5% a year on your investments at the same time that you are paying 19% on your credit card balance.

The tax aspects of debt are worth thinking about, but don't get so hung up on them that you squander time and energy finding ways to profit from having debt. The peace-of-mind issues are as important as the numbers.

Are You Counting Your Chickens Before They Hatch?

Suppose you've watched the property values climb in your neighborhood, and you're considering refinancing your mortgage to take advantage of that appreciation and get some extra cash. Or perhaps you've accumulated a tidy nest egg in your 401(k) account and now would like to borrow on it. Be very careful.

It's true that sometimes these decisions make good financial sense. But keep in mind that borrowing against your house or your 401(k) carries a risk. The appreciation in a house or a 401(k) is just a paper gain, not money in your pocket. You won't truly have real money in your pocket until you sell the house or withdraw money from your 401(k) plan. The risk is that property values or the financial markets will fall, and you'll be left owing money. If you have the misfortune to be laid off from your job and you have borrowed against your 401(k), you will have to keep repaying the loan while unemployed or face additional taxes and penalties.

Know What You Don't Know

The final point about financial planning: Know what you don't know. Yes, there is much that you can do on your own in setting up a financial plan and beginning an investment program, but it's also important to have some humility about other elements of your financial needs. I'll just make a few comments here because so much of it depends on your personal situation.

Life and disability insurance planning is one area in which professional advice is often worth the money, depending on the variables in your life, such as your age, health, marital status, net worth, and whether you have children. The same is true of estate planning. You could use an online tool to create a will or consult an estate attorney. I believe that anyone who expects to accumulate significant wealth should be willing to spend the time and money to make sure his or her will is prepared properly.

Consider the flipside. If you are underinsured, a fire in your home is not just a tragedy for you and your family but a financial calamity as well. If your will is inadequate or not up-to-date, your assets might not be distributed as you desired or you leave your heirs with hefty tax bills. Do a cost-benefit analysis. Often, it pays to obtain professional advice in these instances.

In a Nutshell

As a financial entrepreneur, you need a plan. It is a three-step process:

- **Set your goals.** Determine how much money you'll need to meet your financial, often multiple, objectives.
- **Assess your investment options.** Figure out which kinds of investments are appropriate to reach your goals.
- **Determine how much money you'll need to invest.** Calculate how much money you'll need to set aside.

In addition, as you develop a plan to accumulate wealth, remember that managing debt wisely is key to your success.

4

Save More—Without Feeling the Pinch

M y father was a banker, so he taught me at a young age about the importance of saving money. As a boy, I chipped in some of my lunch money to a savings program at school, and when I earned a few dollars here and there by doing chores, I put that money into an interest-bearing bank account. This was my experience with saving when I entered the investment management business in 1982.

I soon had a great revelation. One day, an older acquaintance who had a sizable account at Vanguard called to ask for help with a transaction. He wanted to move money from his daughter's account to the bank so she could buy a home. When I looked up her account, I was dumbfounded to see that this individual who was my age (under 30) had a six-figure balance. When I commented on it, her father explained matter-of-factly that he'd been investing $50 a month on her behalf in one of Vanguard's stock funds ever since she was born.

It was amazing to see how a modest amount of money, invested with discipline and in an effective vehicle, could grow to such a large sum in less than 30 years. It was a powerful, tangible manifestation of the rewards of disciplined saving and the power of investing in the financial markets. I regularly relay this anecdote to young people who are just beginning their careers or starting families in hopes that it will inspire them as it did me.

In this chapter, I'll discuss how to transform yourself into a disciplined saver and how to make intelligent, focused decisions on where to invest your savings.

Developing the Discipline of Saving

The authors of the bestselling book *The Millionaire Next Door* conducted a study of wealthy Americans and found that frugality was the most common personality trait among them. Authors Thomas J. Stanley and William D. Danko wrote:

> How do you become wealthy? . . . It is seldom luck or inheritance or advanced degrees or even intelligence that enables people to amass fortunes. Wealth is more often the result of a lifestyle of hard work, perseverance, planning, and most of all, self-discipline.[1]

At Vanguard, we noticed that people from all walks of life are represented among our clients who have $1 million or more invested in the funds. In addition to the highly paid celebrities, business executives, and professionals you'd expect to find in such a group, these millionaire investors include many people of more modest income, such as teachers, office workers, and construction workers. Quite simply, they have been highly disciplined savers who invested wisely.

You're likely to earn an impressive amount of money in your lifetime, and you don't have to be a movie or NBA star to do it. Consider that over a 45-year career, an annual income of $75,000 amounts to $3 million. The thought of earning $3 million and spending every cent of it seems monumentally wasteful, doesn't it? Realistically, a considerable amount of that sum will be consumed by taxes and living expenses, but there will be plenty left for you for discretionary spending or saving. With a plan for saving, you can keep your hands on a good chunk of what remains from the $3 million you earned. And if you invest that remaining chunk, you can turn it into much more with time.

Most people feel a strong temptation to spend any money that's in their pockets. To overcome that urge, try not to let it get into your pocket—save it before you see it. If your employer has a retirement savings plan, participate in it as soon as you can. (As noted in the previous chapter, most employers automatically enroll employees in their plan at a predetermined rate. The rate may be lower than desired, so increase it.) The money you contribute will be automatically subtracted from your paycheck, so you won't even notice that you're saving it. Do this with any windfalls, too. If you inherit some money, earn a raise, or receive a tax refund, add at least some of the cash to your nest egg. If you really want to accumulate wealth, live by this precept: "When in doubt, save it."

Need help developing good savings habits? If so, you'll want to take advantage of programs that force you to save. Automatic investment programs enable you to funnel a portion of every paycheck into your investment account or make regular transfers from your bank account. They are worthwhile because they offer a painless, systematic way to invest. I have always relied on the convenience of payroll deductions; money from my paycheck has always gone right into my investment accounts.

Tax-advantaged vehicles offer additional incentives to save, along with penalties for taking the money out prematurely. With traditional 401(k) plans and other employer-sponsored retirement plans, your contributions come out of your pay before taxes are taken out. (Roth contributions are made with after-tax dollars.) The advantages of a tax-advantaged account are astounding, as shown in Figure 4.1. Over 45 years, a $6,000 annual contribution (only 8% of a $75,000 salary) to a tax-advantaged account earning an average annual return of 8% becomes more than $2.5 million. Contributing the same amount to a taxable account would net you a tidy sum of $1.8 million after 45 years, but far less than the tax-advantaged account. (We assume an 8% average annual total return. One-half of the earnings of the taxable account were taxed annually at 24% before reinvestment.)

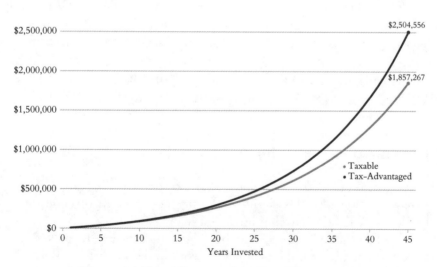

Figure 4.1 Tax-Advantaged vs. Taxable Investing

Source: Vanguard

As I noted, there are disincentives for pulling money out of tax-advantaged accounts, and these disincentives can be, paradoxically, valuable. If you invest money in an IRA, a 401(k) plan, or a 529 plan, there are generally penalties for making premature withdrawals, except under special circumstances. It sounds crazy to think that adults need to have a lock on their piggy banks, but the fact of the matter is that some of us do. Thus, the tax benefits of these accounts serve as the "carrot," while the penalties serve as the "stick." Both have value.

The Magic of Dollar-Cost Averaging

There's another advantage to automatic investment programs. When you invest a set amount in the markets on a regular basis, you are using a strategy known as *dollar-cost averaging*. This has two great advantages. First, it takes the emotion out of investing because you don't spend time agonizing over the "right" moment to invest. Second, with the fixed amount invested, you buy more mutual fund or exchange-traded fund (ETF) shares when the price is low and fewer when the price is high.

To reap the advantages of dollar-cost averaging, you must maintain the discipline to make regular purchases through thick and thin. It's easy to do that when the markets are climbing, but it can be very hard to keep on buying when the markets are heading down. Of course, dollar-cost averaging is no guarantee of wealth. It does not eliminate the risks of investing. It does not ensure that you'll make gains, nor does it protect you against a loss in declining markets. But if you patiently invest those fixed amounts in regular installments, you'll avoid a sharp loss and the accompanying angst of making a large investment at a single point in time only to see a steep drop in the market immediately afterward.

Portfolio Pitfall: Trying to Choose Time

Vanguard published an educational booklet in the 1980s that equated dollar-cost averaging to "using time instead of choosing time." It's a good way to think about it.

As I've noted, some individuals get stuck trying to pick the best moment to put their money to work in the market. They wait, fearing the market is "too high" or will continue a steep slide. As a result, they sit on the sidelines and miss out on giving their assets time to grow and compound.

This "paralysis by analysis" becomes particularly acute when an individual receives a windfall, such as a bonus, an inheritance, tax refund, and lawsuit settlement. The idea of committing a sizable sum to the stock market in one fell swoop seems imprudent. That's why dollar-cost averaging can be a good approach, as it minimizes feelings of regret by providing downside protection against sizable decline in a portfolio's value.

While I am a big fan of dollar-cost averaging, an immediate lump-sum investment has outperformed systematic investing strategies. Vanguard analyzed systematic investing versus lump-sum investing over rolling 12 month periods from 1926 to 2015 in a 60% stock/40% bond portfolio and found the latter outperformed roughly two-thirds of the time, with the magnitude of outperformance of 2.39% per year.[2]

This is another trade-off in investing. Risk a short-term loss for longer-term gain with a lump sum, or sleep better at night with dollar-cost averaging. The overriding point is to get the money in the markets, in the way you're the most comfortable. You can't win any game by sitting on the sidelines.

How to Become a Super-Saver

Saving is a combination of being disciplined with the money you earn and being watchful about spending. Here are a few tips.

Sock away salary increases. Saving money doesn't have to be painful. You may feel a bit of a twinge when you start, but you will quickly adjust your lifestyle, and you have to do it only once. Figure 4.2 illustrates a scenario that I like to share when people tell me they just can't get started saving money. This basic approach is something that anyone should be able to accomplish.

Suppose you're earning an annual salary of $75,000, and you're spending it all. Your income in Year 1 is $75,000 and you have $75,000 in expenses, which we'll define as $45,000 in fixed expenses (e.g., mortgage or rent, taxes, car payments, Social Security withholding, etc.) and $30,000 in variable expenses (e.g., food, clothing, entertainment, etc.). With $75,000 in income and $75,000 in expenses, your net profit (to save or invest) is zero in Year 1.

Year	Income	Fixed Expenses	Variable Expenses	Added to Retirement Savings	Available Cash
1	$75,000	$45,000	$30,000	0	$0
2	$77,250	$45,000	$30,000	$2,250	$0
3	$79,568	$45,000	$30,900	$2,387	$1,281
4	$81,955	$45,000	$31,827	$2,459	$2,669
5	$84,414	$45,000	$32,782	$2,532	$4,100

Figure 4.2 A Personal Cash Flow Statement

Source: Vanguard

In year 2, suppose you get a 3% raise. That takes your income to $77,250. Let's assume your fixed and discretionary expenses have not changed. With your raise, your personal income statement has just gone from break-even to a $2,250 profit. Will you choose to spend it or save it?

Let's say you are fortunate enough to have a 401(k) plan. And let's say you decide to take your $2,250 raise and contribute it to your 401(k) plan. Your income statement shows that your available cash is back to break-even. But you don't really have a profit of zero. At the end of the year, you still have $2,250 in savings. (We're ignoring whatever return that amount is earning in order to keep things simple.)

In Year 3, suppose you get another 3% raise. This raise, applied to your $77,250 salary, takes you to $79,568. Since your salary has grown, your contribution rises to $2,387 a year. To look at it another way, without lifting a finger you're saving $137 out of your second raise. Even if we assume a 3% increase in your variable expenses to $30,900, you'll have $1,281 still available to spend or invest as you wish.

Let's assume that the salary raises and variable expense increases continue at the same 3% rate for the remaining two years. At the end of five years, you'll have saved $9,628. If your 401(k) investment earns an average of 8% a year during that time, your nest egg will have grown to more than $11,000.

As this example shows, once you establish a saving routine, you'll hardly notice the portion of future salary increases going into your savings plan. The lesson: Adjust your lifestyle once by saving your first raise and you will never have to change it again in order to save reasonable amounts of money. That may seem too good to be true. Believe me, it is true.

By the way, the same approach can be used to pay down debt. Suppose you set a date for when you would like to be free of debt. You can use your *free cash flow* (i.e., the money left over after you pay your expenses) to pay off credit cards or to pre-pay your mortgage.

Defer big-ticket purchases. A young colleague walked into my office one day many years ago and said she had just received a raise of $250 a month. When my eyebrows shot up, she was quick to explain: "I just made my last car payment, so I consider myself as earning a $250-a-month raise. It's going straight into my savings." Wise woman!

Cutting your expenses is a great way to boost your savings. Every dollar of expenses that you reduce is actually worth much more to you than an additional dollar of income. That's because of the bite of taxes. Think how much you had to earn for every after-tax dollar you spend. If you are typical, you take home only 66 cents of every dollar you earn, after Social Security (7% of your pay) and federal taxes (24%, if you are in the 24% bracket) and state taxes (3%, on average). Another way of looking at it is that you have to earn $1.55 before taxes for every after-tax dollar that you spend.

If you keep your car for five years after paying it off and invest the savings, you will make solid progress toward your goals. My colleague was looking forward to saving that $3,000 a year in car payments. Even if you acknowledge the additional maintenance and repair expenses that go with owning an older car, you have to admit that she would still be better off than if she bought a new car and assumed a new set of payments. It's reasonable to think that she could have saved $10,000 over the ensuing five years.

Put away those extra paydays. If you're like many workers who get bi-weekly paychecks, you know that there are two months in every year when you get three paychecks instead of two. Another co-worker told me that he circles those dates on his calendar as a reminder to deposit those extra checks into his investment accounts. It's a great idea. If you're accustomed to supporting yourself on two paychecks a month, isn't there a chance you don't need to spend that additional chunk of money?

Add up the small leaks. You'll be surprised at the other potential savings you'll discover if you carefully monitor your spending over a few months. Your monthly subscriptions, whether for magazines, satellite radio, or video streaming services, are worth reviewing.

Be sure to keep track of each purchase you make, no matter how small. Look especially at those that hit your credit card and are paid automatically. At the end of the period, look at what you spent your money on and decide what is necessary. As Ben Franklin said, "Beware of small expenses; a small leak will sink a great ship."

As shown in Figure 4.3, modest savings, invested judiciously, can increase your wealth by amazing amounts. You don't have to live like a miser—just consider the trade-offs you're making every single day. Is a $5 cup of specialty-shop coffee each morning more worthwhile than a secure retirement? If you like coffee, buy it at the convenience store for cheaper or brew it at home for even cheaper still.

One of my teaching tricks that I use with people is what I call, for fun, the "best investment I've ever made." It relates to the last item above. My wife loves lattes. Rather than incur the $5 daily cost highlighted above, I bought her a very nice home latte maker for $300. For that price (and the $0.60 cost of her capsules bought in bulk) I save $4.40 per cup. The return on my investment is more than 200% a year. Not bad!

Examine your big bills. Here, I am talking about the sizable payments associated with your home and car insurance, cell phone, and cable TV. If you are in the habit of automatically paying these from a bank account, you can become numb to how much is actually going out the door.

	Annual Cost	Pre-Tax Value If Saved Each Year and Invested for 20 Years*
One takeout dinner a week for four ($50)	$2,600	$118,981
$7.00 to buy lunch each work day (240 days)	$1,680	$76,880
Interest on credit card debt	$900	$41,186
Daily coffee: Homebrew $0.60 (240 days)	$144	$6,590
Daily coffee: Convenience store $2.00 (240 days)	$480	$21,966
Daily coffee: Specialty shop $5.00 (240 days)	$1,200	$54,914

*Pre-tax value is the sum if saved and invested each year at 8%.

Figure 4.3 Little Expenses Add Up Over Time

Source: Vanguard.

Many banks and credit card issuers provide a year-end summary of your spending. It's a great way to get a handle on your spending habits and the opportunity to look for judicious cuts. You can also use your credit card's automatic bill pay service. It is a convenient way to pay bills, plus you can rack up points, or miles, or whatever incentive is associated with your card.

It pays to periodically review how much you are shelling out to providers, and then call your insurance company, streaming service, or cell phone provider to see if you can negotiate your bill. You'll be surprised how amenable the provider is to offer a better deal to you to retain your business. A co-worker recently told me he saved more than $1,000 on his annual home and auto insurance with a brief phone call. That's real money!

Saving versus Investing

No matter where you put the money, saving is an effective way to accumulate wealth. I'm not the only one who grew up equating saving with bank accounts, not investment portfolios. And salting away money in an interest-paying bank account or certificate of deposit (CD) is not a bad way to accumulate capital. The advantage of keeping your savings in a CD is that your interest rate is assured and the principal is generally guaranteed. Your success in accumulating wealth will depend on discipline since it's primarily a matter of how much you put into the account rather than what it earns in interest.

Setting Your Savings Priorities

Once you've decided to become a disciplined saver, the next question is where to invest that money. Some investors feel overwhelmed because there are so many different tax-advantaged ways to invest long-term savings. There are different kinds of IRAs, as well as 401(k) plans or other employer-sponsored retirement plans, and a range of annuity products.

What's the best investment strategy for you? It depends, again, on trade-offs. For example, look at the two major types of IRAs. Investing in a traditional IRA will get you an instant tax deduction if you meet the eligibility rules, but later in life you'll have to pay income taxes on the proceeds when you begin withdrawing your money. The assumption is that by then you'll be retired and in a lower tax bracket. But perhaps you'd prefer to forgo the up-front tax deduction and invest in a Roth IRA. Then you will owe no taxes when you start withdrawing the money in retirement.

For most people, the Roth IRA is better choice due to tax-free appreciation over the course of a lifetime, tax-free withdrawal in retirement, and no required minimum distributions. These benefits far outweigh the taxes paid on the contributions to a Roth account.

If faced with a choice, how do you prioritize investing in tax-advantaged accounts? For most, here is the optimal order:

1. Contribute to your Roth 401(k) plan up to the employer's matching contribution percentage.
2. Contribute to a Roth IRA up to the contribution limit.
3. Contribute to your Roth 401(k) plan up to the contribution limit.
4. Once you've maxed out on the tax-advantaged opportunities, consider putting your additional savings in a combination of tax-efficient funds, such as ETFs and index funds. (I'll discuss tax-efficient investing in greater detail in Chapter 10.)

One More Incentive to Start Saving Early

The key variables in your investment program are how much you invest, how much time your investments have to grow, and how much return your investments earn. You can control how much you invest and how early you start. But you can't do much to influence your return—or can you?

Here's something interesting that you should recognize as fundamental: **The more time you have in your investment program, the more risk you can afford to accept.** The converse is equally true: The less time your investments have to compound, the less risk you can afford to accept. A person who begins saving for retirement at age 50 probably would not want to risk losing any of her principal by investing in aggressive stock funds. She would be likely to choose lower-risk investments, such as a more conservative balanced fund that will likely provide a lower return. But a teenager who begins investing in an IRA as soon as she is old enough to earn money by mowing lawns or babysitting can afford to invest aggressively. After all, she won't be tapping that money for 45 years or more. Who cares if the account has a bad year and loses 20% of its value? She has decades to let the market and her account recover.

Why is it good to take on more risk? Simply put, the potential to earn higher returns. And over a long period, just a percentage point or two in added return makes a difference much larger than you might expect. Suppose you contribute $6,000 a year to an IRA for 25 years, and you earn an average return of 6% a year. In the end, you'd have $349,000 in your account. Not bad? Well, now assume that you invest a bit more aggressively and get an average return of 8% a year. This time you wind up after 25 years with $474,000. And if your investments should bring you an average of 10% a year, you will end up with $649,000.

Longer investment periods magnify the benefits of taking on increased risk. You have sufficient time to recover from down years and extra time to allow the outsized returns of good years to compound. As you can see, over long periods, the advantages are impressive.

In a Nutshell

You can transform yourself into a disciplined saver by:

- **Signing up for automatic investment programs.** If you funnel money from your paycheck right into your investment accounts, you're paying yourself first.
- **Participating in a 401(k) or other tax-advantaged retirement plan at work.** Tax deferral and the convenience of having the money withheld from your paycheck are two powerful forces in growing your nest egg.
- **Capturing additional savings opportunities.** Direct extra paychecks and windfalls into your investments instead of spending them. Identify expenses—large and small—that are undermining your efforts to accumulate wealth.
- **Understanding the risk/return trade-off and the benefits of time.** The more time you have in your investment program, the more risk you can afford to accept, so directing your savings to more aggressive investments like stocks will be fruitful over the long term.

Notes

1. Thomas J. Stanley and William D. Danko, *The Millionaire Next Door: The Surprising Secrets of America's Wealthy* (Atlanta: Longstreet Press, 1996), pp. 1–2.
2. *Financial Planning Perspectives: Invest Now or Temporarily Hold Your Cash* (Vanguard, 2016), p. 2.

5

Hope for the Best—But Prepare for Something Less

ow that I've discussed how to save, the next question
to consider is: How do you know whether you're saving enough?

People don't tend to ask themselves that question when making
decisions about saving. They decide how much they think they can
afford to save and then hope that they'll end up with sufficient money
for their goals. Or, they only put away any money that remains after
spending. But your notion of what you can afford to save could change
if you make some quick calculations.

If you're really serious about accomplishing a specific goal, you'll
want to first identify the goal and then figure out how much to save to
get there. To obtain the answer, you have to work backward. The factors
in your equation: (1) the amount of your goal, (2) the amount of time
you'll have to save for that goal, and (3) the amount of investment return
you can reasonably expect to achieve. Then, you do a little math.

For instance, say you hope to amass $100,000 for your child's college
education over the next 18 years, and you expect to earn 8% a year on your
investments. A calculator or a spreadsheet will tell you that you'll need to
invest about $207 at the start of every month to accomplish your goal. This
projection assumes that you reinvest all your income on the investment and
do not make any withdrawals from the account during the period.

Is 8% a fair projection for your investment returns? It depends.

Over the very long term—the 94 years from 1926 to 2019—U.S. stocks have gained an average of 10.3% a year. Bond returns have averaged 5.3% a year. Annual returns on cash investments have averaged 3.4%. You'll hear those numbers again and again as you read about investing, and it is reasonable to expect similar returns from those asset classes over the course of many years.

Most investors hold a balanced portfolio comprising the three asset classes, with a mix that reflects their tolerance for risk and, very importantly, time horizon. A 60% stock/40% bond portfolio averaged 9% over the same period cited above.

Importantly, you should not think of any of these figures as guaranteed. The particular 5, 10, or even 15 years when you are investing to meet a goal may diverge considerably from the long-term average. Inflation will be a factor, as will the timing of your contributions. And you cannot know in advance what the markets will be like when it's time for you to draw on your investments.

In this chapter, I'll discuss making the financial assumptions that are the foundation for your investment program. I'll share some stories from my own experience, as well as some hypothetical scenarios based on real market events.

When Inflation Rears Its Ugly Head

When they look to the future, many people forget about inflation, but don't let yourself make that mistake. Inflation is the general increase in the prices of goods and services that tends to occur over time. It reduces everyone's purchasing power—meaning, literally, that a dollar this year doesn't buy as much as a dollar did last year. High rates of inflation are an investor's greatest enemy. Bond investors are particularly vulnerable because much of their return consists of interest payments, which are worth a little less each year in an inflationary period. That's why most long-term investors need to hold a significant stake in stocks, which provide dividends and the potential to increase notably in value.

No measure of inflation is a perfect match for your exact spending habits, but the one that's relied on most for financial planning is the U.S. Consumer Price Index, which tracks the prices of goods and services purchased by consumers in eight major categories (e.g., food and beverages, housing, apparel, transportation, medical care, recreation, education and communication, and other goods and services).

In the 1990s and the first two decades of the twenty-first century, inflation was low and many people seemed to have forgotten that it was a threat. However, veteran investors will remember that in the late 1970s inflation reached double-digit levels. For the 1973–1982 period, the annual inflation rate averaged 8.7%. When inflation is running at 8.7%, the car for which you paid $20,000 costs $21,740 one year later. Five years later, that price is $30,351! And, of course, it's not just the big-ticket items that are affected by inflation. Virtually everything you buy costs more—from a gallon of milk to a pair of running shoes.

The long-run average for U.S. inflation, going back to 1926, is about 2.9%. That sounds low, but look at the results: At a 3% annual inflation rate, something that costs $10,000 now will cost $24,300 in 30 years. At a 5% inflation rate, that $10,000 item would sell for $43,200 in 30 years.

It's safe to assume that inflation will be a factor to one degree or another during the years in which you are accumulating assets or spending them. During your working years, your salary increases are likely to keep up with inflation. But your investment returns may take a hit. For these reasons, it's vital to think about inflation when you calculate how your investments will grow with time.

When you check the historical returns on different kinds of investments, be sure to look at figures that are adjusted for inflation. These are called *real returns*. Figures that haven't been adjusted for inflation are called *nominal returns*. Most of the historical investment returns you'll see are given in nominal terms, so if you are using them for your projections, you will need to adjust for inflation on your own. It's simple to do: You just choose a hypothetical inflation rate and subtract it from the average return figure. You could use a 3% to 4% inflation rate, or if you are very conservative, you could project inflation at a slightly higher level.

Figure 5.1 shows the differences between nominal and real annual returns of the three asset classes over various time periods. As you can see, stocks offer the greatest protection from inflation (i.e., positive real returns), while the real returns on cash are negative.

Figure 5.2 demonstrates the corrosive effect of 4% inflation rate on an investment program over 40 years. (This chart assumes that a person invested $6,000 in a tax-sheltered account at the start of each year for 40 years. It also assumes that the account earned an annual investment return of 8% after expenses and before adjusting for inflation at 4% a year.) The short story told by this picture is that your real purchasing power after these 40 years was slightly more than one-third of what it seems if you looked merely at your account balance. It's an important

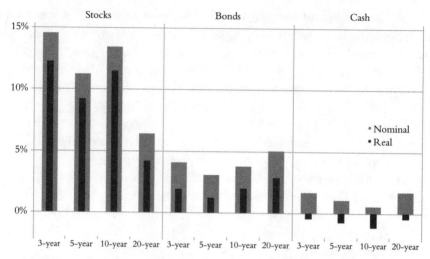

Figure 5.1 Returns on U.S. Asset Classes Before and After Inflation

Source: Vanguard calculations. U.S. stocks represented by Dow Jones U.S. Total Stock Market Index through April 22, 2005; MSCI US Broad Market Index through June 2, 2013; and CRSP US Total Market Index through 2019. U.S. bonds represented by Bloomberg Barclays U.S. Aggregate Bond Index through December 31, 2009, the Bloomberg Barclays U.S. Aggregate Float Adjusted Bond Index through 2019. Cash represented by the FTSE 3-Month US T-Bill Index. Consumer Price Index used for inflation. All data through December 31, 2019.

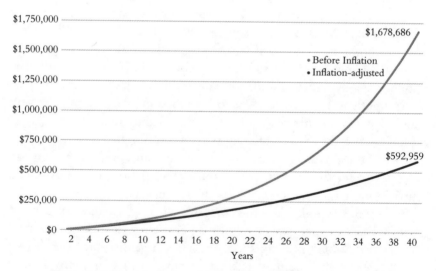

Figure 5.2 How Inflation Affects a Long-Term Investment

Source: Vanguard

reminder of why investing in volatile assets like stocks is important to offset the effects of inflation over the long term.

Future Investment Returns

None of us have crystal balls, so we can't know with any certainty which numbers will provide the most accurate projections of future investment performance. Recognize that even small differences in the assumptions can have a sizable effect on your calculations. If your projections are too rosy, you could end up far short of your goal, as the next case study shows.

Suppose an investor named Andrew decided to open an account in a stock fund with the goal of accumulating $50,000 in 10 years. He chose an index fund designed to match the returns of the S&P 500 Index. To figure out how much he'd need to invest at the start of each year, Andrew tested a set of different assumptions about market performance. He found that if he assumed that the S&P 500 experienced robust 18% gains on average for the period, he would need to invest $1,801 at the start of each year to reach his goal. But if Andrew was a little more reasonable and assumed future average annual returns of 10%—a return closer to the long-term average—he would need to invest an additional $1,051 a year, for a total of $2,852. And if he were more conservative, assuming an 6% annual return, he would need to invest an additional $1,395 a year—a total of $3,196.

Plainly, the ending values based on different projections are fairly dramatic on a 10-year investment scenario, as shown in Figure 5.3. Imagine how the projections would vary if extended over 30 or 40

	Projected Average Annual Total Return	Annual Investment Needed at Start of Year to Reach $50,000
Conservative	6.00%	$3,196
Reasonable	10.00%	$2,852
Robust	18.00%	$1,801

Figure 5.3 Annual Investment to Reach a $50,000 Goal in 10 Years

Source: Vanguard

years. While our example is based on investments made in a lump sum at the beginning of the year, the lesson also holds true if you are making biweekly or monthly contributions, as is common with most investors.

Don't Count on Present Investment Conditions Continuing

When I entered the investment business in 1982, the conventional wisdom was that stocks could be expected to return 9% or 10% a year over the long run. This was the prevailing "wisdom" despite the fact that stocks had returned only 7.7% for the prior 20 years, which seemed to me to qualify as a long run. So, 7%–8% per year seemed like a reasonable expectation. But stocks then proceeded to compound at an astounding average rate of 15.2% a year for the next 20 years. Assuming a 7.5% return, an investor who began 1982 with a $100,000 nest egg could would end up with $425,000 after 20 years. Not bad. But, again, at the actual figure of 15% a year, he or she would amass $1.6 million. What an incredible effect those outsized returns had on investors' returns over that period!

Amid those booming bull market years, I received a sobering note from a long-time business acquaintance. On the occasion of my 10th anniversary at Vanguard, in July 1992, he wrote:

> Congratulations on your first 10 years at Vanguard. It won't always be that easy. The stock market's average annual gains were 19% during the past decade. They were 3.5% during my first 10 years in the business (the mid-1960s to the mid-1970s).

The note was a striking reminder of how deeply an investor's perspective is colored by personal—and often recent—experience. My friend had endured a very different investment climate and, as a result, he had a markedly different take on the present. (As an aside, I would rather have had those 15% returns over the past 10 years. Why? I have considerably larger balances in my personal investment accounts to grow and compound.)

Investment experts often treat historical returns from periods as short as 10 years as a basis for future projections, but returns from a decade can be distorted by prolonged market downturns (such as the 2007–2009 drop in stock prices of 57%) or strong surges like the ones we experienced in the 1990s and 2010s. During the prolonged 1982–2000 boom in the stock market, people began to think that a permanent change had occurred in the economy, and that long-term returns going forward would be much better than ever before in the past. Indeed, the standard measurement of long-term investment results—the past 10 years' returns—was 14% at the end of 1990, much higher than the 8% it had been in 1980. As a result, we saw many naïve investors pile into the stock market in the mid-to-late 1990s with the mindset that the stock market only moved in one direction—up!

At Vanguard, we wanted to discourage investors from using past, short-term performance as a baseline and being unrealistically optimistic about future stock returns. In our client communications, we began discussing long-term investment performance in terms of 15-year returns, which were lower than 10-year returns. Frustrated shareholders wrote to us, "Now you are changing the rules of the game, and you're telling me that long-term is 15 years, not 10 years?" That's a fair observation, of course, but we were merely trying to provide perspective that most investors didn't have on their own.

By 1997, even 15-year historical returns averaged 18% annually, so it became even more difficult to convince investors that the stock market's turbo-charged performance was unsustainable. As ludicrous as it seems now, many investors began to believe that the historical very-long-term averages were no longer relevant and, equally worrisome, negative years were no longer possible. Then the stock market went on to lose more than 49% on a price basis between March 2000 and October 2002—a sobering and painful lesson for those who believed that the markets had evolved to an entirely new state.

The lesson here is that the stock market is highly cyclical, experiencing eye-popping upswings that make investors confident and exhilarated. Then, the proverbial bottom falls out and the market drops precipitously, inducing concern, if not fear, among investors and making them reticent to continue investing in the stock market, or worse, sell. We've seen this boom-and-bust cycle play out in the first 20 years of this century in dramatic fashion. Here's an old Wall Street adage: The market takes the stairs up and the elevator down.

The Problem with the Long-Term Averages

When you are making projections about the growth of your investment portfolio, even the long-term historical averages need to be taken with some level of skepticism. Long-term averages are a mathematical construct. In real life, people don't earn a constant rate of return year after year. The reality is that no risk-based investment appreciates at a steady rate. If you were to chart the value of your portfolio over decades, you would have a bumpy line, not a smooth line, with your balance experiencing considerable of ups and downs while (we hope!) following a generally upward trend over time.

While stock returns averaged 10.3% a year from 1926 through 2019, there have been just a handful of years when the actual return came close to matching that figure. Returns have also varied for 5-, 10-, and even 20-year periods of the entire period. Figure 5.4 shows the ranges of total returns for a variety of rolling 5-, 10-, and 20-year periods, such as the 5-year periods from 1926–1930, 1927–1931, and so on. You'll note that over any 20-year period, stock returns were positive. Time has served as a great risk reducer.

In your own investment program, you will earn good returns in some years and not-so-good returns in other years. There's no way of knowing when the market will be up and when it will be down, but one thing is true: The timing of the ups and downs that occur in your life cycle will be important to your success in reaching your goal. As shown in Figure 5.5, anyone who was investing over the 25-year period from 1995 to 2019 experienced a wide range of returns. But let me emphasize the short-term returns—whether up or down—amount to "noise" and should be ignored.

Let's assume that you are investing for a period of four decades and your portfolio of stocks and bonds has an average annual total return of 10% over that period. Let's also assume that you are contributing regularly to your savings, so that your portfolio starts out small and nears $1 million over time.

Duration	High	Low
1-Year Periods	54.2% (1933)	−43.1% (1931)
5-Year Periods	28.6% (1995–1999)	−12.4% (1928–1932)
10-Year Periods	19.9% (1949–1958)	−1.38% (1999–2008)
20-Year Periods	17.9% (1980–1999)	3.1% (1929–1948)

Figure 5.4 S&P 500 Index Annualized Returns for Rolling Periods (1926–2019)

Source: Vanguard calculations using S&P data.

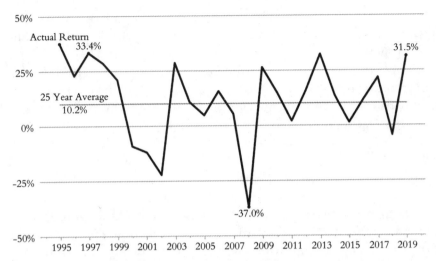

Figure 5.5 S&P 500 Index Annual Total Returns (1995–2019)

Source: Vanguard calculations using S&P data.

If your portfolio had an unexpected gain of 40% in the early years, you would probably be very pleased. But wouldn't you be even happier to receive that 40% gain in the fourth decade, when the balance in your account has grown much larger? A gain of 40% on an $800,000 balance ($320,000) is much more pleasing than 40% of an $8,000 balance ($3,200).

Losses are a different issue. If you had a 40% loss on your $8,000 portfolio in the early years, your portfolio would still have many years to recover. But suppose that the 40% loss occurred in the fourth decade. A 40% loss on $800,000 is a huge setback, and you'd have little time to recover. (This is why it's generally wise to transition to a more conservative mix of investments as you get older.)

Because you have no way of foreseeing the path that your investments will take, you may consider enlisting professional help. You can pay a financial planner to perform what's called *Monte Carlo analysis*. Using sophisticated software, she can run simulations and tell you possible outcomes and success rates for your portfolio, depending on a range of projected financial returns, tax and savings rates, inflation, portfolio construction, and other variables. For example, your planner might tell you that in 60% of the scenarios she tested, you would have met your financial goals, but in the other 40% you would have come up short. If that doesn't satisfy you, you could ask her to assume you'll invest more and re-run the numbers, continuing this until you arrive at a monthly investment contribution that results in your desired probability of success.

But you don't have to pay someone to do elaborate scenario testing to protect yourself from unfavorable conditions. You can be very successful with a do-it-yourself approach. Just be sure to use very conservative planning assumptions.

Scenario-Planning Tools

Your financial planning can be as unsophisticated as punching in numbers on a hand-held calculator and jotting down projections on the back of an envelope. But you can also find plenty of tools to help you project how much you need to save at a given rate of return in order to reach the goals that you have set. A number of calculators are available from investment providers and financial services firms. Or, you can use one of the many financial planning apps or software packages available.

The benefit of these planning tools is that you can compare different what-ifs: What if inflation is 5% instead of 3%? What if your investments earn 6% a year instead of 9% on average? What if you want to retire at 62 instead of 65? All of those factors will affect the answer to the big question: Will you have enough money for your goals? This scenario planning is particularly useful in figuring out how to deploy your savings for retirement. The good news is you don't have to be an economist or investment pro to undertake this homework exercise, and this small investment of your time can pay big dividends in peace of mind for decades to come.

Not-So-Great Expectations

Conservative assumptions about future investment performance are inherently safer than assumptions based on recent market performance. By definition, the lower your assumptions about future returns, the more money you will need to supply to your investment program to reach the same end point. If you assume that your experience won't be all roses, you will become a disciplined saver and a conservative investor. If it turns out that you were too conservative, the worst thing that happens is that you're pleasantly surprised. You'll have more money in your portfolio than you expected.

You face a very different set of potential consequences if you're overly optimistic in your assumptions and turn out to be wrong. If you take the rosy view about future returns, you will conclude that you don't need to supply as much money to your investment program because the market's bounty will get you to your goal. If the market isn't as fruitful as you anticipate, or if the timing of the market's ups and downs isn't favorable, you could end up with much less money than you expected.

Just remember that it's always tempting to use the most optimistic assumptions. That's why you shouldn't conduct your financial planning by first deciding how much to save and then figuring out how much it will earn for you. You can always come up with assumptions to justify an acceptable answer. Want to be able to "find out" that you'll be okay if you save only a little for retirement? Just assume that you'll be earning 20% a year and inflation will be negligible. But will that optimistic scenario occur? I don't think so. (One of the best investment minds I know calls this "torturing the data until it confesses." In other words, working the numbers until you get the answer you want!) In most of the hypothetical scenarios in this book that involve stock investments, I have based my projections on 8% average annual total returns—a slightly more conservative number than historical data suggest.

In my own personal planning, I am even more conservative. To stay on the safe side, I have always assumed that my income might increase at a slow rate, and I project investment returns that will stay only slightly ahead of inflation—real returns of about 3.5%. Back in the 1980s, when I was deciding how much money to save for my children's college educations, very few sophisticated financial planning tools were available. So I did my number crunching by hand on a calculator. I always made conservative assumptions, projecting an investment return of 1% to 3% a year after inflation. When the reality proved to be better than that, as is usually the case when assumptions are as conservative as mine, I felt very lucky.

This is an important truism: If you take a conservative approach to your financial planning, you'll be the one who wins in the long run. Conservative projections will drive you to save more. You will consume less. As a result, you'll be a more satisfied investor because the surprises will usually be on the positive side. If you're too conservative and you end up with more money than you expected, well, that's not so painful a prospect, is it? Look at it this way: You have more to live on or to give.

I believe in planning according to Murphy's Law: "Anything that can go wrong, will." But I believe even more strongly in O'Toole's Corollary: "Murphy was an optimist." Remember O'Toole's Corollary if you want to accumulate wealth.

In a Nutshell

It's wise to be conservative about future investment returns when deciding how much money you'll need to invest to achieve your goals. Some considerations:

- **A dollar won't buy as much in the future.** Inflation will eat away at the purchasing power of your investments, so you're likely to need more money than you think.
- **There is no guarantee that your investments will earn returns that match the historical long-term averages.** If you're overly optimistic about future returns, you may fall short of your objectives.
- **The sequencing of the returns earned by your portfolio is critical.** A period of strong returns (or sharp decline) at the end of your investing period will have greater impact than at the outset. Why? You'll have more money in your investing program to reap gains (or suffer losses).
- **Conservative-versus-aggressive return expectations.** More conservative assumptions about future market returns will help you become a disciplined saver and focused investor. If you assume the market will do most of the work, you might not reach your long-term goals.

PART II
CONSTRUCT
A SENSIBLE PORTFOLIO

6

Balance and Diversification Help You Sleep at Night

L et's say you've identified your goals and decided to develop an investment program to achieve them. Now, you're probably ready to hear about how to select investments. I'll tackle that very topic soon, but first we need to address a major strategic issue. To construct a sensible portfolio, you must first decide on the types of investments you'll need. In this chapter, I'll be talking about building a portfolio using some basic, commonsense principles. Choosing specific stock funds and bond funds will come later.

In truth, you can do pretty well as an investor by keeping just two fundamental principles in mind: balance and diversification. *Balance* means owning different types of investments—assets that typically behave differently from each other so that they are unlikely to all disappoint you at once. *Diversification* means spreading your money around so that no individual investment within the types of assets can hurt your portfolio significantly if it takes a dive. **Balance and diversification help to manage the risks that are inherent in investing.** Notice that I said managing risk and not minimizing risk. As you'll know if you've stayed with me so far, you have to take on some level of risk to get any meaningful reward in investing. With balance and diversification, we're talking about strategies for making sure you don't take on more risk than you intend.

If you hold a portfolio that is balanced across the asset classes and diversified within those asset classes, you'll avoid the risk that accompanies pinning all your hopes on one company's stock or bond, or the stocks or bonds of even a few companies. Your balanced, well-diversified portfolio will be less volatile than one that has concentrated among single stock or bond holdings. A concentrated portfolio will zig and zag between highs and lows. On the other hand, a balanced, diversified portfolio will provide a smoother ride, and you'll be likely to sleep easier at night. This isn't just academic theory. It's a real-life strategy that works.

Balance and diversification are often tossed around as if they were interchangeable, so let's look at the terms more closely:

- A balanced portfolio is invested across at least two of the three major asset classes—stocks, bonds, and cash investments.
- A diversified portfolio is invested in a variety of securities issued by different kinds of companies (or other issuers like states and cities) across different sectors. A diversified stock portfolio is not concentrated in any single stock or industry. A diversified bond portfolio is not concentrated in debt from any single bond issuer or type of bond issuer.

Balance and diversification are a powerful combination when they are both employed. They're the team of oxen you want to have pulling your investment wagon.

Let's apply these principles to a hypothetical portfolio that is invested in individual securities. Suppose your assets are split evenly three ways: A third in Company A's stock, a third in Company B's bonds, and the remainder in Bank C, in which you have an interest-bearing savings account and some short-term certificates of deposit. That's certainly a balanced portfolio, because it is invested in all three of the asset classes. It is not diversified, however. If a major business reversal struck Company A or Company B, you could lose a great deal of money.

Suppose you diversified your portfolio by buying the stocks of 100 companies, not just one, and owned bonds from 100 issuers as well. Then you'd be much less likely to be hurt financially if one of those companies ran into trouble.

Why Balance Really Works

Even if you are new to investing, chances are you already understand the value of balance in other aspects of life. If given the choice, most people would probably rather eat ice cream than kale. But we know that wouldn't be very healthy. We know we will have more energy and probably live longer if we consume a prudent variety of nutritious foods every day.

Balance is equally important to your financial health. Whether the portfolio is a multi-billion-dollar endowment fund or a modest-sized IRA account, investing across the three major asset classes is a good way to reduce risk. Stocks, bonds, and cash investments typically don't rise or fall at the same time. When one type of asset has a bad year, it's likely that at least one of the others will fare better.

Let's look at some historical performance statistics to understand why you need to invest with balance. While U.S. and international stocks tend to outperform bonds and cash over the long haul, there have often been extended periods—sometimes lasting years—in which stocks came in last. Figure 6.1 shows that U.S. stocks did better than bonds and cash during 17 of the 25 years during the 1995–2019 period. But there were 8 years in which stocks were outperformed by either bonds or cash—or both. In those years, if you had all your money in stocks, you might have felt pretty badly about it, especially if you unexpectedly had to draw on your investments. (As an aside, there were times when international stocks outperformed domestic stocks, particularly between 2002 and 2007. That's a point in favor of diversifying the stock portion of your portfolio to markets abroad.)

One of the main reasons for having balance in your portfolio is that it helps you to keep your emotional balance when one part of your portfolio is doing poorly. Knowing that stocks have historically produced long-term returns of 10% a year isn't much comfort in a period like 2000–2002, when stocks lost 49% of their value. Or 2008, when stocks dropped a stunning 37% in a single year. Or in early 2020, when stocks quickly gave up 34% over several weeks.

The key thing to remember about balance is that at any given point in time, it will look like a dumb strategy. In 2019, you might have thought, "I should have had all my money in U.S. stocks!" In 2018, it might well have been: "I should have had all my money in money market funds!" In 2011, you might have asked yourself, "Why in the world am I holding anything but bonds?"

	Cash – 90-Day Treasury Bills	Bonds – Broad US Bond Market	Non–US Stocks	US Stocks - Broad US Stock Market
1995	5.74%	18.47%	9.94%	36.45%
1996	5.25%	3.63%	6.68%	21.21%
1997	5.24%	9.65%	2.04%	31.29%
1998	5.05%	8.69%	14.46%	23.43%
1999	4.74%	−0.82%	30.91%	23.56%
2000	5.96%	11.63%	−15.09%	−10.89%
2001	4.09%	8.44%	−19.50%	−10.97%
2002	1.70%	10.26%	−14.67%	−20.86%
2003	1.07%	4.10%	41.41%	31.64%
2004	1.24%	4.34%	22.32%	12.62%
2005	3.00%	2.43%	17.54%	6.08%
2006	4.76%	4.33%	28.36%	15.72%
2007	4.74%	6.97%	17.39%	5.59%
2008	1.80%	5.24%	−46.15%	−37.04%
2009	0.16%	5.93%	44.63%	28.76%
2010	0.13%	6.58%	12.98%	17.28%
2011	0.08%	7.92%	−14.25%	1.08%
2012	0.07%	4.32%	17.60%	16.44%
2013	0.05%	−1.97%	15.59%	33.51%
2014	0.03%	5.85%	−3.39%	12.58%
2015	0.03%	0.44%	−4.29%	0.40%
2016	0.27%	2.75%	4.72%	12.68%
2017	0.84%	3.63%	27.41%	21.19%
2018	1.86%	−0.08%	−14.61%	−5.17%
2019	2.25%	8.87%	21.80%	30.84%
Average annual return	2.38%	5.58%	5.93%	10.24%

Figure 6.1 Returns of Major Asset Classes (1995–2019)

Source: Vanguard calculations. U.S. stocks represented by Dow Jones U.S. Total Stock Market Index through April 22, 2005; MSCI US Broad Market Index through June 2, 2013; and CRSP US Total Market Index thereafter. U.S. bonds represented by Bloomberg Barclays U.S. Aggregate Bond Index through December 31, 2009, the Bloomberg Barclays U.S. Aggregate Float Adjusted Bond Index thereafter. Non–U.S. stocks represented by MSCI All Country World ex U.S. Index through 2003; FTSE Global All Cap ex U.S. Index thereafter. Cash represented by the FTSE 3-Month U.S. T-Bill Index.

Whenever you find yourself questioning the wisdom of balance, remember the difference between tactics and strategy. Tactics focus on short-term benefits; strategy looks to the long term. Tactics may win you a battle, but you need strategy to win the war. With a balanced portfolio, it's true that you'll never be earning as much as you would if you managed to put all your money in the asset class that was destined to be the year's top performer. The problem is, there is no way to know in advance which one it's going to be. A balanced strategy keeps you from kidding yourself about your ability to predict the future.

You'll see the upside and downside of balance in Figure 6.2. As shown, the three balanced portfolios underperformed U.S. stocks for the 25-year period from 1995 through 2019. But during 5 years out of the 25, stocks lost money, and although the balanced portfolios also lost money during those years, they lost far less. During those tough times, holding a balanced portfolio could have given you the courage to stay the course and keep investing.

There will be times when you are sorely tempted to abandon balance. Over the years, many investors have told me stories about giving up on a balanced portfolio when one asset class got so far ahead that they just couldn't stand it anymore. They shifted all of their money into the hot-performing class. Then, invariably, the performance on that type of asset soon reverted to returns much more in line with the long-term averages, and the investors found that their portfolios had shrunk.

In the early 1980s, money market funds—which historically have returned about 4% a year on average—suddenly began providing 14% and 15% yields. Money poured in. But those outsize yields lasted only for a period of months. Investors who sank everything into money market funds would have had to move fast in order to benefit when stocks rallied suddenly and continued to outperform throughout most of the 1980s and 1990s.

Many investors assume that they'll be able to recognize the point at which one market cycle ends and another begins, but in my experience, virtually no one can do so consistently over time. Market shifts tend to happen very suddenly, and when they are occurring, they are nearly imperceptible—often to professionals and non-professionals alike. The fact that we've seen a major change becomes obvious only after the fact.

	US Stocks Broad US Stock Market	Balanced Portfolio 80% Stock, 20% Bond	Balanced Portfolio 60% Stock, 40% Bond	Balanced Portfolio 40% Stock, 60% Bond
1995	36.4%	32.9%	29.3%	25.7%
1996	21.2%	17.7%	14.2%	10.7%
1997	31.3%	27.0%	22.6%	18.3%
1998	23.4%	20.5%	17.5%	14.6%
1999	23.6%	18.7%	13.8%	8.9%
2000	−10.9%	−6.4%	−1.9%	2.6%
2001	−11.0%	−7.1%	−3.2%	0.7%
2002	−20.9%	−14.6%	−8.4%	−2.2%
2003	31.6%	26.1%	20.6%	15.1%
2004	12.6%	11.0%	9.3%	7.7%
2005	6.1%	5.4%	4.6%	3.9%
2006	15.7%	13.4%	11.2%	8.9%
2007	5.6%	5.9%	6.1%	6.4%
2008	−37.0%	−28.6%	−20.1%	−11.7%
2009	28.8%	24.2%	19.6%	15.1%
2010	17.3%	15.1%	13.0%	10.9%
2011	1.1%	2.4%	3.8%	5.2%
2012	16.4%	14.0%	11.6%	9.2%
2013	33.5%	26.4%	19.3%	12.2%
2014	12.6%	11.2%	9.9%	8.5%
2015	0.4%	0.4%	0.4%	0.4%
2016	12.7%	10.7%	8.7%	6.7%
2017	21.2%	17.7%	14.2%	10.7%
2018	−5.2%	−4.1%	−3.1%	−2.1%
2019	30.8%	26.4%	22.1%	17.7%
Ending value of a $10,000 account	$114,315	$99,237	$82,824	$66,635

Figure 6.2 Returns of Balanced Portfolios (1995–2019)

Source: Vanguard calculations. U.S. Stocks represented by Dow Jones U.S. Total Stock Market Index through April 22, 2005; MSCI U.S. Broad Market Index through June 2, 2013; and CRSP U.S. Total Market Index thereafter. U.S. bonds represented by Bloomberg Barclays U.S. Aggregate Bond Index through December 31, 2009, the Bloomberg Barclays U.S. Aggregate Float Adjusted Bond Index thereafter.

The first such change I encountered was the beginning of a long bull market, which happened just a month after I joined the mutual fund business in the summer of 1982. No one could see that the market was about to enter one of the longest bull runs in its history. Friends made it plain that I must be crazy to join the fund industry at a time when no one was making money in stocks. I thought I was making a good career move because of the fine company I was joining, but I'd never have guessed that my firm and many others would soon be growing apace as the markets soared.

It's no wonder that people were pessimistic about stocks in the summer of 1982. Stocks had returned an average of 6.5% a year from 1972 to 1981, a period when the annual inflation rate averaged 8.6%. Subtracting inflation, you were actually losing 2.1% a year by investing in stocks! Why would anyone have wanted to own a risky investment like that when money market funds were yielding 15%? But the bull market took root on August 13, 1982, and for the next 10 years, stocks would gain 17.5% a year and money market funds 7.3% a year, on average.

With the benefit of hindsight, we can see that there have been plenty of other times when the performance momentum suddenly shifted from one asset class to another. Here are several dramatic examples from the past 50 years:

- January 11, 1973. Stocks returned 18% in 1972, but as 1973 began, the worst bear market of the post–World War II era was just around the corner. Stock prices peaked on January 11. The bear market would last until October 1974, with stocks declining 45%. For the 1973–1982 period, stocks would return 7.6% a year, on average, below historic norms.
- December 31, 1981. Investment-grade corporate bonds, as measured by the Barclays U.S. Corporate Investment-Grade Index, had returned 0.8% a year, on average, for the 5 years ending in 1981. But the New Year was bringing good news, and bonds went on to gain 39% in 1982 and would produce average annual total returns of 15% for the next 10 years.
- August 25, 1987. Stocks had been booming when prices peaked on August 25, having returned over 35% for the previous 12 months. But the crash of October 1987 was about to occur. The stock market would lose more than 20% of its value in a single day on October 19, erasing $500 billion in investor wealth. (The total loss from August

25 was more than 33%, which would pull down historical averages for a decade.)

- March 24, 2000. Stocks began to recover from the October 1987 crash in December of that year, igniting a run-up of more than 750% over the 12-plus years. The later stage of the bull market saw extraordinary returns for growth stocks, and technology stocks in particular. The bubble burst in 2000, and stocks would go on to lose more than 49% over the next two and a half years.

- October 9, 2007. Following the tech bubble, stocks gained 133% from October 9, 2002 through October 9, 2007. Then, the Global Financial Crisis hit and stocks lost 57% between October 9, 2007 and March 3, 2009.

- February 19, 2020. Stocks returned an extraordinary 530% on a cumulative basis from March 9, 2009 through February 19, 2020. Then, in one of the most stunning reversals in stock market history, stocks dropped nearly 34% over the course of the next 23 trading days. Bonds served as a cushion, returning −1% during the period.

The lesson from these pivotal moments is that it's very, very difficult to recognize a shift in momentum from one type of asset to another, or from one industry sector to another. If you decide to try to pick the right time to move your portfolio from stocks to bonds or from bonds to stocks, you are unlikely to get it right. And think of the wasted energy and the emotional toll when you look back and regret your wrong move. Better to commit to a balanced strategy and save your energy for more rewarding pursuits.

Diversification Is Good for You—But Sometimes It Hurts

Diversification is the other principle to remember when constructing your portfolio. If you are invested in a broad variety of stocks, bonds, and money market securities, your portfolio is not only balanced, but diversified. Diversification reduces the risk associated with having too much of your assets invested in a single company's stock or bond. The term *specific risk* is used for the risk associated with such an investment. An academic could give you a long, sophisticated presentation on specific risk, but in my view it's as simple as that old warning about not putting all your eggs in one basket.

Investors sometimes ask whether certain companies are safer invest-ments than others and can be held in concentrated amounts. If you think about it for a moment, you'll see why the answer is no—unless you have the benefit of hindsight! Though a company may be active in many different industries, the whole enterprise is still in the hands of one leadership team. And all of those leaders are human beings who can make mistakes. People often cite Berkshire Hathaway as an example of a very diversified, extraordinarily well-run company. While Berkshire Hathaway is invested in many different lines of business, don't forget that it has just one chairman and one board of directors. It's a fine company, but you would be taking on a great deal of specific risk if you invested a significant portion of your money in its stock.

Over the years, many companies have been hailed as supremely sure things, only to hit the skids for one reason or another, such as a drop in profits or exposure to legal liabilities. Large, well-established compa-nies have been known to suffer drastic declines even though business is booming for everyone else. In the years after the oil crises of the 1970s, many companies that were used to operating in a cheap-energy environ-ment struggled to adapt to a new set of circumstances. Other compa-nies have been disrupted by upstart rivals. Think how Blockbuster fared when Netflix and Redbox gained momentum in the marketplace. (Hint: It went out of business.)

Some investors own stock in their employer's retirement plan. While there are valid reasons for investing in your employer's stock, it exposes you to specific risk. I advise owning no more than 10% of your overall portfolio. Consider, too, that if your company hits a really rough patch, you may not only suffer a loss in your portfolio, but your job could be in jeopardy, too.

The virtues of diversification also apply to bonds. If you own one company's bonds, you are vulnerable to changes in its credit quality due to management mistakes or other factors. That could mean you'd lose money if you had to sell the bonds—or, worse, you could lose all of your investment if the company defaulted on its debt. Surprises do happen! Consider Lehman Brothers during the start of the global financial crisis. The company's debt was quite highly rated (A2) on September 10, 2008, and five days later the company entered bankruptcy and bond holders suffered severe losses. Holding the bonds of a variety of issuers reduces your risk. In a mutual fund that holds bonds from hundreds of issuers, the failure of one issuer to pay interest or principal has only a minimal impact on investment performance.

Baseline Basics: The Enduring Appeal of Balance

Balance in investing is like a navy blue blazer. You can joke about it being stodgy, but over and over again, it has demonstrated its reliability. Let me tell you the story of Vanguard® Wellington™ Fund. If funds had clothes, Wellington would be attired in a blue blazer and gray flannels.

You could say that a balanced mutual fund was out of step the day it began operations on July 1, 1929, near the top of the Roaring Twenties boom. As a balanced fund, Wellington Fund reduced risk by investing in a sensible mix of high-quality stocks and bonds. Its founder, Walter Morgan, was a conservative investor in an era of rampant speculation. Who cared about bonds? Who cared about risk? Speculating in stocks had become the national pastime. But the stock market peaked that summer, and the worst stock market crash in history was just three months away. Thanks to Mr. Morgan's prudence, the new fund would survive both the crash and the horrific Great Depression that followed.

Wellington Fund, initially named the Industrial and Power Securities Company, went on to weather World War II, the upheaval of the 1960s, the recession of the 1970s, the boom of the 1980s and 1990s, and the turbulence of the 2000s. It has outlasted nearly all of the 677 other funds that were in business in 1929. Most of them were aggressive stock funds that invested with borrowed money, and their share prices sank like stones after the crash.

Today, Vanguard Wellington Fund is the nation's oldest balanced mutual fund, and with $103 billion, one of the largest. It has gone in and out of favor over the years as the concept of balance has fallen in and out of favor with investors. From 1970 to 1984, for example, more money left the fund than came in each year. But its story proves that a conservative, balanced approach is a strategy for all times.

Over a 30-year period, from 1990 to 2019, Wellington Fund produced an average annual return of 9.5%, compared with 10% for the S&P 500 Index for the period. Not bad for a fund that maintains a roughly 65%/35% ratio of stocks to bonds—meaning that it's only about 65% as volatile as the S&P 500 Index. Someone who made a $10,000 IRA contribution into Wellington Fund at the start of that period and left it there untouched for 30 years would have had a balance of $152,256 at the end of 2019. Even if you factor in inflation over those 30 years, the account would have been worth

$74,719 in real dollars. My point is not to brag about Wellington Fund specifically (or to encourage you to invest in it, necessarily) but to demonstrate that balance and diversification are proven strategies over time in practice, not just theory.

Keep in mind that there will be many times when you regret holding a diversified portfolio, just as you sometimes will regret pursuing a balanced strategy. By definition, diversifying means that you give up some of the gains you could get if you had the ability to foresee which of your holdings were going to do best over the next year or so. In a diversified portfolio, there will always be a few star performers, just as there will be a few laggards. How you handle your emotions in those situations will be critical. You could smack yourself in the head and say, "I wish that I (or the manager of my fund) had the sense to put all my money in Amazon, Apple, or Tesla" (or whichever company is the current star). Try this instead: Look at your fund's worst performers and be glad you didn't put all your money there.

Of course, just as diversification is relevant to an individual's or a mutual fund's portfolio, it also applies to an investment program made up of several mutual funds. Funds concentrating on just part of the market carry significant risk. Some technology-sector funds posted triple-digit gains in 1999, only to decline significantly in 2000 and 2001. But at the height of the bubble, plenty of people—professionals as well as ordinary investors—scoffed at diversification as an outmoded idea. Indeed, an investor who stuck with balance and diversification missed out on most of the short-term boom in technology stocks. But when the dust had cleared, the balanced investor was far better off. Even today, I see articles that declare the traditional 60% stock/40% bond portfolio as dead. I assure you that the death of the balanced portfolio is, to paraphrase Mark Twain, "greatly exaggerated."

Here's a tragic example of giving up on diversification. In the months after the bursting of the dot-com bubble, I spoke to a remorseful investor near retirement who had moved her entire account out of a broadly diversified Vanguard stock fund and into a technology fund at another firm in 1999 at the height of the dot-com frenzy. When the tech sector and growth stocks in general tumbled, she lost 80% of her money. If she had stayed in the broad stock market fund, the loss would have been only about 15%. She went on to say, "Mr. Brennan, as soon as my technology fund gets back to even, I'll move the money back to Vanguard." Sadly, she was waiting for that moment for many years. It's dangerous to hope that a bad investment will get back to even, as we'll discuss later.

A Case Study

Let's take a closer look at how diversifying a stock portfolio reduces risk. For this example, we developed a series of 11 hypothetical stock portfolios and examined how they would have performed during the five-year period ending June 30, 2020. In terms of diversification, they ranged from Portfolio 1, which was invested in just one sector, to Portfolio 11, which had holdings evenly spread across all of the stock market's 11 sectors. Portfolio 1 was devoted entirely to the Energy sector, the most volatile industry group for the five-year period. Portfolio 2 was evenly split between the Financials sector and the Energy sector, the second-most-volatile sector in the period. And so on through Portfolio 11, which had exposure to the entire stock market.

As shown in Figure 6.3, diversifying the portfolios significantly reduced volatility. As more sectors added to the portfolio, volatility became more muted. To compute this type of risk, we used a measure called *standard deviation*, which is based on the extent of up-and-down swings in returns over a given period. (I'll discuss standard deviation in more detail in Chapter 11.) Portfolio 11 experienced about half the volatility as Portfolio 1 and produced a better five-year return of (+8.23% vs. −9.18%). Higher returns with less risk is a great combination.

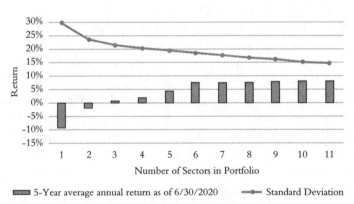

Figure 6.3 How Diversifying Your Portfolio Reduces Volatility

Source: Vanguard calculations using S&P 500 sector returns from FactSet.

In a Nutshell

Balance and diversification are investment principles that pay off in the long run if you commit to them and stick to them when the going gets rough.

- **Balance smooths your ride.** Holding a balanced portfolio of stocks, bonds, and cash can make it easier to endure the inevitable ups and downs in the markets.
- **Diversification reduces risk.** Holding a diversified portfolio of securities of a variety of issuers protects you from the risk that goes with putting all of your eggs in one basket.

7

You Need a Personal Investment Policy Whether You're Starting with Zillions or Zip

The very first step in assembling an investment portfolio is to decide how to spread your dollars among stock, bond, and cash investments. This is your asset allocation plan and it is the most critical investment decision you will make. That's right—**your asset mix will be a bigger factor in your investment returns than any selections you will eventually make of individual mutual funds or exchange-traded funds (ETFs).** This statement may sound odd—after all, many people in the financial business want you to believe that your success depends on shrewd stock-picking or buying the right funds. But they're wrong. (I am purposely keeping real estate out of the discussion, as many individuals have exposure to real estate through home ownership but don't consider it an investment as such. I will note, too, that many broad stock market index funds offer exposure to real estate through holdings of real estate investment trusts [REITs].)

Think of your asset allocation plan as one of the most critical components of your personal investment policy. Just as multi-billion-dollar pension and endowment funds adopt investment policies based on a target asset mix, so should you. The idea is to develop a simple policy that you can stick with over time, modifying it only as your situation changes—not in response to the ups and downs of the financial markets. Be sure to put your policy in writing and file it away with your important financial records to reinforce the commitment you're making to yourself. I provide a representative investment policy later in this chapter.

One caveat: Many investment providers will present a snapshot of your allocation when you review your account balances online. It is a useful tool, but don't check your asset mix too frequently and let short-term changes compel you to make frequent alterations to your portfolio. We'll talk more about periodic rebalancing and its benefits in Chapter 15.

Should you invest your entire portfolio in stocks? Or, should you divide it among stocks and bonds? Or, perhaps, stocks, bonds, and cash investments? It depends. Your asset mix should suit your investment objectives, your time horizon, and, very importantly, your risk tolerance, with consideration to your overall financial situation. In this chapter, we'll again encounter that familiar risk/reward trade-off as we examine how to go about determining and formulating an investment program that is right for you.

Why You Should Care . . . a Lot

There's an important reason for focusing intently on asset allocation. It really matters! A landmark 1986 study examining broadly diversified portfolios that engaged in limited tactical asset allocation found decisions about asset mix had a far greater influence on investment results than decisions about specific funds. As a result of this study—"Determinants of Portfolio Performance," by Gary P. Brinson, L. Randolph Hood, and Gilbert L. Beebower[1]—it's now widely accepted in the investment industry that the first step in constructing a portfolio is to make a conscious, deliberate decision about how to apportion your assets among stocks, bonds, and cash investments.

Unfortunately, some investors don't spend much time thinking about their asset mix. They ignore it or allow their underlying investment selections to create it for them. They may change the mix willy-nilly every time the investment climate shifts, moving their money into stocks when the market is rising and then into bonds when the stock market slumps. Or, they may waste time and energy agonizing over whether to invest in a technology ETF or a utility ETF, or over which of the hundreds of large-cap growth funds to buy, without giving a thought to their overall investment policy. These approaches are likely to lead to disappointing results. Asset allocation is a strategic decision. If you get the strategy right, the tactical decision about which mutual funds and ETFs to buy is made easier.

Kicking the Tires on Some Different Portfolio Models

Before you can decide on your asset mix, you need to understand the trade-offs involved. Each possible weighting of stocks, bonds, and cash carries a different level of risk and potential reward. We've already discussed the fact that riskier assets tend to provide higher, but more volatile, returns over time, while less-risky assets provide lower, but more stable, returns. Accordingly, it will come as no surprise to you that returns from stock-heavy portfolios have historically been higher and more volatile than those of bond-heavy portfolios over the long term. Conversely, portfolios dominated by bonds have provided lower returns with less volatility.

Figure 7.1 illustrates the trade-off in practical terms. It shows, for example, that a conservative growth portfolio composed of 40% stocks and 60% bonds provided average yearly returns of 7.8% from 1926 to 2019. Along the way, this portfolio posted losses in 17 of the 94 years—roughly 1 year in every 5. In contrast, an all-stock portfolio returned 10.3% a year, on average, while enduring losses in 26 out of 94 years—a decline roughly every 3 1/2 years. (Both portfolios had their worst years in 1931, when the conservative portfolio lost −18.4% and the aggressive portfolio lost −43.1%.) Obviously, if you were the owner of the aggressive portfolio, you needed strong nerves to stick with it long enough to earn that higher long-term return.

Developing a Personal Investment Policy

You can design your own investment program to achieve the level of risk/return that suits your needs. To determine your needs, you'll want to consider a few key factors.

Goal of Mix	Components	Average Annual Return	Worst 1-Year Loss	Number of Years Out of 94 with Losses
Stability	10% stocks 80% bonds 10% cash	5.8%	−6.7% (1969)	9
Income	20% stocks 80% bonds	6.6%	−10.1% (1931)	13
Conservative Growth	40% stocks 60% bonds	7.8%	−18.4% (1931)	17
Balanced Growth	50% stocks 50% bonds	8.3%	−22.5% (1931)	18
Moderate Growth	60% stocks 40% bonds	8.8%	−26.6% (1931)	22
Growth	80% stocks 20% bonds	9.6%	−34.9% (1931)	24
Aggressive Growth	100% stocks	10.3%	−43.1% (1931)	26

Figure 7.1 Asset Mixes and Their Past Performance (1926–2019)

Source: Vanguard. U.S. stocks represented by S&P 500 from 1926 through 1974, the Dow Jones U.S. Total Stock Market Index from 1975 through April 22, 2005, the MSCI U.S. Broad Market Index though June 2, 2013, and the CRSP U.S. Total Market Index through 2019. U.S. bonds represented by the Standard & Poor's High Grade Corporate Index from 1926 to 1968, the Citigroup High Grade Index from 1969 to 1972, the Lehman Brothers U.S. Long Credit AA Index 1973 to 1975, and the Bloomberg Barclays U.S. Aggregate Bond Index from 1976 to 2009 and the Bloomberg Barclays U.S. Aggregate Float Adjusted Bond Index through 2019. Cash represented by the Ibbotson 1-Month Treasury Bill Index from 1926 through 1977, and the FTSE 3-Month U.S. Treasury Bill Index from 1978 through 2019.

Financial Situation

How secure is your job? How much money have you saved? How much debt do you carry and when is it due? Those are the kinds of questions that will help you to clarify the priorities in your overall investment program. If you are tucking away a significant sum, you won't need to take on as much risk to reach a particular goal as you would otherwise. For instance, if you were investing a lump sum of $100,000 and hoped to reach a $500,000 goal after 20 years, you would need average annual gains of 8%. But if you had only $50,000 to invest, you would need to receive an exceptional 12% average annual return to get to $500,000 in 20 years.

There are additional issues to consider. It would be unwise to focus all your energy on developing a stock portfolio if your job is not very secure and you don't have an emergency fund. Your first step is to get that fund in place by building up short-term bond and cash investments. Those reserves would come in handy if you lost your job. If you put your rainy-day money into stocks, you run the risk of being forced to draw on them at an inopportune time, such as in the midst of a market downturn.

Baseline Basics: A Sample Personal Investment Policy

Think of your personal investment policy as a GPS, providing a map and giving directions on your investment journey. Your policy statement need not be complex, but it might contain several basic components as outlined below.

Financial Situation
Age: ____
Portfolio Value: $____
Monthly Income: $____
Monthly Expenses: $____
Debt: $____
Tax Bracket: ____

Investment Objective
Replace up to ____ % of final working income via portfolio distributions. Estimated portfolio need of $____ in today's dollars at retirement.

Time Horizon
45–55 years (30 years to retirement)

Risk Tolerance
Moderate

Target Asset Allocation
Overall: ____% stocks/____% bonds
Workplace retirement plan: ____% stocks/____% bonds
Taxable accounts: ____% stocks/____% bonds
IRA: ____% stocks/____% bonds

(continued)

Baseline Basics: A Sample Personal Investment Policy   (*Continued*)

Asset Location

Place tax-inefficient assets, such as active funds and taxable bonds, in tax-advantaged accounts; put emergency savings and tax-efficient investments (index funds, ETFs, and individual securities) in taxable accounts.

Savings Target/Hierarchy

$____ per year, allocated as follows: $____ to 401(k) plan, $____ to Roth IRA, $_____ to taxable accounts.

Projected Return

____ % average annual return

Inflation Assumption

____% per year

Glide Path

Reduce equity exposure by ____% every five years, starting at age 60.

Liquidity

Hold $____ in cash outside of investment portfolio, equal to ____ months of spending.

Other Considerations

Rebalance annually.

Favor tax-exempt bond funds in taxable accounts, if advantageous.

Time Horizon

How soon will you need the money you hope to accumulate? Will you have to withdraw it as a lump sum or can you draw on it gradually over a long period? Questions like these will further guide you in allocating your dollars. Generally, the longer you have until you'll need to tap your money, the greater your ability to seek a higher return by holding volatile investments like stocks.

Two general rules of thumb apply:

1. If you have an investment horizon for a goal that is less than 5 years away, you probably should not be investing in stocks. That's because of market risk; stocks may decline just when you need to sell your holdings. For instance, if you are saving up to make a down payment on a house in 5 years or less, you should play it safe and invest the money in short-term bonds or a money market funds rather than in stocks. There were three 5-year rolling periods in the last 25 years in which stocks posted negative returns (2002, 2004, and 2008). If you were in the market for a house in the early 2000s and invested the down payment in stocks, you probably remained a renter for a bit longer than desired.

2. If you have a very long time horizon of 20 years or more and can tolerate the interim volatility, then you probably should invest predominantly in stocks. While money market funds and other very short-term investments are good for preserving capital, they typically don't grow as much as stocks over long periods, and they may even lose ground to inflation.

If you're somewhere in the middle of these two extremes—say, with a time horizon of 10 to 15 years—a mix of bonds and stocks is probably appropriate. But other factors in your situation will help guide your asset mix for these intermediate-term goals.

One more comment about your time horizon: It may be longer than you think. After all, you're unlikely to be withdrawing every cent from your retirement account or your child's college savings on a certain day. The retirement phase of your life could last 30 years or more, and college payments could take 4 or more years.

Risk Tolerance

Do you find yourself worrying a lot about things you cannot control? Or do you just take events as they come, accepting bad news as inevitable from time to time? Questions like these will help you assess your tolerance for risk. Quizzes to assess risk tolerance are plentiful on the internet, so if you are so inclined, you can take a few minutes to complete one, which will help you determine your personal temperament for risk. Be honest with yourself as you complete the quiz and consider the current environment. If stocks have been on a strong run, you might be more confident in your ability to assume risk than if stocks are in a downward spiral.

While your current financial situation and time horizon are fairly straightforward factors to assess, your risk tolerance is very subjective. No one else can know how much or how little you'll be distressed if one of your investments suffers a loss or your portfolio is down for a considerable period of time. Many people don't even know for themselves until they have experienced the distress of distressed markets. Try this: Imagine that you get your next account statement and it shows that half of your account has vanished, due to a sharp decline in the stock market. In fact, some people experienced this very situation in the 2008–2009 period. If your stomach churns at the mere thought of such a loss, you would not be comfortable with a portfolio that's entirely invested in stocks.

Although other factors may seem to point you toward an aggressive portfolio, your tolerance for risk should trump everything else. While you will probably want to hold some stock investments to reach your long-term goals, you should balance them with a sufficient amount of bonds and cash investments to let you sleep soundly at night, even when the markets are volatile. Holding bonds can give you the courage to hold stocks. (We'll examine bonds in the next section and delve into risk tolerance in greater detail in Chapter 11.)

The Role of Bonds

Long-term investors are often quick to embrace stocks but sometimes less interested in bonds. Some people simply think bonds are boring; others are intimidated by them. The next chapter goes into more detail about bonds. But since I've been discussing the role of bonds in a portfolio, I want to say a few words on their behalf here.

Bonds are frequently seen as an investment for retirees or other investors seeking a regular source of income. It's true that the regular interest payments do make bonds an attractive choice if you are looking for a steady source of income, which is a goal of many retirees.

But you don't have to be a retiree to benefit from investing from bonds. As I've discussed previously in this book, holding bonds in a portfolio helps to offset the volatility of stocks. When the stock market plunged in early 2020, plenty of investors found that their boring old bond funds were very reassuring investments. As shown in Figure 7.2, bonds offered a buffer to the decline in stock prices in the early part of 2020. And, as you can see, the balanced portfolio of 60% stocks/40% bonds offered a smoother ride than stocks.

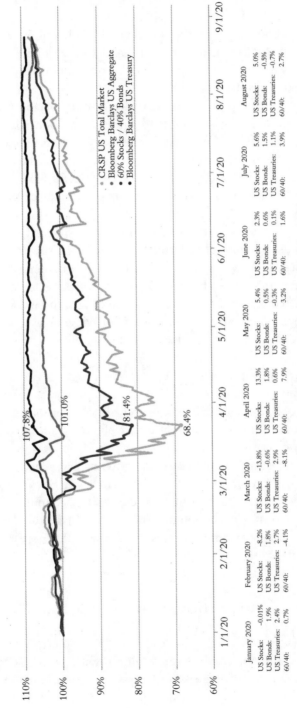

Figure 7.2 Bonds Buffered Stock Volatility in 2020

Source: Vanguard calculations using data from FactSet. 60% stock/40% bond portfolio consists of 60% CRSP U.S. Total Market Index and 40% Bloomberg Barclays U.S. Aggregate Bond Index. Data through August 24, 2020.

Bonds are, admittedly, somewhat complex. A very smart person I know insists that she'll never be able to understand how bonds work because she was born without the "bond gene." You don't have to understand, however, all of their intricacies in order to use them effectively in your portfolio. In other words, you don't have to have the bond gene to invest in bonds or bond funds.

If you've ever hopped on a seesaw, you can understand how bonds behave. The most important thing to understand about bond investments is that bond prices and interest rates move in opposite directions. When interest rates are rising, bond prices are falling. And when rates are falling, bond prices are rising. This is a confusing concept to new investors, but you'll remember it if you think of bond prices and interest rates as a seesaw.

Why does it happen? Suppose you invest in a 30-year Treasury bond that pays 3% in interest. If prevailing interest rates rise to 4%, other investors will be able to buy new bonds that pay a higher rate. No one in their right mind would be willing to pay full price for a 3% bond, so if you wanted to sell your bond you would have to take less than its face value. But if interest rates fall instead, and new Treasury bonds are offered with a 2% rate, you'll probably be able to sell your bond for more than you paid.

Long-term investors should ignore the bond seesaw. If you are investing in bonds as part of a long-term strategy, you shouldn't worry too much about any price declines. In fact, although it may seem counterintuitive, bond fund investors should celebrate when bond prices—especially long-term bond prices—are falling. Bond prices fall when interest rates are rising, which means the interest payments you reinvest will earn a higher return. Over the long term, those reinvested interest payments will be the source of most of the wealth accumulated in your bond fund account. At higher interest rates, you'll accumulate wealth faster. An investment earning 7% a year doubles in 10 years. One earning 6% doubles in 12 years.

The Role of International Stocks

So far, we kept our discussion to U.S. (or domestic) stocks and bonds. There are potential rewards, along with risks, to broadening your horizons, so to speak. U.S. stocks account for 60% of the global equity market (as of December 31, 2019). Non-U.S. equities, including those of developed countries such as Germany, Japan, and the United Kingdom, plus those of emerging countries such as South Korea and India, account for the remaining 40%. Dare I say, there may be a world of opportunity in investing in international stocks?

If you invest in the stocks of U.S. companies, you already have significant exposure to those overseas markets. Many U.S. companies derive a significant portion of their sales and profits from markets around the world. However, there are some worthwhile reasons to invest directly in international stocks. A major one is the growth opportunity offered by businesses abroad. Many leading companies in important industries are based outside the United States. In addition, there are growth possibilities of emerging-market economies in Asia, South America, and Africa.

Investing in international stocks can also add a degree of diversification to your long-term portfolio. The returns of foreign stocks can move in different directions from those of U.S. stocks. Thus, holding international stocks can help to offset the ups and downs of U.S. stocks in your portfolio. To capture the benefits of portfolio diversification without taking on too much risk, limit your international stock holdings to no more than 30% of your overall stock holdings.

At the same time, international stocks carry additional risks. One risk is that currency movements will have an effect on your investments. A stronger U.S. dollar diminishes the value of foreign assets owned by U.S. investors, while a weaker U.S. dollar will increase their value. (Some international funds offset this risk by employing currency hedging strategies.) A second factor to consider is political risk, the possibility that events in other nations could lead to problems for your investments. Political risk is of heightened concern in the markets of less-established, developing nations.

International funds typically charge higher fees than other types of stock funds. Research may be more expensive, and transaction costs are higher in smaller markets. The average expense ratio for international stock funds in 2019 was 0.69%, compared with 0.56% for the average U.S. stock fund, but there are low-cost funds and ETFs charging far less (Source: Morningstar).

International stocks can be more volatile than U.S. stocks. History shows that single country and regional funds, in particular, can suffer serious severe declines.

If you want to obtain exposure to foreign markets, the best way is through very broadly diversified low-cost mutual funds or ETFs. Indexing works in international markets just as it does domestically. You can find index funds that track the major foreign markets in Europe and Asia, as well as emerging and frontier markets.

Also, resist the temptation to buy or sell international funds based on your views or the views of experts about where the dollar is headed. That's another form of market timing.

I am less convinced that you need to earmark a portion of your portfolio to international bonds. In my mind, the additional costs and risks, along with added complexity to your portfolio, outweigh the marginal diversification benefits offered by the asset class.

Portfolio Pitfall: Beware the Allure of Gold, Commodities, and Other Risky Investments

In this book, I am focusing on stocks, bonds, and cash—the three major asset classes. From time to time, you'll hear people tout investments in other assets, such as commercial real estate, gold and precious metals, timber, collectibles, and so forth. It's true that these investments can provide strong returns from time to time. Also, I suppose you could argue that they help with portfolio diversification because they may behave very differently from stocks, bonds, and cash. But they are very risky, and certainly not essential to a solid investment program.

While these assets can add diversification to a large portfolio, they also add complexity, and they may be expensive in terms of management fees or your time. Your best bet is to leave them out entirely. Broad stock and bond funds will give you exposure to those sectors, so you'll benefit from any booms in timber or commercial real estate or gold mining without being overly exposed to the risks. If you feel that you must invest in them, never weight them as heavily as you would stocks, bonds, or cash investments.

Asset Allocation Models for Retirement Investing

Let's close this chapter by covering asset allocation for your retirement portfolio, since it likely represents the largest part of your investment program. Financial advisors have devised various model portfolios geared to the typical investor. Similarly, target date funds (TDFs) offer ready-made portfolios for retirement-minded investors of all ages. Most target-date series offer funds in five-year increments;

you simply pick the one that is the closest match to your intended retirement year.

Model portfolios and TDFs generally assume that the investor's allocation should change over time, with the level of risk dropping as retirement approaches. Portfolios for investors in their 20s invest entirely, or almost entirely, in stocks, and then gradually add bonds over the years. For example, a portfolio might start you with 100% stocks in your 20s, move to 80% stocks/20% bonds in your 30s, go to 70% stocks/30% bonds in your 40s, and so on. As you approach retirement, you own more bonds than stocks.

Although I am a fan of TDFs, they have some drawbacks. Prepackaged portfolios geared to a typical investor won't suit every individual. They focus solely on age, whereas you must also consider your objectives, time horizon, and risk tolerance. If you are 55 and investing for retirement, but you plan to work well past 65, your age won't tell the full story about your time horizon. You may differ from the average retirement investor in other ways as well. For instance, if you have other means of financial support and won't need as much retirement savings on which to live, you may want to invest more aggressively in order to build an estate for your heirs or charitable interests. In this case, you could increase the stock component of your portfolio above what the models suggest. It all comes down to your specific goals and financial circumstances.

Your risk tolerance may be another factor that sets you apart from the typical retirement investor. Suppose you are not comfortable with risk. Then you would want to choose a more conservative asset mix than the models or TDFs recommend. For instance, instead of 70% stocks/30% bonds in your 40s, you might prefer a 50%/50% mix or even a 30%/70% mix. It's quite possible that two investors with different risk tolerance levels would choose different asset mixes even though they had identical goals and time horizons. A close college friend and I were born on the same date in 1954, and when we got a chance to compare notes when we were in our 40s, we discovered that while we had a lot of commonality in our lives, we had a radically different approach to investing—he being more conservative while I was more aggressive. The great thing about living below your means and being a disciplined saver is that you'll have the flexibility to be either more conservative or more aggressive with your investment portfolio.

One caveat for those who are getting a late start on saving for retirement: Be very, very careful about taking on extra risk in an effort to make up for lost time. Yes, you can sometimes score big by investing aggressively, but you can also lose big. You can't afford to gamble with your retirement savings. Rather than taking on extra risk, the more certain route to financial security is to work longer, save more, or adjust your lifestyle in retirement.

In a Nutshell

You're establishing a personal investment policy when you decide how to spread your dollars among stock, bond, and cash investments. This is a critical first step in constructing an investment portfolio. Should your stock/bond mix be 80%/20%, or 60%/40%, or some other blend? Take the "OTROC" approach to deciding:

Objectives. What is your purpose in investing?

Time horizon. How soon will you need to use the money? Some investments are better suited to short-term, mid-term, or long-term purposes.

Risk tolerance. How much nerve do you have for the risks of volatile markets?

Other investments. What holdings do you already have, and what do they offer in terms of balance and diversification?

Choose. Decide your portfolio's asset mix accordingly.

Note

1. Brinson, Hood, and Beebower, "Determinants of Portfolio Performance," *Financial Analysts Journal*, 1986, 1991.

8

Mutual Funds and Exchange-Traded Funds: The Easy Way to Diversify

There is an old saying that the three most important words in real estate are *location, location, location*. If there are three most important words in investing, they are *diversification, diversification, diversification*. Diversification will help you manage the risk that's an inevitable part of investing in stocks and bonds.

You can choose to diversify by selecting a variety of individual securities, or you can diversify by investing in a packaged investment product like mutual funds. As I have said previously, I'm an unapologetic believer in funds—both mutual funds and exchange-traded funds (ETFs)—as the vehicles of choice for your serious money. For simplicity's sake, I'll use the term *fund* in this chapter to describe the traditional mutual fund and its younger sibling, the ETF.

Securities or Funds?

How do you best participate in the financial markets? Buy individual securities or invest in funds? Which approach is the right one for you? Which approach is likely to lead to long-term investment success? I'm going to be blunt. Despite all that you read on the internet about people striking it rich by investing in individual securities, I strongly urge you not to follow suit. Why? It's too risky, and, frankly, very few of us have the ability to trade stocks repeatedly and successfully. Study after study has proven that to be the case.

When professional investment managers select securities, they pore over extensive research on a company, analyze reams of financial data, and weigh competitor metrics, industry trends, among many other factors. Even so, successful results aren't guaranteed. The pros who spend their entire careers—40 to 60 hours a week—studying these factors don't bat a thousand. In fact, most stock pickers fail to beat the performance of the broad market for two reasons. First, it is extremely difficult to identify winners in advance. Second, it is extremely difficult to overcome the investment management and transaction costs that can substantially cut into investment returns. Chances are that your own batting average won't be any better. And non-professionals cannot match the time, resources, and experience of a professional investment manager.

It's challenging to make the right decisions and avoid the wrong decisions when you are managing a portfolio of many different securities. Suppose you're evaluating a company with a new CEO that has just spun off a division at a time when the industry is going through major upheaval. You need to decide whether those developments bode well or ill for the company. Better hurry with the analysis because it's just one of dozens of companies you are investing in, and the investment climate and business outlook are constantly changing for all of them.

Baseline Basics: Exchange-Traded Funds Explained

Introduced in 1993, exchange traded funds (ETFs) were still in their formative stage at the writing of the first edition of this book, and as a result, little attention was paid to discussing them. ETFs have since become the fastest-growing product among regulated investment companies (i.e., mutual funds, closed-end funds, and unit investment trusts) and are increasingly being used by investors and financial advisors as the product of choice to assemble balanced, well-diversified portfolios. Meanwhile, mutual funds remain mainstay offerings in employer-sponsored retirement plans, such as 401(k) plans.

To be clear, ETFs are mutual funds, but with an important distinguishing characteristic—they can be purchased and sold throughout the day like a stock at the then-current price, whereas mutual funds are priced at the end of the trading day. In my view, the appeal of ETFs are these traits: diversification, ease of access, tax efficiency, and low cost. Unlike some commentators, I won't list intraday trading flexibility, for the serious long-term investor should care little about buying and selling at the latest price of the minute.

If that's not enough to juggle, remember that you've got to be managing your emotions, too. Investors tend to make emotional decisions; even the experts sometimes do the same. It's tough to resist the temptation of momentum, betting that the markets and even individual stock prices will continue to move in a certain direction. When markets are climbing, the temptation is to buy in. When markets are falling, the temptation is to bail out.

The idea of a quick and considerable gain through individual stock investments is alluring to many investors. Pick a few winning stocks and ride them up to riches. But history shows that even the high-flying stocks eventually settle down to earth. Consider two fine companies and technology stocks like Cisco and Intel. Cisco was trading at less than $2 per share in the early 1990s, but by 2000, it rocketed to a record high of $77 per share. Then, the tech bubble burst, and the stock fell to a low of $19.80 in 2002. While the stock has regained some luster in recent years, 18 years later it has never regained its former high. Intel has faced a very similar, volatile ride. Both companies have fared very well; the stocks simply have never regained their turn-of-the-century euphoric, and unsustainable, valuations.

Today, as I write this, investors appear enamored with a handful of top-performing technology companies. Without naming names, these stocks seem like no-brainers. While I am not predicting tremendous future losses for any of these stocks, you should recognize the potential for hot stocks to eventually cool. It has happened for as long as stocks have been traded.

For all of the reasons I've outlined, most individuals will find that the best way to achieve diversification is by investing in funds. Many funds hold securities from hundreds or even thousands of issuers. In fact, it's possible to obtain exposure to the entire universe of U.S. stocks and bonds very efficiently with just two funds—a total stock market index fund and a total bond market index fund.

The virtues of diversified funds are regularly demonstrated by market events. In March 2020, when the stock market took a dive at the beginning of the coronavirus pandemic, mutual fund investors fared better than investors in hundreds of individual stocks. One set of data makes that point. During March, 345 stocks out of a total of 3,476 in the CRSP U.S. Total Market Index lost 50% or more of their value—approximately 10% of the total number of stocks. In sharp contrast, just 1% of equity funds had losses of 50% or more during the month of March—4 of the 3,683 U.S. equity mutual funds in existence for the period.

How Funds Work

In my view, funds are the greatest invention ever in financial services because they provide ordinary people with easy access to diversified, professionally managed investment pools at a relatively low cost. Today, millions of investors from virtually every walk of life entrust their savings to funds to reach their financial goals. The existence of these investments has been a key reason for America's evolution from a nation of savers to a nation of investors. The U.S. fund industry started with the introduction of a single mutual fund in 1924 and today manages more than $26 trillion in assets. Nearly half of all U.S. households invest in mutual funds (Source: Investment Company Institute).

The idea behind the funds is simple: Many people pool their money and provide it to a professional firm to invest it for them in a particular market or market segment. Every fund has a portfolio manager (or team of managers) who invests the pooled assets in accordance with the objective stated in the fund's prospectus. (A prospectus is a required legal document that provides details on the investment offering.) The objective could be, for example, long-term growth, current income, or reasonable income along with stability of principal. Depending on its objective, a fund may invest in common stocks, bonds, cash securities, or a combination of all three. Each investor shares proportionately in the fund's investment returns.

I'll discuss mutual funds and ETFs in more detail in a forthcoming chapter. But if you haven't invested in a fund before, you should know some of the key points that make them different from other investments.

- Funds pass along all their earnings—after expenses—to their shareholders.
- Each fund is a distinct investment company owned by its shareholders. However, funds are usually offered by a sponsor company, which provides investment management and administrative services to the fund and is paid by the fund to do so.
- Share prices of mutual funds are established once a day following close of the markets. That's 4:00 p.m. Eastern time for U.S. stocks. By comparison, an ETF is priced throughout the day based on the value of the fund's underlying securities.
- A fund's performance is expressed as *total return*. Total return has two components: 1) any interest and dividends earned by the fund and paid to shareholders and 2) any change in the share price and capital gains from the sale of securities that the fund passes along to shareholders. (See the Baseline Basics box later in this chapter for more information on the components of total return.)
- A fund is required to report performance in a standardized fashion. When mutual funds report their performance, they are required to state total returns for 1-year, 5-year, and 10-year periods. For each multiyear period, the fund must calculate a yearly average, which is generally labeled the *average annual total return*. This standardized reporting helps you make like-to-like comparisons of a fund's performance to peer funds and market benchmarks.

The Advantages of Funds

The mutual fund industry has enjoyed a very high of level of public trust for its near 100-year history. One reason is that funds and ETFs offer tremendous value and utility. Another reason is that mutual funds are the most strictly regulated segment of the U.S. securities industry. Funds are highly transparent, required to provide full disclosure of their policies, objectives, and risks; security holdings; operating costs and account fees; and any sale charges or commissions.

A key reason for this tradition of integrity is a strong regulatory framework. The two primary watchdogs are the U.S. Securities & Exchange Commission (SEC) and the Financial Industry Regulatory

Authority (FINRA). The primary law regulating funds is the Investment Company Act of 1940—a comprehensive, thoughtful piece of consumer-protection legislation whose effectiveness has stood the test of time. The law contains numerous provisions designed to ensure that funds are operated in the interests of the shareholders rather than the interest of the fund sponsor. I won't list them all, but one example is that mutual fund boards must include independent directors whose duty is to serve only the interests of fund investors. It's a subtle, but very important aspect of the investor protections inherent in the fund structure.

For investors, the advantages of funds can be summed up succinctly:

- **Diversification.** Combining your money with that of thousands of other shareholders makes it possible to invest in far more securities than you could buy as an individual. That reduces your risk of loss from problems affecting the securities of any single company or other issuer.
- **Professional management.** You don't have to make decisions about which securities to buy and sell. An experienced investment manager who has access to extensive company and market information makes those decisions for you and works with skilled securities traders to make security transactions effectively and cost efficiently.
- **Liquidity.** You can sell your shares back to the fund on any business day or sell your ETF at any time during the day at prevailing prices, so you have easy access to your money.
- **Convenience.** Most fund sponsors have websites and apps that enable you to access your investment portfolio, monitor your funds, conduct transactions, and obtain tax information. Or, if you prefer, you can conduct business over the phone or at a local branch office.
- **Low costs.** Compared with other means of investing, most mutual funds are quite cheap. Economies of scale enable them to hold down management, servicing, and transaction costs. **That said, costs can vary widely, from minuscule to onerous, so knowing what you're paying is an important key to investment long-term success**.

How You Make Money as a Fund Investor

You invest in a fund to make money. So before you put up any cash, you should understand exactly how a fund proposes to make money for you. The way a fund produces earnings can make a big difference to you in several respects.

The first thing you need to understand is that there are three potential ways to make money by investing in stocks, bonds, and other securities.

- **Interest.** You earn interest on bonds, money market instruments, and other debt securities.
- **Dividends.** You earn dividends on stocks when a company distributes some of the profits it makes to its shareholders. Not all companies pay dividends; some have no profits to pay out to shareholders, while others retain all of their earnings to reinvest and keep the business growing.
- **Capital appreciation.** You can benefit when the price of an investment that you hold goes up in value.

Funds earn money in the same ways: They get income—dividends or interest—from stocks or bonds they own. And they can realize capital gains when they sell securities at a profit. The fund is obligated to pass these earnings along to you, the owner. It does so by making distributions, usually expressed in terms of a dollar amount per share.

But that's not the whole story about how you can make money from a fund. You also can sell your fund shares or exchange them for shares in another fund—which is, in effect, a sale. If your fund shares are worth more when you sell them than for what you've purchased them, you've made a profit. Selling those shares locks in your profit and gives you a realized capital gain.

Baseline Basics: Total Returns and Its Components

A performance of a mutual fund is expressed by its total return over a specified time period—typically presented on an annualized basis over one, five, and ten years. Total return is the percentage change in a mutual fund's net asset value, taking into account the reinvestment of all income dividends and any capital gains distributions made by the fund and after the deduction of expenses.

It is also useful to know the components of the total return of a fund. Total return can be split into its capital return (i.e., the change in net asset value [NAV] and any capital gains distributions) and income return (i.e., interest and dividend distributions). Capital returns tend to fluctuate based on the underlying performance of the stock and bond markets. This is most pronounced in stock

(continued)

**Baseline Basics: Total Returns and Its
Components   (*Continued*)**

funds, moderate in bond funds, and nonexistent in money market
funds. The income component of total return tends to be more
stable for stock funds but more volatile for bond and money market
funds based on changes in prevailing interest rates.

Figure 8.1 shows the return components of various types of funds.
You'll note that there is a considerable difference on how different
types of funds achieve their returns. There are differences among stock
funds, too. Over the past ten years, 87% of the total return for growth
funds can be attributed to capital return; the corresponding figure for
value funds is 66%. Dividend-producing funds (such as equity income,
dividend growth, and balanced funds) tend to produce a higher percentage of their total return via income. Growth-oriented funds, on
the other hand, derive most of their returns via NAV appreciation and
gains from the sale of stocks in the underlying portfolio.

Unless you hold the fund in a tax-advantaged retirement account
(i.e., an IRA or 401(k) plan), you'll owe taxes on income or capital
gain distributions from a fund, as well as any gain reaped on a sale of
fund shares. The IRS taxes income and capital gains differently, and the
amount of taxes you'll owe also depends on your tax bracket. (Income
from tax-exempt bond and money market funds usually is free from
federal income tax. But capital gains distributions are taxed, even if
they're from a tax-exempt fund.)

We'll discuss tax issues in Chapter 10, but for now, just remember
that you generally won't keep all the money you make from your investments in funds, just as is true for investments you make directly. Even if
you reinvest your earnings in additional shares of a fund instead of taking
them in cash, you'll owe taxes.

Caveats to Consider

Funds aren't perfect. Like any other investment, they have some short-
comings or, in a more positive light, trade-offs. These are the major ones:

- **You can lose money in a mutual fund.** Unlike bank accounts,
  mutual fund accounts are not insured or guaranteed by the Federal

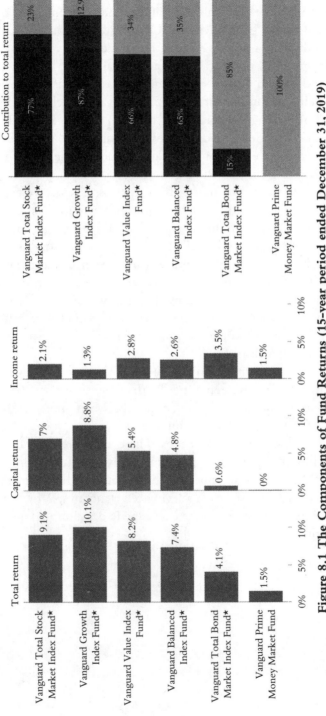

Figure 8.1 The Components of Fund Returns (15-year period ended December 31, 2019)

Source: Vanguard calculations using Admiral Shares of the respective funds denoted by asterisk.

Deposit Insurance Corporation or any other government agency. Your share price can go down, and so can your income from dividends or capital gains payments. Of course, you could run those risks with individual securities as well. The trade-off is you take the risk of losing money in order to have your capital grow.

- **Diversification has a trade-off.** Just as diversification keeps you from being seriously hurt by the problems of a single security, it keeps you from making the "big score" that you might get by piling everything into a single stock or bond whose value then shoots up. Again, a risk/reward trade-off. You get a far less bumpy ride with a diversified fund than in trying for the big score.

- **Costs can vary.** As I noted above, it's possible to invest more cost-effectively with mutual funds. However, you must be careful about where you buy your funds and what you're charged. Paying high operating expenses and taxes will reduce your investment returns significantly. In the end, your performance as an investor will be measured after all costs are incurred. There will, of course, be a few high cost funds that perform well by that measure, and if you focus solely on cost, you might have missed out. That's a trade-off, but the odds are so far in your favor by choosing the low-cost investments that the trade-off is worth it.

  At the same time, don't be "basis point wise and dollar foolish." The difference between funds with expense ratios of 0.03% and 1.03% is meaningful; the difference between funds with expense ratios of 0.03% and 0.05% is minute.

- **A confusing array of choices.** There are more than 16,000 funds offered by 800-plus fund sponsors from which to choose, according to 2019 Investment Company Institute data. Further, some funds offer multiple share classes with varying fee structures. While choice is a good thing, too much choice can impede decision making—another trade-off.

In a Nutshell

It's extremely difficult for an investor to construct and manage an adequately diversified portfolio made up of individual securities. Funds offer multiple advantages as the building blocks of your portfolio:

- **Diversification.** You can invest in hundreds or even thousands of individual securities through a single mutual fund.
- **Professional management.** Funds are managed by experienced, trained investment professionals.
- **Convenience.** Services like account recordkeeping and tax reporting are provided to you. Funds are a low-hassle way of obtaining exposure to the financial markets.
- **Cost efficiency.** You can invest more cost effectively through mutual funds than individual securities. Just be sure to avoid high-cost funds.
- **Liquidity.** You can sell your shares back to the fund on any trading day, so you have easy access to your money.

9

How to Pick a Mutual Fund (and How Not To)

Once you have decided how to allocate your assets among stocks, bonds, and cash, you are ready to consider selecting specific investments. In this chapter, I will show you a straightforward way to go about selecting mutual funds and ETFs. I won't recommend specific funds, although I would love to! Rather, my objective is to give you guidance on evaluating funds and assembling a balanced portfolio, as well as an understanding of the trade-offs that are involved in choosing one fund over another.

The goal is to "buy right and sit tight"—that is, pick funds that will suit your needs and serve as durable components of your portfolio for a long time. You don't want to be changing your investments as frequently as you change the oil in your car (or the tires, for that matter) because that would be counterproductive. By choosing funds judiciously, you can construct a portfolio that will serve your needs for years—even decades—and require relatively few adjustments. That's the route to building a solid investment portfolio, which, as I noted in the previous chapter, is critical to long-term investment success.

First, just to be clear, here's how not to select funds:

- Don't buy whatever is recommended on a financial website, on television, or in magazine articles without further due diligence.
- Don't buy a fund purely because it topped the performance charts over the past 12 months, or over any shorter time period, for that matter.
- Don't buy a fund simply on the recommendation of a friend or colleague.
- Don't buy a fund because you've heard the manager interviewed on TV or a podcast and he or she sounded very smart.

I recall a little bit of a pickle I caused Vanguard telephone representatives by recommending a specific fund on a television program. I appeared on *Wall $treet Week* one Friday night, and when asked about my own personal investing, I responded that I simply buy our global index fund every two weeks. The problem was that Vanguard didn't offer a global index fund at the time. What I meant was that I bought index funds representative of the U.S. and international markets. But that didn't deter thousands of investors from calling Vanguard's 800 number over the weekend and asking for the prospectus for a nonexistent global index fund, leaving the skeleton crew manning the phones over those two days somewhat befuddled about what their "fearless leader" recommended on television. This anecdote underscores the wisdom in the last bullet above—the funds owned or recommended by a so-called expert are not necessarily right for you.

Plenty of less discerning investors rely solely on "top ten" lists, but they are often disappointed by the results. The trouble with most fund rankings is that they are based heavily on past investment returns and ignore cost and risk. And here is a very important point: Past performance is not predicative of the future. There's a required boilerplate phrase in mutual fund prospectuses: **"Past performance is not a guarantee of future results."** This boilerplate is one of the eternal truths of investing. If necessary, make it your mantra so you'll remember it when you are tempted to act simply on the basis of performance-based rankings.

Of all the ratings and rankings, Morningstar's star-based system is perhaps the best known. The star rating is a quantitative, backward-looking measure of a fund's past performance, measured from one to five stars. The star ratings are intended to help investors assess a fund's track record relative to its peers. Morningstar complements the star ratings with a forward-looking assessment of a fund's ability to outperform its peer group or a relevant benchmark on a risk-adjusted basis over a full market cycle. The rating of Gold, Silver, or Bronze denotes a fund's potential for outperformance. Morningstar provides excellent data and insight-ful commentary on funds and can serve as a resource as you evaluate potential candidates for your portfolio. Yet people too often treat a high star ranking as a seal of approval just as they might rely on the appliance ratings in *Consumer Reports* to select a new washing machine. Note, too, many fund providers—recognizing the allure of the star ratings—pro-mote them in advertisements and websites.

If you use rankings, I advise you to consider them as merely one data point in a more comprehensive analysis of the fund. There's just too much risk in putting too much stock in a fund's past performance. Why? There are a variety of reasons: Markets change. Managers change. Bad news happens. Investment strategies or sector allocations that succeeded in one period may do poorly in the next. And these factors aren't just theoretical; the real force behind the warning comes from long, hard experience. Anyone who has spent significant time in the investment management industry has seen, over and over again, how quickly and completely the tide can turn for a fund or particular investment style.

Suppose you were making an investment in December 1999, and you decided to choose between a growth stock mutual fund and value stock fund on the basis of their 10-year performance records—you'd probably have sunk all your money into growth. Growth funds far out-performed value funds at that point—up 504% on a cumulative basis versus 316% for value. But starting in March 2000, the wind changed and value-oriented stocks took the lead for the next 8 years. As shown in Figure 9.1, following the global financial crisis of 2008–2009, growth

Date	Russell 3000 Value Index	Russell 3000 Growth Index
11/30/1980–8/31/1988	213%	89%
8/31/1988–12/31/1991	50%	103%
12/31/1991–9/30/1993	36%	5%
9/30/1993–2/29/2000	141%	317%
2/29/2000–3/31/2007	97%	−28%
3/31/2007–6/30/2020	88%	311%

Figure 9.1 Stock Market Leadership: Cumulative Returns for Value and Growth (1980–2020)

Source: Vanguard calculations using Russell data.

	2010	2011	2014	2019
Fund A	1	1374	2109	1976
Fund B	2	123	2124	216
Fund C	3	2054	640	1862
Fund D	4	76	1855	709
Fund E	5	1743	1778	1849
Fund F	6	147	2003	2027
Fund G	7	2105	1355	11
Fund H	8	1867	NA	NA
Fund I	9	1571	1487	1217
Fund J	10	219	1861	714
Number of funds evaluated	2200	2163	2178	2052

Figure 9.2 Hot Funds Turn Cold

Source: Vanguard calculations using Morningstar data. Data includes all U.S. stock funds classified with Morningstar style box categories.

then assumed the market leadership position, which continues today. (Interestingly, over the past 25 years ended December 31, 2019, growth and value stocks have been in a virtual dead heat—returning 10.13% and 10.07%, respectively.)

Similar pivots have occurred between large-cap and small-cap stocks, as well as between the U.S. stock market and non-U.S. markets. And there's just no telling when these changes might occur.

Past performance is a poor predictor of future returns at the individual fund level, too. By way of example, in Figure 9.2, we examined how the top ten performing domestic stock funds in 2010 performed in subsequent years. If you bought them because of their performance, you would have been disappointed in the results.

A Process for Constructing a Portfolio

Constructing a long-term portfolio is a four-step process:

1. Decide how to allocate your money among stocks, bonds, and cash.
2. Choose where to invest within each asset class.
3. Decide whether you want index funds, actively managed funds, or both.
4. Evaluate and select specific funds.

The remainder of this chapter examines each step in greater detail.

Step 1: Stocks, Bonds, Cash? It's Time to Decide

By now, you recognize the importance of making a deliberate decision about how to allocate your dollars among stocks, bonds, and cash. To get started, you need to settle on an asset allocation—be it 100% stocks; 80% stocks/20% bonds; 60% stocks/30% bonds/10% cash; or any other combination that considers the factors covered in Chapter 7. Specifically, your goals, time horizon, personal financial situation, and tolerance for risk.

Once you decide on your target asset mix, you can put together a portfolio without much more effort if you want to keep things simple. The easiest way to set up a balanced, broadly diversified portfolio is to buy a target date fund. These funds start off with a large percentage in stocks and gradually decrease that amount in favor of a greater weighting in bonds as the stated target date approaches. This is known as a *glide path*—the predetermined rate at which a fund changes its asset allocation over time, becoming more conservative as the investors come closer to retirement.

Target-risk funds, sometimes called life-cycle funds, are another possible single fund solution. These funds typically invest in stocks and bonds by holding other mutual funds, but unlike target-date funds, the allocation among asset classes remains static. Funds can feature a range of allocations, from aggressive (80% stocks/20% bonds), to moderate (60% stocks/40% bonds), to conservative (20% stocks/80% bonds).

Another, more traditional, option is choosing a balanced fund that matches your target allocation. A balanced fund is one that invests in both stocks and bonds; some employ cash investments as well. You can choose a balanced fund that holds more stocks than bonds, or the reverse; or you can find one that is divided 50% stocks/50% bonds. Some balanced funds enforce their allocations fairly strictly, while others may change the proportions to take advantage of market trends, which is an approach that's far riskier but has the potential for greater reward.

Target-date, target-risk, and balanced funds enable you to gain exposure to stocks and bonds with a single investment. It's a simple, but very sound, low-maintenance strategy. Of course, you don't have to take the single-fund route. You could decide to build a portfolio with several funds selected to create a more tailored strategy, starting with a core of two or three mutual funds that offer broad exposure to the markets. A broad stock market index fund, a broad bond market index fund, and a money market fund will give you everything you need. If you are seeking a 60% stock/30% bonds/10% cash asset mix, you would set up your savings program to funnel 60% of your money to the stock fund, 30% to the bond fund, and 10% to the money market fund.

I'll give you some guidelines for choosing funds, with just this word of warning first: No one should need more than ten funds. In the case of owning funds, less is frequently more.

Step 2: Where to Invest Within an Asset Class?

If you want to go beyond a broad market fund to represent stocks or bonds in your portfolio, you need to look at subcategories of these funds. There are also different types of money market funds. Here, I'll describe in general terms how to consider specific categories of funds within the major asset classes. In choosing among funds representing these sectors, you will be establishing your sub-asset allocation.

Money Market Funds

Money market mutual funds are among the safest places to put your money. I must emphasize that they are not insured by the Federal Deposit Insurance Corporation or any other government agency, so they can't boast the same protection as bank accounts. That said, money market funds are highly regulated and must adhere to rigorous diversification, maturity, and liquidity standards. They seek to maintain a stable price of $1 per share by investing in very-short-term debt securities from very-high-quality issuers, such as major corporations, banks, and the federal government.

Of course, the trade-off of the safety of money market funds is lower yields compared with other fixed-income investments. Your money will not experience sufficient growth in such a fund to keep you comfortably ahead of inflation. That's why, as I noted earlier, a money market fund shouldn't be used as the core of your long-term portfolio, but as a complementary, convenient cash management tool.

Money market funds generally fall into three categories:

- U.S. Treasury funds. These funds are the most conservative since they invest principally in direct U.S. Treasury obligations, possibly the safest investments in the world.
- U.S. government funds. Also called *federal* funds, these funds invest in securities from government agencies other than (or in addition to) the

U.S. Treasury. These funds may also buy issues from non-government agencies that are backed by the U.S. government.
• General funds. These are often called *prime* funds. They invest principally in high-quality issues from large corporations and banks.

What trade-offs do you make in choosing among these three groups? It's mainly a matter of risk versus yield. Treasury funds, being the safest, usually pay the least in income. Government funds pay a bit more. Prime funds, which are considered the riskiest since they invest in corporate securities, typically provide the highest yields among money market funds.

If you are in a high tax bracket, you may want to look at a fourth type of money market fund—the municipal money market fund. Such funds are also called *tax-exempt* money market funds. The income on these funds is exempt from federal income taxes and sometimes from state and local income taxes as well. But there is a trade-off: The pre-tax yields are typically lower than those provided by taxable money funds, so some analysis is required to determine if they make sense given your tax bracket. (Chapter 10 features additional discussion about tax-exempt funds, including an explanation of how to calculate taxable-equivalent yields.)

Since the first edition of this book, a long-standing, but formerly obscure, fund category—ultra-short-term bond funds—has gained prominence. Ultra-short-term bond funds invest primarily in investment-grade bonds that mature within one to two years and tend to have a higher yield than money market funds. Some investors will be tempted by the yield premium offered by these funds and think of them as a substitute for money market funds. They are not, so be wary of firms promoting them as such.

Ultra-short-term bond funds are subject to principal risk (i.e., prices of the bonds in the portfolio could decline in value) and credit risk (i.e., the bonds in the portfolio could experience losses due to credit downgrades or default). Unlike a money market fund, the price of an ultra-short-term bond fund will fluctuate. This is not to say that such funds should be avoided, but, as always, remember the trade-off that the potential for higher return comes with higher risk.

Bond Funds

Before deciding among bond funds, you need to be clear about exactly what role you want bonds to play in your portfolio. That's because with bonds, the aforementioned risk/reward trade-off can lead to very different results. Here's the simple version of a somewhat more complex story: If you're looking for the highest current income available from bonds, you will have to expect some notable ups and downs in your account value. If you'd rather have more price stability, then lower your expectations for income from bonds.

With that in mind, let's look at the major types of bond funds. If you're new to these funds, you'll first need to have a firm understanding of these categories:

- Tax status: Taxable or tax-exempt?
- Credit quality: High, medium, or low?
- Maturity: Short, medium, or long?

Taxable bond funds include those investing in U.S. Treasury, government agency, and corporate issues. The income generated and distributed to you is taxable. Municipal bonds are issued by state and local governments and governmental authorities. The income is exempt from federal taxes (and, in many cases, state taxes for the state that issues the bonds).

A word to the wise: Never pick tax-exempt funds for an IRA, a 401(k) plan, or any other account that already is sheltered from taxes. And you shouldn't consider a tax-exempt bond fund for your taxable accounts unless you are in a relatively high tax bracket and have made the calculations to ensure the fund is a wise choice. That's because tax-exempt funds typically have lower yields than similar taxable funds.

Credit quality and maturity are directly related to the question of risk versus reward. You should not buy any bond fund—taxable or tax-exempt—until you understand how it fits within these categories.

The style box shown in Figure 9.3 provides an easy way to visualize taxable bond fund classifications. For example, a fund that invests primarily in long-term Treasury bonds, considered to have unimpeachable credit quality, would occupy the top-right-hand box. A fund that invests primarily in short-term "junk" bonds, which are considered low in credit quality, would occupy the lower-left box. Just keep in mind that style boxes illustrate the primary investment emphasis of a fund. They're not perfect tools because there are some funds that straddle the categories.

Credit quality. The credit quality of a bond relates to the issuer's ability to pay interest on the bond and, ultimately, to repay the principal upon maturity. A bond with a lower credit rating typically will pay higher interest to compensate for the greater risk that principal and

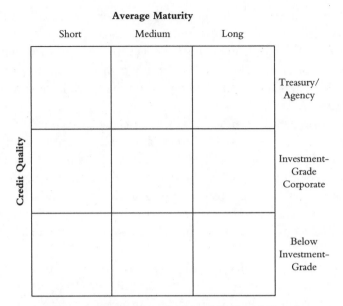

Figure 9.3 Style Box for Taxable Bond Funds

interest won't be repaid on time. Conversely, a bond with a higher credit rating can be expected to pay lower interest.

Major sources of credit ratings include Moody's Investors Service and Standard & Poor's Corporation. These rating firms conduct analysis to determine the creditworthiness of entities (e.g., companies, states, universities, etc.) that issue bonds. You don't need to know the intricacies of these alpha-numeric ratings, but it's helpful to have a general awareness of the bond credit levels. U.S. Treasury bonds have the highest quality because they are backed by the "full faith and credit" of the United States government. At the bottom of the credit list are high-yield or "junk" bonds, issued by companies viewed as having the potential to default. Funds typically display the distribution of credit quality of their portfolios on the sponsor's website.

Average maturity. This is the average time until all of a fund's bond holdings reach maturity. For a short-term fund, average maturity is generally less than five years; for an intermediate-term fund, five to ten years; and for a long-term fund, more than ten years. As you might imagine, bond funds with longer average maturities are more sensitive to changes in prevailing market interest rates. A statistic called *duration* (see Appendix) is a handy way to judge this interest rate sensitivity. The longer the fund's duration, the steeper a fund's share-price swings tend to be when rates change. But longer-term bonds typically pay higher interest rates than shorter-term bonds to compensate investors for the risk that future events (rising interest rates or inflation, for example) will erode the value of the bond investment. Maturity and duration figures can be obtained by calling the fund sponsor or visiting its website.

Selecting bond funds. Let's deal with the credit-quality trade-off first. My advice is to stick with higher-quality bonds for the vast majority of your long-term bond allocation. That means investing in broadly diversified funds that hold U.S. Treasury bonds, high-quality corporate bonds, and/or insured mortgage-backed bonds. If you're in a higher tax bracket and tax-exempt bonds make sense for you, stick to funds focusing on high-quality bonds issued by financially strong municipalities.

I suggest higher-quality bonds as your main focus because the whole idea of owning bonds is to balance out the risks of owning stocks and to obtain regular income. You don't want to use the core of your bond allocation to gamble on significant price appreciation or to stretch for higher income through low-quality bonds. You can take similar risks, with generally higher return potential, through your equity allocation.

With respect to average maturity, if your investment time horizon is long term (i.e., more than a decade), base your bond allocation on an intermediate- or long-term fund. In doing so, keep your eyes open to the fact that the fund's share price will be more volatile than would be the case with a shorter-term bond fund. You'll be putting up with that volatility for the sake of the added income you'll get from the intermediate-term or long-term fund.

If your time horizon is shorter than ten years, don't use a long-term fund. You won't be paid enough to offset the risk that the share price will fall just at the time you need the money. Instead, find an ultra-short-, short-, or intermediate-term fund for your bond allocation.

Stock Funds

To be a thoughtful investor, you need to know something about the way stocks are classified. Frankly, some of the terms you'll hear are jargon. Terms such as *growth* and *value* have acquired a financial meaning that isn't always in sync with what most people assume or the way fund managers think about stocks. But such terms are so commonly used that you should be familiar with them if you're going to understand what you read and hear about stock mutual funds.

Stock funds are typically classified according to two criteria: market capitalization and investment style.

Market capitalization. This category tells you about the size of the companies in which a fund invests. For an individual stock, market capitalization (or *cap* for short) is equal to the number of shares outstanding multiplied by the current share price. For a fund, the term refers to the median market cap of all the stocks it owns. Stock funds are typically grouped as large-cap, mid-cap, or small-cap. While there is no industry standard for the dollar amounts associated with those terms, fortunately they are fairly intuitive. For example, you can assume that most of the holdings of a large-cap fund will be familiar, big company names. But the fund may also own mid- and small-cap companies. Why should you care about market capitalization? One reason is that it's a risk indicator. As a group, small companies have historically been much more volatile than big companies, and mid-size companies fall in between. So, you're unlikely to want your core stock allocation to consist only of small-cap funds. The other reason to care about market caps is diversification: you want to have some exposure to small-caps and mid-caps because there are times that these smaller stocks perform considerably better than large-cap stocks.

Investment style. Stock funds are also classified in terms of whether they invest primarily in growth or value stocks. If they invest in both, they are called *blend* funds. Growth stocks have the prospects for greater revenue and earnings growth than the average company and generally pay little or nothing in dividends. They are said to have high price-to-earnings ratios (think of this as the *price*, not the share price, but the amount of earnings you buy for each dollar of share price), so investors who buy them are willing to pay a higher price, expecting the company to grow fast enough to warrant an even-higher price in the future. Value stocks, in contrast, represent companies that the market as a whole doesn't expect to grow very fast. These stocks generally have lower price-to-earnings ratios. The idea in value investing is to find companies that are underappreciated or temporarily out of favor with the market and purchase them at a good price.

There are a variety of categorization schemes for stock funds, but the one you'll encounter most often is the style box model depicted

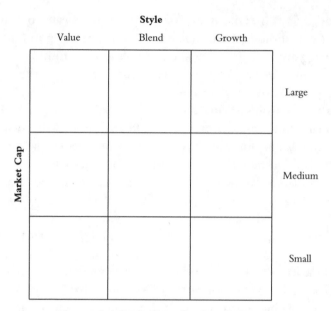

Figure 9.4 Style Box for Stock Funds

in Figure 9.4. I think of the style box categories as fish ponds. If you are investing in stocks for the long term, you'll want to fish in all the ponds. The reason for this is that there will be times when large-cap stocks outperform small-cap stocks (or vice versa) and times when value stocks outperform growth stocks (and vice versa). The idea is to maintain some exposure to all sectors at all times. To keep a hook in every pond, pick a single stock fund that invests broadly across all sectors of the stock market or a number of funds that invest in different sectors.

Some investors have strongly held convictions about value investing or growth investing and will passionately argue the long-term merits of the respective approaches. But over the long run, the returns of growth and value stocks have been pretty similar. I wouldn't recommend a strong bias in either direction. Stay broadly diversified across market capitalization and styles.

So far, we've been focusing on *domestic funds*—those that invest in U.S. stocks. You should consider diversifying your investment program with international funds. These funds invest in the stocks of markets outside the United States, enabling you to gain exposure to the growth opportunities in the rest of the world. Categories of international funds include:

- Global funds, which invest both in the U.S. stock market and in international markets.
- Emerging markets funds, which invest in companies based in developing nations or in countries.
- Regional funds, which emphasize stocks from one part of the world, such as Asia, Latin America, Africa, or Europe.
- Single-country funds, which invest in securities of only one country. Frankly, investing in a single foreign market is really more a form of speculating than investing.

International stocks carry additional risks, including political risk and currency risk. Therefore, I'd suggest that you limit your holdings of international stock funds to no more than 30% of the stock portion of your portfolio.

The final category of equity funds that I'll cover is specialized funds, such as market sector funds, factor, and environmental, social, and governance (ESG) funds. Sector funds invest in a single industry or economic sector, such as real estate, utilities, health care, technology, or gold. These funds are concentrated, so their returns tend to be especially volatile. Therefore, they're not suitable as core holdings in a long-term portfolio. Use sector funds only in moderation, and only if you have carefully researched the risks, and you can stomach volatility and periods of underperformance relative to the broad market.

Bear in mind that there are always one or two sectors doing much better than the stock market as a whole. You probably will feel tempted, because when a particular sector is in favor, its returns will be excellent. But industry sectors inevitably cool off, and, unfortunately, it's usually soon after investors begin to pour large sums into the sector.

Factor funds invest in stocks exhibiting similar characteristics or factors (e.g., momentum, quality, liquidity). Factor funds may be marketed with alluring names, such as *smart beta* or *alternatively weighted index* funds. As with sector funds, investing in factor funds requires patience and fortitude. Performance is typically inconsistent across different economic and market conditions. Further, investors must be able to endure potentially extended periods of underperformance relative to the broad market, much like traditional active funds. Factor funds typically feature higher expense ratios and portfolio-level transaction costs relative to index funds, but lower expense ratios and portfolio-level transaction costs relative to traditional active funds.

Baseline Basics: ESG Funds

ESG stands for environmental, social, and governance, and you'll increasingly encounter this acronym as you do your legwork on evaluating and selecting funds. You might also come across socially responsible investing (SRI), values-based investing, green investing, sustainable investing, and impact investing, among other terms. It is a confusing category, with no universally accepted definitions or consensus among regulators, asset managers, special interest groups, and academics on ESG processes and principles.

For simplicity's sake, I'll use Vanguard's definition: ESG investing is an investment-related activity that accounts for some type of environmental, social, or governance consideration. Let's look at each:

- Environmental criteria: How a company performs as a steward of the natural environment, such as energy use and conservation; emissions and air quality; and waste management.
- Social criteria: The impact of a company on its employees, suppliers, clients, and communities, including its business operations and how it manages and addresses labor and diversity practices, gender equality, and human rights.
- Governance criteria: How a company is governed with respect to executive pay, board diversity, voting rights, financial controls, and risk disclosure.

How ESG manifests itself in the management of funds and ETFs varies. Some index funds and ETFs seek to follow a benchmark that excludes specific stocks (or bonds), such as alcohol distillers, tobacco companies, gun manufacturers, and fossil fuel producers. Some active funds seek to outperform the market by integrating ESG-related risks and opportunities of companies into their selection process. A fund, for instance, might follow ESG guidelines prescribed by the Principles of Responsible Investment, an organization that advocates for ESG investing. Other funds employ an inclusionary strategy—investing in securities that the manager (or index) provider identifies as possessing leading ESG practices or high ESG ratings. For example, a fund that focuses on companies with a demonstrated commitment to sustainable business practices.

If you wish to align your values, beliefs, and/or preferences with your investment program, ESG funds should be in your consideration set. As with other investments, you need to consider a fund's investment objective and strategies, and past performance, cost, tax efficiency, among other factors. There are conflicting opinions on whether ESG funds help or hurt investment performance, but one thing is for certain: Such funds will deliver performance that deviates from the broad market.

Step 3: Actively Managed Funds, Index Funds, or Some of Each?

You can build an investment portfolio using either actively managed funds or index funds—or a mix of both. There are some interesting differences between the two strategies, and their relative merits have provoked a great debate ever since index funds first appeared in the 1970s. Here's my position: Index funds have advantages so powerful that you should use them for the core of your portfolio. Indeed, an all-indexed portfolio can work very well. If you want to invest in actively managed funds, let them play a supporting role. And then, only invest in below-average cost active funds to give yourself a head start on beating the market. Let's look at the differences between the two approaches.

Portfolio Pitfall: Don't Buy a High-Cost Index Fund

I am going to give you a "two-fer" here. First, pay attention to the expense ratio of an index fund. Not all are low cost! You can find a broad market stock index fund charging an expense ratio of under 0.05% ($5 for every $10,000 invested). But some charge ten times that amount. I found two with expense ratios of 0.50% ($50 for every $10,000 invested) or more. Be discerning.

Second, don't buy a higher cost actively managed fund that produces a portfolio that is difficult to distinguish from the benchmark. The industry term for such a strategy is *closet indexing*. While the fund's portfolio may closely resemble the market average, you are destined to receive below-average returns once the higher fees are factored in. Check the fund's R-squared value, which I cover

(continued)

Portfolio Pitfall: Don't Buy a High-Cost Index Fund   (*Continued*)

in the next chapter. R-squared measures the correlation of the fund's returns to the benchmark's returns. If you want to match the market, buy an index fund—not an active fund masquerading as the market.

The manager of an active fund tries to beat the market by selecting specific stocks or bonds. The manager bases decisions not only on education, experience, and market savvy but also on sophisticated security analysis and research on economic, demographic, or other trends.

In contrast, an index fund tries to match—not beat—the market. To do so, the fund buys and holds all (or a large, representative sample) of the securities in an established market benchmark. That might be the S&P 500 Index for domestic stocks, the FTSE Developed All Cap ex U.S. Index for international stocks, the Bloomberg Barclays U.S. Aggregate Bond Index for domestic bonds, or any of dozens of other well-known indexes tracking markets or market segments.

What's so great about index funds? Why do I recommend that you do without the shrewd selection, market savvy, extensive research, and all that? It's because history has shown that, despite those advantages, collectively, active managers don't beat the indexes even half the time. The most obvious, and irrefutable, reason that they don't is costs—the money that active funds have to spend on research, analysis, and trading fees. Index funds have no research expenses and do relatively little trading, so they have a big cost advantage over actively managed funds. That cost advantage translates into a big head start for the investors in index funds. A fund that takes less of a cut from its gross returns to cover its expenses is passing along a bigger portion of the market's return to you.

It's pretty hard to argue against the logic of indexing for a meaningful portion of a serious investment program, but some die-hard proponents of active investing still seek to refute the academic underpinnings and real-world success of the indexing strategy. You may hear them say that index investors are settling for average or mediocre returns. They'll ask you: Why not reach for something better than average by investing in an actively managed fund that tries to beat the indexes? In fact, very few actively managed funds manage to beat their benchmark indexes over meaningful periods of time, as shown in Figure 9.5. The facts suggest that there's a great deal of wisdom in aspiring to be "average." And frugal.

	Blend	Growth	Value
Large	13%	23%	17%
Mid	4%	42%	10%
Small	5%	22%	17%

Performance data reflect periods ending December 31, 2019 (Sources: Vanguard calculations, using data from Morningstar, Inc.). Equity benchmarks are represented by the following indexes—Large blend: MSCI U.S. Prime Market 750 Index through January 30, 2013, CRSP U.S. Large Cap Index thereafter; Large growth: S&P 500/Barra Growth Index through May 16, 2003, MSCI U.S. Prime Market Growth Index through April 16, 2013, CRSP U.S. Large Cap Growth Index thereafter; Large value: S&P 500/Barra Value Index through May 16, 2003, MSCI U.S. Prime Market Value Index through April 16, 2013, CRSP U.S. Large Cap Value Index thereafter; Mid blend: S&P MidCap 400 Index through May 16, 2003, MSCI U.S. Mid Cap 450 Index through January 30, 2013, CRSP U.S. Mid Cap Index thereafter; Mid growth: MSCI US Mid Cap Growth Index through April 16, 2013, CRSP U.S. Mid Cap Growth Index thereafter; Mid value: MSCI U.S. Mid Cap Value Index through April 16, 2013, CRSP U.S. Mid Cap Value Index thereafter; Small blend: Russell 2000 Index through May 16, 2003, MSCI U.S. Small Cap 1750 Index through January 30, 2013, CRSP U.S. Small Cap Index thereafter; Small growth: S&P SmallCap 600/Barra Growth Index through May 16, 2003, MSCI U.S. Small Cap Growth Index through April 16, 2013, CRSP U.S. Small Cap Growth Index thereafter; Small value: S&P SmallCap 600/Barra Value Index through May 16, 2003, MSCI U.S. Small Cap Value Index through April 16, 2013, CRSP U.S. Small Cap Value Index thereafter.

Source: Vanguard calculations, using data from Morningstar, Inc. Fund classifications provided by Morningstar. Data as of December 31, 2019. The figures are not adjusted for survivorship bias and include only funds that survived the entire time period.

**Figure 9.5 Percentage of Actively Managed Stock Funds
Outperforming Indexes (2000–2019)**

Baseline Basics: The Major Market Indexes

You've probably heard the closing figures of the Dow Jones Industrial Averages quoted on the car radio or nightly news programs. The Dow, as it as frequently shorthanded, measures the performance of the stocks of 30 large U.S. companies and covers all industries except transportation and utilities. While the Dow is a widely followed gauge of the U.S. stock market, it is not used commonly as a target benchmark for index funds and ETFs due to its price-weighted construction methodology. The largest and most popular index funds follow benchmarks that are market-capitalization weighted.

(continued)

Baseline Basics: The Major Market Indexes *(Continued)*

This simply means that an index ranks company stocks according to the total market value of their outstanding shares. Here are some common target benchmarks for index funds:

Stock Indexes

Standard & Poor's 500 Index (S&P 500). Tracks large-capitalization stocks, representing about 82% of the value of all U.S. stocks.

Standard & Poor's Completion Index. Tracks the portion of the U.S. stock market not included in the S&P 500 Index.

CRSP U.S. Total Market Index. Tracks the entire U.S. stock market.

Russell 1000 Index. Tracks large-company U.S. stocks.

Russell 2000 Index. Tracks small-company U.S. stocks.

FTSE Global All Cap ex U.S. Index. Tracks stocks of companies located in developed and emerging markets, excluding the United States.

FTSE Developed Europe All Cap Index. Tracks stocks of companies located in 16 European countries, mostly in the United Kingdom, Germany, France, and Switzerland.

FTSE Developed Asia Pacific All Cap Index. Tracks stocks of companies located in Japan, Australia, South Korea, Hong Kong, Singapore, and New Zealand.

S&P 500 Growth Index. Represents a segment of the S&P 500 Index that comprises stocks with higher-than-average ratios of market price to book.

S&P 500 Value Index. Represents a segment of the S&P 500 Index comprising stocks with lower-than-average ratios of market price to book.

Bond Indexes

Bloomberg Barclays U.S. Government Bond Index. Tracks U.S. government agency and Treasury bonds.

Bloomberg Barclays U.S. Corporate Bond Index. Tracks fixed-rate, non-convertible, investment-grade corporate bonds.

Bloomberg Barclays U.S. Mortgage-Backed Securities Index. Tracks fixed-rate securities of the Government National Mortgage Association (GNMA), Federal National Mortgage

Association (FNMA), and Federal Home Loan Mortgage Corporation (FHLMC).

Bloomberg Barclays U.S. Aggregate Bond Index. Tracks the entire taxable U.S. bond market, including Treasury, agency, corporate, mortgage-backed, asset-backed, and international dollar-denominated issues.

Bloomberg Barclays U.S. Corporate High Yield Index. Tracks corporate bonds with credit ratings that are below investment-grade.

Bloomberg Barclays Municipal Bond Index. Tracks investment-grade tax-exempt bonds that are issued by state and local governments.

Step 4: Evaluating a Fund

Let's assume you've determined that you want to invest in a particular fund category. Perhaps it's an intermediate-term Treasury bond fund or a large-cap value stock fund. Now you need to know how to identify and evaluate some funds that could fit the bill.

One sensible approach is to choose a few well-known, reputable fund families and then compare similar funds offered by those firms. Here are some things to keep in mind when you compare.

- **Make sure you understand what you are buying.** Double-check that the fund or funds you are considering are "fishing in the right pond" for your investment objective. There are truth-in-labeling rules for mutual funds, but opinions can differ about what terms like *growth* or *value* mean, or how *high level of income* or *capital appreciation* are defined. You can verify that a fund is doing what you expect by looking at the holdings listed in its latest shareholder report or on the fund pages of the sponsor's website. Make sure that you understand where it invests. Does it also hold U.S. securities? Foreign securities? A combination of both? And make sure that you understand the various risks an investment in the fund entails.

  You can find essential information about a fund's investment policies, strategies, and risks in its prospectus. The prospectus is a legal document, so it is not exactly a breezy read. An abridged version, called a summary prospectus, is also available. I strongly encourage reading the summary prospectus, if not the full prospectus, before investing in any fund. For getting the most out of the effort, see the accompanying Baseline Basics, "Reasons to Read the Prospectus."

- **Choose low-cost funds.** Costs are a drag on your investment returns—the more you're paying, the more of a drag on your returns. We'll talk more about costs in a future chapter. The key point here is that you should always examine a fund's costs before investing in it. You don't have to buy the lowest-cost fund, but you should be very selective in evaluating annual operating costs (called an *expense ratio*), commissions, transaction fees, and account fees.

  I honestly can't think of any reason to invest in any type of fund with above-average expense ratio. Expenses are especially important when you're choosing bond and money market funds. Indeed, with money market funds, it's by far the dominant factor in achieving competitive returns. Since all such funds have to invest largely in the same groups of securities, it's hard for any one of them to pull far ahead of the pack in terms of returns. If you are choosing between two very similar funds, look at their costs.

  Multiple research studies have underscored that high costs lead to inferior returns for investors. Further, a 2002 seminal study by Financial Research Corporation analyzed the predictive value of fund metrics (e.g., alpha, beta, past performance, Morningstar rating, and expense ratio). The researchers concluded a fund's expense ratio was the most reliable predictor of future performance.

- **Gauge the quality of management.** Check to see who manages the fund and how long they've been at it. Experience matters. Throughout the modern era of professional money management, there have always been flashes-in-the-pan who fare incredibly well in a bull market, or make a single prescient call about a bear market, or guess right on a hot market sector. It is actually pretty easy to be right once, but it's much harder to be right consistently over time. To make sure you are entrusting your hard-earned money to fund managers who have proven themselves over time, look up their tenure, experience, and educational background in the prospectus or on the fund sponsor's website.

- **Verify that the fund has pursued its strategy consistently over time.** Has the fund recently changed its manager, portfolio, or basic investment policies? If it has, be sure to find out why. A fund can make money by following any of a number of investment strategies, but it has to follow that strategy consistently and over a long time to succeed for its long-term investors. In the process, the fund will have to weather periods in which its investment approach produces good results and periods when its results are subpar. Sometimes a rocky spell will provoke a fund to change its strategy or manager, but such a shift can prove to be ill-timed. One way to check is to consult Morningstar, whose fund snapshots include the investment style history. (Sometimes funds are reclassified even though they didn't change, so you do need to inquire further.) If you see that a fund's practices or portfolio appear to have changed, feel free to call the fund company and ask why.

- **Is the fund sponsored by a broad and deep and credible organization?** As a prospective investor, you are in effect considering entering into a partnership with a fund provider. Since your goal is establishing a satisfying, long-lasting partnership, you should decide whether you are comfortable with how the company does business before buying any of its funds. There are many fine companies that provide mutual funds and ETFs, but they're certainly not all the same. It can be needlessly risky to buy an off-brand fund when you can obtain the same product from established, high-quality fund sponsors. Might there be an occasion when you would do business with a small or new fund provider because of the specialty products it offers? Sure. But to buy a core bond fund, money market fund, index fund, or balanced fund from a non-mainstream provider makes no sense whatsoever, in my view. You will most likely pay higher costs and receive limited services, and you won't be absolutely sure that the fund provider has the kind of stability a long-term investor needs.

- **Look at past performance.** I began this chapter by saying that past investment performance shouldn't be your first criterion for choosing a fund. But at some point, you'll definitely want to evaluate the performance history of a fund that you're considering. While past returns are no guarantee of future performance, they do provide an indication of how consistent a fund has been and how well it has performed relative to its benchmark and peer funds.

The SEC requires all fund marketing literature, ads, and website pages discussing performance to report one-, five-, and ten-year total returns as of the most recent calendar quarter. One-year returns aren't very meaningful for determining the relative merits of two funds. If you are comparing two funds, look at their returns over a decade. In addition to the ten-year average annual total return, also examine year-by-year returns to gain an understanding of how the funds' performance varied over time. Keep in mind that the underlying financial and economic environment always has an effect on returns. For example, the majority of stock funds benefited from exceptional absolute gains from 2010 onward, but most of them suffered a severe, albeit brief, setback in early 2020 amidst the COVID-19 pandemic.

You will also want to know how a fund compared to its benchmark index and other similar funds. For the actively managed variety, the fund's return relative to its benchmark will tell you whether the fund manager added value over what you could have earned by investing in an index fund. Two caveats: Be sure to compare a fund to the index that is most relevant. (See the Baseline Basics on "The Major Market Indexes.") And remember that an index fund's return will not exactly match the return of its target index because the fund incurs operating costs and transaction expenses while the unmanaged index does not.

- **Check asset size.** There are a few things to garner from checking the amount of assets in a fund. First, a large fund is likely well established and possesses a track record for you to gauge its performance. At the same time, a fund can grow too large, especially if it is performing well and becomes popular with investors. In the case of actively managed funds, if a fund attracts considerable cash in a short period of time, it may hinder the portfolio manager's ability to put that money to work efficiently and effectively. Similarly, the fund many grow to a size that is unwieldy and the manager may not be able to sustain the performance that attracted attention in the first place. In some cases, bigger is not better. Some responsible fund providers will restrict the sales of a fund or close it altogether in order to enable the manager to better execute the fund's strategy.

  One benefit to size is scale. Large funds can spread costs over a larger asset base and pass along the saving resulting from economies of scale in the form of lower expense ratios. (On the flipside, if a fund is new and has a relatively small asset base, it may have a higher expense ratio than peer funds.) However, not all fund sponsors are magnanimous and may choose to maintain a fund's expense ratio at its current level. After all, many fund providers are publicly traded companies seeking to generate profits for the shareholders of its funds, but also owners of its stock.

Baseline Basics: Reasons to Read the Prospectus

When you buy shares in a mutual fund or shares of stock in a corporation, you're not buying mere pieces of paper. You are becoming part-owner of a company. (Remember, a fund is a company, too.) So, when evaluating a possible investment, it's best to think like an owner.

As a potential owner, start by reading a fund's prospectus. I know, *prospectus* sounds like a Latin word meaning dull and boring. However, becoming familiar with the prospectus, and hence the fund, is part of your homework as an investor. In the event that you don't have the time to read the prospectus from front to back, take 10 or 15 minutes to read through it, looking specifically for answers to the questions below. (You'll locate many of them in the "Fund Profile" section near the front of the booklet or in the summary prospectus.) I guarantee you'll be a more informed investor as a result. You can request a prospectus from the fund sponsor or read a PDF version on the sponsor's website. I also recommend reading a fund's shareholder reports. Here is what to look for in the prospectus:

What is the fund's investment objective? Make sure you understand what the fund is trying to accomplish. A money market fund's objective is to provide principal stability. An aggressive growth fund's objective is growth in capital; it is seeking to buy stocks that will rise in value over time. A balanced fund or an equity income fund is likely seeking to produce both current income and long-term capital appreciation.

How will the fund make money for you? Look for the section on investment strategy to learn how the fund manager will try to reach the stated objective. This should tell you the types of securities the fund typically holds, and some basic information about the methods the manager uses to select the securities. If you find the strategy hard to fathom, don't invest until you have asked more questions and gained at least a general understanding of how the fund works.

What risks will you encounter? Read the section about primary risks and take note of everything the prospectus has to say

(continued)

**Baselines Basics: Reasons to Read
the Prospectus** (*Continued*)

about risks. These risks are real; I assure you that the fund company doesn't list them there on a whim! In fact, it is required. But remember, your goal isn't to avoid all risks, but instead to understand the specific risks you'll face. Every fund has some type of risk.

Who's running the fund? The prospectus will include a section about the fund's portfolio manager. You want to know how long the manager has been running the fund; its past results may be less meaningful if the manager has changed recently. How many years has the manager been in the investment business, and what are his or her credentials?

What are you paying? In the standardized fee table, you'll find a full list of the fees and expenses charged by the fund, including its expense ratio and any sales commissions, purchase or redemption fees, low-balance fees, and the like. To help you see the impact, there will be a table illustrating how much these fees would cost you on a hypothetical $10,000 investment in the fund.

How long has the fund been around? There are plenty of sound, established funds with long track records. A newer fund may be a fine investment, but you should be aware that its track record may not be very telling. Further, its results when new and small may be hard to sustain as it gets older and larger. Generally, very large, actively managed funds have a difficult time outperforming their benchmarks.

What services does the fund's sponsor offer? Make sure that the fund's sponsoring company provides the services you want and that you know what they'll cost you. Do you want to have 24 × 7 access to your accounts? Do you want guidance selecting funds? Do you want other services, such as brokerage and charitable giving options?

How has the fund performed? I listed this item last because past performance really is not a good indicator of how a fund will perform for you going forward. The prospectus will tell you a fund's average annual returns for the past one-, five-, and ten-year periods and provides a helpful comparison of those results against a market index as a benchmark. Look at both the pre- and post-tax returns to get a sense of how the fund's income and capital gains distributions may affect your tax bill.

To sum up, here's what you ultimately want in a fund:

- **Low costs.** You can't predict that a high-performing fund will continue to perform well, but you can predict that a high-cost fund will continue to have a heavy drag on its performance. Avoid high-cost funds and focus on funds with below-average expense ratios.
- **Solid performance.** While it's misguided to think that you have to have the top-ranked fund in its category, it does make sense to limit your selections to funds that have ranked in at least the upper half of funds in their category over meaningful periods of time. A caveat: The very top funds in any given period may have taken on extra risk to get stellar returns. Avoid the true stinkers, too. Bottom-quartile performers tend to stay at the bottom of the long-term performance rankings. The reason is that those funds tend to have the highest operating costs, and those will be an ongoing anchor weighing on performance.
- **Consistent performance.** You want a fund that has relatively predictable relative returns in the past. If a fund's returns seem erratic compared with those of peers having similar investment objectives, it could signal a lack of discipline in adhering to the fund's stated policies and strategies.

In a Nutshell

To construct a sensible portfolio, follow this four-step process:

- **Determine your asset mix.** How will you allocate your dollars among stocks, bonds, and cash?
- **Allocate your dollars within those asset categories.** What kinds of stock funds, bond funds, and money market funds will you pick?
- **Weigh indexing and active management.** Will you invest in index funds, actively managed funds, or some of both?
- **Compare and evaluate specific funds.** Of the funds that are in the categories you're seeking, which offer low costs, a solid record of long-term returns, and consistent performance?

10

It's What You Keep That Counts

I nvesting is an inherently risky activity and full of uncertainty. In truth, we, as individual investors, have no control over the market forces and economic cycles that affect the performance of our investments. But we do have control over a few important things, and those will be the focus of this chapter and the next.

In investing, it is what you keep that counts. And what you keep has everything to do with three simple things: (1) what your investments earn; (2) the costs you pay your investment provider; and (3) the taxes that you pay on your earnings. Figure 10.1 demonstrates the considerable impact of costs and taxes on a hypothetical fund account. It underscores that the bottom line is your profit after costs and after taxes.

All investments have costs. Most gains get taxed sooner or later. You can't avoid costs and taxes altogether, but there are some steps you can take to minimize the bite, and you don't need an accounting or law degree to do so. If you keep a few simple things in mind when you structure your investment program, you'll be able to keep more of your returns. In this chapter, I'll explain:

- How to choose low-cost, tax-efficient funds.
- How to avoid behavior that hurts you on taxes and costs.
- How to be judicious about which kinds of funds you hold in your tax-advantaged accounts and which ones you hold in your taxable accounts.

	Income
Gross investment gain (10% before expenses)	$1,000.00
-Fund expenses (0.63% of $10,500 average account balance)*	−66.15
Net investment gain	$933.85
− Income tax (30%)	−280.16
After-tax profit	**$653.69**

* 0.63% was the average asset-weighted expense ratio for all mutual funds (excluding ETFs) in 2019 according to Morningstar.

Figure 10.1 How Costs and Taxes Impact Investment Returns on Hypothetical $10,000 Investment

Source: Vanguard

The Lowdown on Lower Costs

When I entered the fund business in 1982, it was commonplace for mutual funds to charge sales commissions of 5% or more on share purchases. Back-end loads, when you get nicked 1% or 2% for selling fund shares, were also common. The average expense ratio for stock funds (not counting the sales loads) was 1.07% ($107 on a $10,000 investment)—very high by today's standards when you can own a broad stock index fund for as low as 0.03% ($3 on a $10,000 investment).

Over the past 40 years, costs have fallen dramatically and—for the sharp and more discerning investor—pose much less of a formidable obstacle today. Why? Among the reasons: competition among fund firms, a more educated consumer, and the growing adoption of lower-cost products like index funds and exchange-traded funds (ETFs). As a result, the majority of investors' assets are now in lower cost funds. At year-end 2019, equity mutual funds with expense ratios in the lowest quartile held 80% of the total assets of equity mutual funds' net assets, while those with expense ratios in the remaining quartiles held only 20% (Source: Investment Company Institute).

And mutual fund investors usually pay "below sticker" price (Figure 10.2). The simple average expense ratio of equity mutual funds (the average for all equity mutual funds) was 1.24% in 2019. The asset-weighted average expense ratio for equity mutual funds (the average shareholders actually paid) was far lower, at 0.52%. That's a tribute to investors

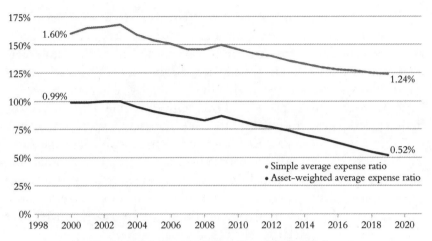

Figure 10.2 Investors Pay Less Than Sticker

Source: Investment Company Institute

and their continually growing awareness of cost as a core part of the investment equation.

Costs: Are You Leaving Too Much on the Table?

Despite costs coming down across the industry and the broad availability of low-cost funds, you, as a financial entrepreneur, need to be vigilant about costs. Many investment firms want you to ignore what they charge you. Their marketing campaigns dwell on investment performance or star rankings, as if these have value beyond price. Meanwhile, some investors lose track of the total amount they're paying as their financial provider layers on charges, or lures them in with low costs on some offerings, only to charge much higher costs on other products. Many individual investors don't give nearly as much attention to costs as other factors. It's unfortunate to see people work so hard to get the money to invest and then be so careless about costs. They might as well be walking around with big holes in their investment buckets.

If someone tells you that costs don't matter, ask him or her why institutional investors—pension funds, endowments and the like—negotiate so fiercely with investment firms to keep management expenses and advisory costs low. Institutional investors have long understood that costs eat into investment returns and that the effects are magnified over time by compounding.

There's plenty of other proof that costs matter. Returning to the study cited in Chapter 9 by the Financial Research Corporation, expense ratios are the only factor that can be reliably linked to the future performance of mutual funds. Researchers examined ten characteristics of mutual funds to determine whether they could have been used to predict how the funds actually performed over a given period. The characteristics included past performance, Morningstar ratings, expenses, turnover, manager tenure, net sales, asset size, and four risk/volatility measures. The researchers examined five broad fund categories and found that funds with lower expenses delivered "above-average future performance across nearly all time periods." The study called lower expense ratios an "exceptional predictor" for bond funds and a "good predictor" for stock funds.

It's a fact of life that all funds have costs, but some funds are much more expensive to own than others. The average mutual fund expense ratio was 0.63% in 2019, but there were funds out on the market charging as much as 2.00%. Some funds also levy sales charges or other fees on top of their expense ratios. According to the Investment Company Institute, 45% of equity funds feature a share class with a sales charge.

Examine Fund Expense Ratios

All the fees and expenses you pay reduce your investment returns directly because they are deducted before you receive your return. Every mutual fund has an expense ratio, which it has to report publicly. The ratio represents the percentage of the fund's assets that were used to pay operating expenses in a given period. The expenses covered include legal and accounting services; telephone service, postage, printing, and other administrative costs; and investment management expenses. All of these expenses are subtracted from the fund's gross investment return before you, the shareholder, see any of it.

Most actively managed funds have an expense ratio between 0.50% and 1.5%, which translates into $50 to $150 a year on an investment of $10,000. You should expect to pay slightly above-average expenses for actively managed funds that require significant investment management resources and research, for example, aggressive, small company funds and international funds. But be skeptical about any fund whose expense ratio is higher than its category average. You can expect to pay much lower expense ratios for index funds and ETFs, some as low as 0.02% or 0.03% (or $2 or $3 on a $10,000 investment).

Baseline Basics: Rules of Thumb on Expense Ratios

Here are general rules when it comes to the expense ratios of fund categories:

* Stock funds generally have higher expense ratios than bond funds.
* Small-cap stock funds generally have higher expense ratios than large-cap funds.
* International and global funds generally have higher expense ratios than domestic funds.
* Actively managed funds generally have higher expenses than index funds and index-based ETFs.
* Mutual funds generally have higher expense ratios than ETFs.

"But It's Just a Few Percentage Points . . ."

Perhaps you're tempted to think that a difference of a percentage point or so is hardly worth worrying about. Many investors likely paid little attention to their funds' expense ratios during the 2010s when stocks experienced double-digit gains in seven of ten years. When you're seeing double-digit returns, an expense ratio of 1% or 1.5% may well seem trifling. Costs become more punitive as returns become more average. On a gross gain of 20%, a 1% expense ratio is eating up one-twentieth of your return. On a gross return of 5%, a 1% expense ratio is consuming one-fifth of your return. Costs matter at all times, but especially in a lower return environment and lower return investment categories like money markets and bonds.

Over the long run, even small costs have a big impact. Remember compounding? It magnifies not only returns, but the damage of costs, too. Figure 10.3 shows the impact of costs over time on a hypothetical $10,000 investment in three funds:

* Fund A is an index fund with an expense ratio of 0.05%.
* Fund B is an actively managed fund with an expense ratio of 0.65%.
* Fund C is a higher cost actively managed fund with an expense ratio of 1.25%.

After 20 years, Fund A would have grown to $46,146, more than accumulated in the moderate cost Fund B ($40,910) and considerably

	Fund A	Fund B	Fund C
Initial investment	$10,000	$10,000	$10,000
Value after. . .			
5 years	$14,657	$14,222	$13,798
10 years	$21,482	$20,226	$19,037
15 years	$31,485	$28,766	$26,267
20 years	$46,146	$40,910	$36,242

Figure 10.3 How Costs Affect Returns Over Time

Source: Vanguard, using the SEC Cost Calculator (https://www.sec.gov/investor/tools/mfcc/get-started.htm). This example assumes an 8% annual return, reinvestment of dividends, and annual compounding of net expenses.

more than Fund C ($36,242). Which of the three funds would you rather have entrusted your money? The low-cost fund produced extra returns approximately equal to the original investment. Costs matter.

As an investor, you put up the capital and you take the risk. It makes sense to minimize costs so that you—not the investment provider—will earn the bulk of the returns. The bottom line: Choose low-cost funds.

You Can Look It Up

How do you find out about fees, expense ratios, turnover rates, and other salient fund characteristics so that you can make a thoughtful comparison? Fortunately, it's easy. You can look all of these up in the fund's prospectus, in its annual and semi-annual reports to shareholders, or in information provided by companies such as Morningstar. You can also check the fund sponsor's website or app. Or, call the company and ask. The SEC offers a helpful cost calculator for you to make comparison of fund costs (https://www.sec.gov/investor/tools/mfcc/get-started.htm).

As noted in the previous chapter, prospectuses are a particularly good source because the SEC requires mutual funds to disclose all fees and expenses in a standardized table placed near the front of the document. The fee table shows all expenses that an investor would pay on a hypothetical $10,000 investment at the end of one, three, five, and ten years, assuming a 5% annual return.

Baseline Basics: Understanding Costs

The expense ratio is likely going to be the single largest cost associated with owning funds and ETFs. But there are other costs associated with fund investing, especially if you are investing in funds through an intermediary, such as a broker, an investment advisor, a financial planner, an insurance agent, or a bank representative. All these professionals deserve to be paid, of course, but sometimes they get their money indirectly.

- **Front-end load.** A sales commission paid when you buy shares of a fund. For example, if you invest $20,000 in a fund that charges a 5% front-end load, it means in effect that you are starting out with a $1,000 loss. Only $19,000 of your $20,000 is invested for you, and you'll need to earn 5.3% on that $19,000 in the first year just to get back to your initial investment. (Some firms also charge commissions to buy ETFs, although these have largely been eliminated at the largest brokerage firms.)
- **Back-end load.** A sales commission paid when an investor sells mutual fund shares and sometime referred to as a *contingent deferred sales charge*. Some funds gradually phase out back-end loads for investors who remain in the fund for several years.
- **Transaction fee.** A purchase or redemption fee is used to cover the transaction costs incurred by the fund when investors buy or sell shares. These fees, which are typically modest, are not compensation paid to the professional selling the fund. Instead, they compensate all fund shareholders for fund transaction costs and fairly charge them to investors causing those costs. Thus, they can be a good thing.
- **12b-1 fee.** A 12b-1 fee is a method of charging marketing and distribution-related expenses directly against fund assets. (The term refers to the SEC rule that permits the practice.) Nearly half of all mutual funds charge 12b-1 fees, typically keeping a chunk of the money themselves and passing along a portion of it to the professional who sold the fund to you. You'll see a fund's 12b-1 fee listed as part of its expense ratio, and they normally run between 0.25% and 1% of the fund's net assets. If you are charged a 12b-1 fee of 0.50%, you are paying $50 a year for every $10,000 in your account.
- **Fee waiver.** Some funds waive management fees or administrative costs to make the fund appear more cost competitive and to boost a

(continued)

Baseline Basics: Understanding Costs *(Continued)*

fund's yield and total return. Most of these waivers are temporary. Be careful about pursuing stock and bond funds employing fee waivers; when the waiver ends and you want to move your money out, you could find yourself confronting capital gains taxes that wipe out any savings as a result of the waiver. (Note that money market funds may waive expenses, especially in periods of very low interest rates, in order to keep their yields above zero. In this case, a fee waiver is welcome.)

Figure 10.4 gives an example of a representative fee table. In this case, the fund offers multiple share classes, each with distinct cost structures that feature varying expense ratios and loads. The dollar amounts you'll pay over various time periods are also shown under two scenarios—if you hold onto the fund shares and if you sell fund shares. As you can see, Class I shares, featuring an expense ratio of 0.99% and no sales charge, will be less damaging to your portfolio over time. In general, avoid funds with complicated fee structures and be equally wary of brokers pushing no-load funds with high expense ratios.

The prospectus fee table enables you to compare fund costs; the hypothetical examples enable you to see costs in dollar terms. Note that the prospectus fee table may include compensation paid to an investment advisor or financial planner, such as a commission or 12b-1 fee. It does not reflect other advisor-related fees, such as asset-based fees or hourly charges paid to a financial advisor.

Putting Costs in Perspective

Despite all of the disclosure on fund costs, it may be difficult to determine the dollar amount you are paying on your fund investments. Indeed, mutual funds are not required to send you a monthly bill like your electric company, streaming service, and cell phone provider. But it may help to put your investment costs in perspective by considering them as just another monthly payment.

One challenge in doing so is that your account balance varies from month to month, and each of your funds charge a different expense ratio. You can do the math on your own; simply take your balance and multiply

SHAREHOLDER FEES (Fees paid directly from your
local investment)

	Class A	Class C	Class I
Maximum Sales Charge (Load) Imposed on Purchases as % of the Offering Price	5.25%	None	None
Maximum Deferred Sales Charge (Load) as % of Original Cost of the Shares	None	1.00%	None
		(under $1 million)	

ANNUAL FUND OPERATING EXPENSES (Expenses you pay
each year as a percentage of the value of your investment)

	Class A	Class C	Class I
Management Fees Distribution (Rule 12b-1)	0.68%	0.68%	0.68%
Fees	0.25	0.75	None
Other Expenses	0.42	0.43	0.41
Service Fees	0.25	0.25	0.25
Remainder of Other Expenses	0.17	0.18	0.16
Total Annual Fund Operating Expenses	1.35	1.86	1.09
Fee Waivers and/or Expense Reimbursements	(0.11)	(0.12)	(0.1)
Total Annual Fund Operating Expenses After Fee Waivers and/or Expense Reimbursements	1.24	1.74	0.99

Figure 10.4 Prospectus Fee Table for Hypothetical Equity Fund

by the fund's expense ratio: $50,000 × 0.05% = $25. We show in Figure 10.5 the dollar costs for various funds that comprise a $150,000 portfolio.

Another useful tool is the FINRA Fund Analyzer, which can help you determine the impact of costs on funds and ETFs. You can input your investment amount, rate of return, and holding period; the tool will then calculate your future investment balance and total costs. You can find it here: https://tools.finra.org/fund_analyzer/.

Fund	Balance	Expense Ratio	Your Cost
Equity Fund A	$50,000	0.05%	$25
Equity Fund B	$30,000	0.70%	$210
Equity Fund C	$20,000	0.89%	$178
Bond Fund A	$25,000	0.17%	$42.50
Bond Fund B	$15,000	0.62%	$93
Money Market Fund	$10,000	0.26%	$26
Total			**$574.50**

Figure 10.5 Putting Costs in Perspective

This exercise puts the percentages of expense ratios into real dollars and cents, enabling you to get a better handle on what you're paying your fund provider. If you're working with a financial advisor who charges an asset-based fee of 1% per year, you would pay an additional $1,500 in fees on your $150,000 portfolio. As a result, your total all-in costs would be more than $2,000 (i.e., $575 in fund costs and $1,500 in advice costs).

Be Aware of Transaction Costs Paid by the Fund

Funds incur transaction costs when they buy and sell securities. Brokerage commissions are one type of transaction cost. Another cost occurs as a result of the bid–ask spread, or difference between the bid price and ask price for a particular security. These are not explicitly stated costs like the expense ratio, but they create a drag on investment returns all the same. The costs associated with buying and selling securities are reflected in the fund's performance and are hard to quantify precisely. The more frequently a fund buys and sells securities, the higher its transaction costs are likely to be. Keeping these costs down is one of the advantages of index funds, which do relatively little trading relative to actively managed funds.

There's a simple way get a sense for whether a fund incurs higher than normal transaction costs and, thus, likely produces high taxable capital gains, too. To find out how frequently a fund buys and sells, look up its *turnover rate*, which is a measure of trading activity and reported in fund materials and fund sponsor websites. If a mutual fund has turnover rate of 100%, it means that the average holding period for its stocks was one year. Some funds have turnover rates as high as 300% to 400%. At the other extreme, some funds have turno-ver rates as low as 5%, meaning that, on average, they hold stocks for 20 years. Keep in mind that a high turnover rate doesn't necessarily mean you should skip the fund. Aggressively managed funds may do a considerable amount of buying and selling as part of fulfilling their stated objectives.

The side effect of frequent trading at the fund level is the potential for realizing profits from the sale of fund securities. That sounds great, until you recognize that you're on the hook for paying taxes on the gains distributed by the fund. I'll cover taxes as an investment cost in the next section.

Taxes Are Costs, Too

Most mutual fund managers focus on maximizing the pre-tax returns they provide to their investors, so it's up to you to pay attention to your after-tax returns. As a fund investor, you can minimize your tax bill in three ways, which I cover in the following section.

Resist the Temptation to Trade Frequently

One of the old jokes in the investment business is that the quickest way to make a small fortune is to start with a large fortune and trade it a lot. It's all too true, and taxes are one of the reasons. If you trade your fund or ETF shares frequently, you may be incurring big tax liabilities. A quick refresher: When you sell some or all of your shares at a profit, or you exchange shares of one fund for shares of another, you can reap a capital gain on which you'll have to pay taxes. Just how much you owe will be determined by your tax bracket and the length of time that you held the shares.

For example, if you buy 100 shares of Fund ABC for $20 a share and sell them all 6 months later for $22 a share, you will owe short-term capital gains taxes on your $200 profit. If you're in the 24% marginal tax bracket, that's $48 you must pay to the government. However, if you hold onto the shares for more than 12 months before selling them, your profit is considered a long-term capital gain. Then it will be taxed at a maximum rate of 20%, so you'll owe no more than $40. The current U.S. tax code rewards patience.

Baseline Basics: Taxes and Mutual Funds

As a mutual fund investor, you can incur taxes in three ways:

- When the fund distributes income dividends. These distributions reflect all interest and dividend income earned by the fund's holdings—whether cash investments, bonds, or stocks—after the fund's operating expenses are subtracted.
- When the fund distributes capital gains from the sale of securities. These reflect the profit the fund makes when it sells securities. A fund is said to *realize* a capital gain when it makes such a profit. It realizes a capital loss when it sells securities at a price lower than it paid. If a fund's total capital gains are greater than its total capital losses, it has net realized capital gains, which are distributed to fund shareholders.
- When you sell or exchange fund shares at a profit.

You must pay taxes on distributions regardless of whether you receive them in cash or reinvest them in additional fund shares. There are a couple of exceptions. Interest income from U.S. Treasury securities is exempt from state income taxes, and interest income from municipal bond funds, whose interest income is exempt from federal income tax and may also be exempt from state taxes.

An important factor in how much taxes you owe on these distributions is the holding period—that is, how long the fund held the securities before they were sold. Securities sold for a profit within one year are called *short-term capital gains* and those sold after a year would be *long-term capital gains*.

Your mutual fund will provide you with the information you need to report these distributions properly at tax time. Income (such as interest and dividends) and short-term capital gains are currently taxed as ordinary income at your marginal tax rate, from 10% to 37%, depending on your overall income and your marital filing status in 2020. Long-term capital gains are taxed at a maximum rate of 20%. (A taxpayer with less than $40,000 in adjusted gross income pays no capital gains tax.)

Choose Tax-Efficient Funds

Most investors don't realize it, but a fair portion of their pre-tax returns on U.S. stock funds ultimately goes into federal income tax coffers, not into their pockets, unless those returns are sheltered in a tax-advantaged account. This is a particularly important issue for people in high tax brackets.

How can this be? It's because mutual funds have to distribute to you any income or capital gains they receive from the securities they own, which then become *your* income or capital gains. You don't feel the tax pinch until you file your annual return; that's why many people never make the connection.

Tax-efficiency of mutual funds caught on in the 1990s, when economic researchers first realized that the way a fund was managed could have a big impact on shareholders' taxes. Fortunately, funds are required to disclose the likely effect of taxes on their returns. To report these after-tax returns, a fund applies current tax rates to the income and capital gains it distributed during a given period, and also to the gain (or loss) that an investor would have realized by selling shares. You can find this information on the fund's website, as well as the fund's prospectus or annual report. The tax burden may not matter much to you when fund returns are generally high, but in slumping markets you may find it galling to owe capital gains taxes on distributions from a fund that is losing money.

Figure 10.6 shows the impact of taxes on two Vanguard stock funds: Vanguard Explorer Fund and Vanguard Total Stock Market Index Fund. While it is a somewhat apples-to-pineapples comparison (i.e., matching an actively managed small-cap fund to an all-market index fund), I want to make the point clear on tax efficiency. As you can see, the *returns after taxes on distributions* on the actively managed fund are far lower than the *returns before taxes* over all time periods. You lose far less in the index fund, by comparison.

Though most funds are not managed with the goal of keeping taxes low, some are more tax-efficient, either inherently or by design. There

	1-yr	3-yr	5-yr	10-yr
Vanguard Explorer Fund Investor Shares				
Returns before taxes	13.58%	12.05%	13.61%	13.05%
Returns after taxes on distributions	12.29%	9.53%	11.30%	11.14%
Return percentage retained after taxes on distributions	91%	79%	83%	85%

	1-yr	3-yr	5-yr	10-yr
Vanguard Total Stock Market Index Fund Admiral Shares				
Returns before taxes	14.99%	11.64%	13.68%	13.48%
Returns after taxes on distributions	14.47%	11.13%	13.14%	12.99%
Return percentage retained after taxes on distributions	97%	96%	96%	96%

Data as of 09/30/2020

Figure 10.6 Assessing Pre– and Post-Tax Returns

Source: Vanguard

are two types of funds to consider if you are looking for something that is tax-friendly:

- **Stock index funds and ETFs**—especially those tied to broad market indexes—are generally very tax-efficient because of their buy-and-hold practices. Their turnover is typically very low, but they do distribute capital gains on occasion—for example, when a stock is removed from the target index and thus must be sold by the fund. If this gain cannot be offset by realized losses, a fund is forced to make a distribution. A caveat for the record: In theory, stock index funds could be forced to realize sizable capital gains if hordes of investors decided to redeem their shares, say, during a severe market downturn. Thankfully, most index funds investors are buy-and-holders and this phenomenon has not materialized in any of the challenging markets environments that we've experienced in the past few decades. (Note that bond index funds aren't very tax-efficient because over the long term their returns are based on income, not capital gains.) Stock ETFs benefit from an in-kind transaction feature at the portfolio level that all but eliminates gains in most cases.
- **Tax-exempt funds**, also known as *municipal* or *muni* bond funds, generate income that is exempt from federal income tax, and in some cases from state and local income taxes as well. However, I want to emphasize that muni bond funds are not for everyone. The trade-off is that muni bonds normally have lower yields than taxable bond funds. Generally, you won't benefit from holding munis unless you are in the 30% tax bracket or higher.

To figure out whether to invest in a muni bond fund or a comparable taxable bond fund, you have to do a few simple calculations. Over the years, I've seen a number of investors choose muni funds without bothering to do the numbers, and most of them are hurting themselves by doing so. Those taxpayers were so determined to avoid taxes that they were investing in lower-yielding muni bonds even though they didn't benefit from the tax exemption. They could have earned higher returns for themselves by investing at least some of that money in taxable bond funds.

So, do the numbers for yourself before you invest in a municipal bond fund. You need to look at something called the *taxable-equivalent yield*. You get that by doing a bit of math, using the formula below, that is more complicated to describe than it is to perform.

<u>Muni Bond Yield</u>

$$\text{Taxable Equivalent Yield} = 1.00 - (\text{your tax rate})$$

Let me walk you through it. First, convert your combined state and federal tax rate to a decimal form (a 30% tax rate becomes 0.30, for example). Then, subtract the decimal figure from 1.00 (in our example, $1.00 - 0.30 = 0.70$). Next, divide your result into the muni fund's yield. In our example, if the muni yield was 2%, you would divide that by 0.70: $2\% \div 0.70 = 2.86\%$. This tells us that the muni bond fund has a taxable equivalent yield of 2.86%. You will now have an apples-to-apples comparison when sizing up the yield of a municipal bond fund to yields of taxable bond funds.

Use Taxable and Tax-Advantaged Accounts Wisely

Asset location is a fancy sounding term that has become an increasingly important investment issue over the years. The idea is that you need to think about the tax sensitivity of your overall portfolio and choose the right "location"—a tax-advantaged or a taxable account—in which to hold assets.

The tax laws make it smart to hold certain kinds of investments in taxable accounts and others in tax-advantaged accounts, such as 401(k) plans and IRAs. The first point to make about retirement accounts is that, since taxes are not being paid along the way, your money can grow faster in these accounts. (With a Roth IRA you won't pay any taxes in the future, assuming you follow the rules.) That's one reason you should contribute the maximum you can to such tax-advantaged accounts.

But there's an additional wrinkle to consider if you're interested in minimizing your current taxes. Your overall investment plan may include funds more liable to incur taxes than others. Which funds tend to be less tax-efficient? Remember that income distributions and short-term capital gains are taxed at a higher rate than long-term capital gains. Consequently, bond funds and income-oriented stock funds that pay dividends, as well as very aggressive stock funds with high turnover rates, can increase your tax bill. If possible, hold these kinds of funds in your retirement plan or your IRA.

In a Nutshell

There's little you can do to influence the future performance of your investments, but you can exercise control over what you're giving up in costs and taxes. Follow these tips to improve your bottom line as an investor:

- **Choose funds with low expense ratios.** The average mutual fund expense ratio was 0.63% in 2019, but there are funds that charge much less. Favor funds with lower expense ratios.
- **Resist the temptation to trade frequently.** In a taxable account, frequent trading can carry tax consequences. Even without this tariff, it is difficult to trade your way to wealth.
- **Pay attention to asset location.** Be strategic in deciding which kinds of funds to hold in tax-advantaged accounts and which to hold in taxable accounts.

11

Risk: Give It the Gut Test

I've been talking a lot so far about the long-term rewards that you can reap as an investor if you are willing to accept a prudent and comfortable level of risk. Investing in money market funds instead of keeping your money in the bank is one example of taking a prudent risk that carries worthwhile rewards—the rewards being relatively higher income on your cash investments. In this case, the risk is minimal. But another example of prudence is choosing to invest your long-term retirement assets in a well-diversified stock fund instead of keeping them entirely in a money market fund. Though the stock market is definitely risky, most long-term investors find that the potential rewards are well worth the risk, as long as they take care to diversify and have the fortitude to ride out periods of volatility. In both of these investment scenarios, risk is an ally in your effort to increase your wealth.

Risk can be both friend and foe, so prudent investors pay careful attention to it when they construct a portfolio. In this chapter, I'll focus on two aspects of managing risk:

- How to understand the level of risk in your overall portfolio and to avoid worrying over the risks of specific holdings. The reason for taking a holistic view is that the risk factors of some holdings can be mitigated by those of other holdings. For example, the price stability and income of money market funds serve to offset some of the volatility of stock prices.

- How to assess whether the level of risk is one that you can tolerate. There are a variety of statistical tools and historical data you can use to measure the risks of investments, but ultimately, your gut is the simple, and likely most accurate, test of your risk tolerance.

Your Investment Risk

In its broadest sense, your investment risk is the chance that you ultimately won't have sufficient money to meet your long-term goal of a comfortable retirement or a college education for your kids. But another way to think of risk is in terms of how you tolerate the price declines of your funds and account balance that you'll experience from time to time as you pursue your goals. If you can't bear the inevitable bumps in the road, you won't stick with your investment program long enough to meet your goal. So, you have to weigh the trade-off—the risk of falling short of your goals against the risk of declines along the way.

Risk is not always apparent, but finance experts have sought diligently to define and quantify it. They have come up with all kinds of names for specific aspects of risk; see the Baseline Basics, "The Risk Monster Is a Many-Headed Beast," for a long list of those terms. Researchers have also developed mathematical measurements for certain kinds of financial risk. These measures have daunting names, but they're not really all that complicated to understand and apply. They focus on how volatile a stock or a fund was over a past period of time or how closely its returns matched those of the overall market. While these numbers can be useful when you are comparing funds, they have some flaws, as I'll explain in a moment. So, feel free to skip to the next section of this chapter if you're simply not interested in knowing about them.

- **Standard deviation** measures how much a fund's returns have bounced around its average return over the past three years. Suppose, for example, that Fund A posts annual returns of −5%, +10%, and +25%. Over the three years, that means an average annual return of +10%, with a standard deviation of 15. Fund B returns +5%, +10%, and +15%. It too earns an average return of +10%, but its standard deviation is just 5. Based on standard deviation, Fund A has been three times as risky as Fund B.

- **Beta** measures how sensitive a fund has been to the performance of the broad market. For stock funds, beta is generally measured relative to the S&P 500 Index or the Wilshire 5000 Total Market Index. For most bond funds, the mark is the Bloomberg Barclays Aggregate Bond Index. A beta of 1.0 means that the fund has moved in lockstep with the market. A beta of 1.5 means that the fund has been much more volatile than the market; it has tended to gain 1.5% for every 1% rise in the market and, very importantly, lose 1.5% for every 1% decline in the market. On the other hand, a fund with a beta of 0.50 is notably less volatile than the benchmark. Unfortunately, a fund's beta isn't helpful if the fund has little in common with the benchmark it is being measured against. That's where R-squared comes in.
- **R-squared** measures the degree to which a fund's returns go up and down at the same time as the market. (Again, the market is defined in terms of an appropriate index.) R-squared can range from 0 to 1.00—0 for a fund that doesn't match the market movements at all, and 1.00 for a fund that is always up when the market is up and down when the market is down. An R-squared of less than 0.70 suggests a low correlation between a fund and the relevant market to which it is being compared.

None of these measures should be your primary gauge for investment risk. One weakness they share is that they are based on what happened in the past, and the conditions that existed then may not apply anymore. Another weakness is that they cannot be easily used for assessing the overall risk level of a portfolio, especially one that includes a mix of stock, bond, and money market investments.

Portfolio Pitfall: Don't Let Fear of Loss Keep You Out of the Market

On occasion, I talk to someone who is so risk-averse that he or she is afraid to invest at all. Even during the strong bull market we had after the Global Financial Crisis in 2008–2009, there were investors who knew that they should invest in stocks to reach their long-term goals and had plenty of time to do so, but were paralyzed by the fear that another downturn could wipe them out.

Over the long term, avoiding risk to this degree is itself extremely dangerous if you have any hope to accumulate wealth.

(continued)

Portfolio Pitfall: Don't Let Fear of Loss Keep You Out of the Market   (*Continued*)

If you don't put at least some of your money into stocks or bonds, you won't be able to stay ahead of inflation. You'll wind up with an account balance that looks bigger than it used to be, but buys less.

Many risk-averse investors find a measure of comfort in a balanced fund of stocks and bonds. A balanced fund is a middle-of-the-road investment that seeks to provide a combination of growth, income, and conservation of capital. Another useful tactic is to start out slowly—take risk a sip at a time, so to speak. Time is your friend, a concept we will cover in Chapter 14.

Duration: A Risk Measure for Bonds

In Chapter 9, I discussed the *average maturity* of bond funds. That's a good thing to know, but a statistic called *duration*, while much more sophisticated, is an even better one. Knowing a bond fund's average duration will enable you to get a bead on its interest rate risk—how much the share price will change when market interest rates fluctuate.

Average duration is expressed in years, but it is not really a measure of time. Instead, it tells you how much a bond fund's share price will rise or fall for each percentage point change in market interest rates. For example, if interest rates rise by 1 percentage point, a fund with an average duration of five years will see its share price fall by about 5%. And if interest rates fall 1 percentage point, the fund's share price will rise by about 5%.

Calculating a bond fund's average duration involves computing the cash flows from interest payments on the fund's holdings. In short, it's complex. Fortunately, you don't have to calculate duration; you can get the information from the fund company. Once you have the statistic, you can easily use it to compare different bond funds. And it's smart to compare, as even two funds with similar average maturities can have significantly different average durations.

Following is an illustration of the risk/return trade-off in bonds, based on the actual yields of three low-cost U.S. Treasury funds in June 2020. In reading the table in Figure 11.1, remember that average duration lets you estimate how much a fund's price will move up or down for a given increase or decrease in interest rates. So, if market interest

Treasury Funds	Yield	Average Duration (in years)	Impact of a 1% Rise in Rates on NAV
Short-term	0.30%	2.10	−2.1%
Intermediate-term	0.40%	5.10	−5.1%
Long-term	1.30%	18.50	−18.5%

Figure 11.1 Bond Funds and Duration

Source: Vanguard. Data as of June 30, 2020.

rates were to rise 1 percentage point, the price decline would be about 18.5% for the long-term Treasury fund, 5.1% for the intermediate-term fund, and 2.1% for the short-term fund.

The intermediate-term Treasury bond fund offered 0.10% percentage points more in yield than the short-term Treasury fund, or approximately 33% more income from each dollar invested. But to get that increase in yield, an investor had to take on more than twice as much interest rate risk—a duration of 5.1 years versus 2.1 years. The long-term Treasury fund's 1.3% yield would result in about 225% more income, but the duration figure shows that it has more than triple the interest rate risk of the intermediate-term fund.

Higher interest rate risk may not be a big concern for long-term investors, who can overlook short-term price declines for the sake of earning higher yields from intermediate- and long-term bonds. If interest rates were to rise, and the share price of the bond fund fell, the investor would have the consolation of having reinvested income put to work at higher yields. A $1,000 investment held for 10 years, with income reinvested, grows to $1,030 at a 0.3% annual yield, to $1,040 at a 0.4% yield, and to $1,138 at a 1.3% yield. It is fair to point out that the second and now the third decades of the century have been marked by unusually low interest rates. Some observers would say that there is no place for rates to go but up. When this happens is anyone's guess. (We will address this topic in greater depth in the Postscript.)

As this example clearly shows, most of the opportunity for gaining additional yield came from going from intermediate- to long-term bonds, rather than from moving from short-term bonds to intermediate-term bonds. In any case, the idea is to examine trade-offs so you can make an informed judgment about the balance between risk and reward. Investors who reach for higher yields need to be sure they're comfortable with the significant additional risk involved.

A Simple Way to Check a Fund's Past Volatility

For a simple gauge of a fund's volatility, just look at its past returns, preferably over a long period. Keep in mind that a fund that is volatile when it is experiencing gains is likely to be volatile on the downside, too. I can illustrate this point with Vanguard Growth Index Fund. As Figure 11.2 shows, if you were thinking about investing in this fund at the beginning of 2008, you might have found its previous three years of positive returns very encouraging. But in 2008, the fund suffered a sharp decline, followed in 2009 with a considerable gain. Not all funds are subject to such variations in returns. As a general rule, growth, aggressive growth, and international stock funds are more likely to have more volatile returns.

The Gut Test

Once you've assessed the volatility of the individual funds you're considering, you still need to give your whole portfolio what I call the gut test. The investments you're assembling may look great together on paper, but you are the only one able to say whether you can live with the risk they present as a group. To do this, you need a little knowledge about yourself and your ability to endure volatile periods and short-term losses.

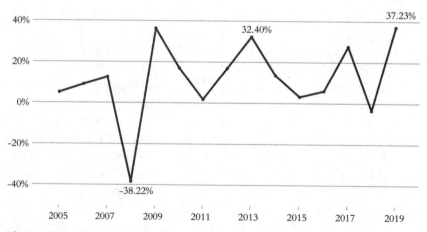

Figure 11.2 Vanguard Growth Index Fund Annual Returns (2005–2019)
Source: Vanguard

Goal of Mix	Components	Average Annual Return	Worst 1–Year Loss	Number of Years Out of 94 with Lossses
Stability	10% stocks 80% bonds 10% cash	5.8%	−6.7% (1969)	9
Income	20% stocks 80% bonds	6.6%	−10.1% (1931)	13
Conservative Growth	40% stocks 60% bonds	7.8%	−18.4% (1931)	17
Balanced Growth	50% stocks 50% bonds	8.3%	−22.5% (1931)	18
Moderate Growth	60% stocks 40% bonds	8.8%	−26.6% (1931)	22
Growth	80% stocks 20% bonds	9.6%	−34.9% (1931)	24
Aggressive Growth	100% stocks	10.3%	−43.1% (1931)	26

Figure 11.3 Asset Mixes and Past Performance (1926–2019)

Source: Vanguard. U.S. stocks represented by S&P 500 from 1926 through 1974, the Dow Jones U.S. Total Stock Market Index from 1975 through April 22, 2005, the MSCI U.S. Broad Market Index though June 2, 2013, and the CRSP U.S. Total Market Index through 2019. U.S. bonds represented by the Standard & Poor's High Grade Corporate Index from 1926 to 1968, the Citigroup High Grade Index from 1969 to 1972, the Lehman Brothers U.S. Long Credit AA Index 1973 to 1975, and the Bloomberg Barclays U.S. Aggregate Bond Index from 1976 to 2009 and the Bloomberg Barclays U.S. Aggregate Float Adjusted Bond Index through 2019. Cash represented by the Ibbotson 1-Month Treasury Bill Index from 1926 through 1977, and the FTSE 3-Month U.S. Treasury Bill Index from 1978 through 2019.

Historical returns can give you a general idea of what to expect based on your broad asset mix. Figure 11.3, which you first encountered in Chapter 7, reveals how various model portfolios have performed in the past. Suppose you are weighing the risk of a conservative growth portfolio with 60% of its assets in stocks and 40% in bonds. As the data show, you could take some comfort in knowing that a hypothetical portfolio with that composition had losses in 22 out of the last 94 years. But you also ought to ask yourself how well you would have endured the year 1931, when such portfolio would have lost −26.6% of its value.

If you suspect you'll lose sleep worrying about a large drop in the value of your investments in tough market conditions, you'd be wise to opt for a more conservative mix of assets that will exhibit less volatility. True, a more conservative asset mix may mean you'll have to save more to achieve your goals, but it is more likely that you'll stick with your program through trying times if you're not scared to pieces.

How much risk is too much? It depends on your own constitution. Some people can shrug off big market swings. Others cannot. When markets turn volatile, they worry themselves sick about losing money and may make emotion-based decisions that they later regret. This is why I counsel investors, especially novice investors, not to review their account balances too frequently. It is too easy to access your balances on your investment provider's app and react to seeing your accounts showing substantial losses. You are investing for 30 to 40 years (or longer); checking your balance on a quarterly (or preferably an annual) basis should be more than sufficient.

Good markets can lull you into thinking you're tougher and more comfortable with risk than you actually are when stormy markets arrive. When the markets are rising, people tend to think of themselves as very risk-tolerant. All they see is the reward side of the risk/reward trade-off. That's just what happened in the late 1990s, when stocks had been rising so long that many investors decided that the climb would never stop—or at least, that downturns would be brief. They saw no reason to fear investment risk. In the months after the spring of 2000, when the market changed course, those investors discovered that they weren't nearly as risk tolerant as they had thought. Downward volatility feels very different from upward volatility. We saw this same movie again in 2008 and in 2020. There's a non-scientific theory that I actually believe in this regard. It says that "the pain of loss is 10 times the joy of gain." It may not be entirely accurate, but I believe it's directionally accurate based on my lifetime of conversations with investors.

It's a common investing mistake to think you can take a "chameleon" approach to risk and change your investment policy whenever the market environment shifts. But as we covered earlier in this book, it is extremely difficult to time the market consistently over time.

Baseline Basics: The Risk Monster Is a Many-Headed Beast

Every investment carries some degree of risk. But there are many types of risk, and they vary with the nature of the investment. These are some of the major ones you'll see mentioned on fund websites and in prospectuses.

- **Market risk.** The chance that the overall securities market will slump, carrying your investment along with it. When you invest in stocks, this is one of the most significant risks you face. It is primarily a shorter-term threat, however. History has shown that, while stock prices have skyrocketed or plummeted during relatively short periods, over decades they have trended steadily upward. That's because corporate profits and the U.S. and global economies have grown over time.
- **Specific risk.** This is the "eggs-in-one-basket" risk. Concentrating your portfolio in a few stocks, or in just one or two market sectors, increases the chance that you'll lose money because of troubles at one company or in a single industry group. Stock market leadership can switch suddenly among sectors—say, from technology to energy to financials. And even fine companies with superb track records can stumble or be affected by an unpredictable development. The best way to reduce specific risk is to invest in broadly diversified exchange-traded funds (ETFs) and mutual funds.
- **Interest rate risk.** The chance that the value of your bond investment will fall if interest rates rise. The longer a bond's maturity, the greater the interest rate risk. You can reduce, but not eliminate, interest rate risk by investing in shorter-term bond funds. Note that interest rate risk and income risk are opposites and, in a sense, offset each other. If your bond fund's price falls because interest rates go up, the income it earns will rise over time, reflecting the higher rates. It is important to recognize that we've been in a multi-decade period of declining interest rates, so many bond investors have become numb to the potential for severe bond price declines.

(continued)

Baseline Basics: The Risk Monster Is a Many-Headed Beast (*Continued*)

- **Credit risk.** The possibility that you will lose money when a bond issuer defaults. Also, the possibility that your investment will lose value if an issuer's credit rating is lowered, which sometimes occurs in tandem with a merger, buyout, or takeover. The reason such events can trigger credit downgrades is that a company may choose to finance the restructuring by issuing a large amount of new bonds, debt that could threaten its ability to pay off existing bonds. For a fund or ETF that invests in many bonds, the credit risk from a single default or rating change is reduced.
- **Manager risk.** The chance that the professionals managing your mutual fund will make consistently poor choices that lead to losses or subpar returns. This risk is a factor in all actively managed funds. You can virtually eliminate it by investing in index funds.
- **Income risk.** The possibility that your income from a bond or money market fund will fall if interest rates decline. Income risk is higher for money market funds than for bond funds and higher for short-term bond funds than for long-term funds. This is because shorter-term investments mature more rapidly, forcing the fund to reinvest the money at whatever interest rates are prevailing.
- **Style risk.** The possibility that a strategy based on particular types of securities will underperform or go out of favor. Market segments (e.g., small-company stocks, for example), investment style (value and growth), and industries (e.g., technology, consumer products, etc.) can experience cycles in which they do either better or worse than the overall stock market. In the past, those periods have lasted for as long as several years. This is the risk that you take if you put all your money in growth funds or value funds. You can reduce this risk by making sure your investments cover small-, medium-, and large-size companies in a wide variety of industries.
- **Inflation risk.** The chance that the purchasing power of your investment will drop. This risk, based on the rising prices of goods and services, is more serious than many people realize. For example, if inflation runs at 3% for five years, the value of a regular $100 interest payment will fall to $86 in terms of actual purchasing power. Inflation risk is a major consideration with money market and bond funds, but you can reduce it by holding some stocks in

your portfolio. Why do stocks mitigate inflation risk? Because they have the potential to gain in value at a rate greater than inflation. Importantly, too, over many decades, dividends paid by companies to their shareholders have grown at a rate that far exceeds inflation, so such dividends are an excellent inflation hedge. In total, as I have noted elsewhere, historical returns show that, over the very long term, returns on stocks have beaten inflation by a wider margin than those of either bonds or cash investments.

- **Liquidity risk.** The chance that your returns will suffer because a fund manager encounters trading difficulties in a market. Sometimes foreign stocks, for example, can be challenging to buy or sell, in part because trading volume on some foreign exchanges tends to be lighter than on U.S. exchanges. You can reduce this risk by focusing on funds that invest in countries with well-established financial markets. Bond funds may also be unable to sell a security in a timely manner at a desired price. Liquidity risk is generally high for long-term bond funds.

International investments carry some additional risks:

- **Currency risk.** The chance that currency movements will hurt your returns from a mutual fund that invests abroad. Investments that are denominated in foreign currencies decline in value for U.S. investors when the U.S. dollar rises in value against those currencies. Conversely, the investments rise in value when the dollar weakens. There have been prolonged periods when the dollar trended one way or the other. But, on balance, currency movements on international investments have not been a meaningful component of long-term returns.
- **Country risk.** The possibility that events in a specific country— such as political upheaval, financial troubles, or a natural disaster— will drive down the security prices of companies whose stocks trade in those markets. You can reduce, but not eliminate, this risk by choosing an international fund that invests in many countries and that focuses on developed nations rather than emerging-markets countries.

Measuring Your Risk Tolerance

The investment industry has developed a variety of diagnostics—quizzes, questionnaires, and the like—to help you measure your tolerance for risk, but it has always seemed to me that there are inherent limitations in trying to use objective measures for something so subjective. Risk tolerance can't be measured as easily as your blood pressure or your cholesterol level. Ultimately, you have to trust your gut. I have often taken online quizzes and ended up with scores that label me as a highly risk-tolerant investor. I knew myself well enough not to believe those scores at face value. But because I have always chosen to live well below my means, I can actually comfortably take more risk (e.g., invest more heavily in equities than an average person my age) than I might naturally otherwise be comfortable taking. I have always done so, however, in a very risk-controlled way with strategies like dollar-cost averaging.

To assess your own risk tolerance, ask yourself these questions:

- How would you feel if your portfolio lost 20% of its value in one day? The Dow Jones Industrial Average lost −22.6% on October 19, 1987—its greatest one-day percentage loss in market history.
- How would you feel if you witness your portfolio steadily shrinking during an extended market downturn? Such things have happened in the past and are very likely to happen again. The 2007–2009 bear market in stocks lasted for 17 months. And bonds were stuck in a slump from March 1971 to September 1975—a period of 54 months!
- How did you react to a −34% plunge in the S&P 500 Index in less than a month, which occurred in the first quarter of 2020? And, conversely, what did you do when prices rebounded to record highs in December?

A prolonged and painful bear market is difficult to simulate. You can take all the tests you want, but if all you know about tough markets is what you've read in books, you don't really know how you will respond.

Managing Investment Risk

I will offer a few final thoughts on risk in the following section.

If you've decided you're truly a risk-tolerant investor, and you intend to invest accordingly, remember the factors that will help you to stay the course when the markets test your mettle: Hold a balanced, well-diversified portfolio. Control your costs. Keep on saving and investing. Time will be your ally, as I'll explain in more detail in Chapter 14.

If you've decided you're truly risk-averse, recognize that being a conservative investor is nothing for which you should feel ashamed. A close friend who is an investment professional was a very conservative investor in his private life. He recognized that he was in a high-earning, but high-risk, profession that was vulnerable to market cycles, and to him that meant he ought to minimize the financial risk in his personal life. He was a far more conservative investor than I. Although he was a highly paid senior partner in an investment management firm, he kept his long-term assets in a money market fund instead of investing them in the stock market. His colleagues teased him about adhering to his no-stocks strategy even amid the bull market of the 1980s and 1990s, but he looked pretty smart when the bull market was followed by a prolonged bear market. When teased, his refrain was: "I sleep really well at night, no matter what happens in the stock market." He is a person who really knows his gut. But, to be clear, given his profession, he had an advantage. He could earn his way to financial security; most people don't have that luxury. The latter need a combination of financial discipline and investment success to get to where they want to go.

In a Nutshell

There are a variety of objective tools you can use to assess risk in your portfolio, but ultimately, the best gauge is a very subjective one: Can you stomach the range of ups and downs that are likely to occur as you journey toward your goal? When you are constructing a portfolio, consider these factors:

- **How much appetite for risk do you have in general?** You know yourself better than anyone else. Choose investments accordingly.
- **How would you have handled (or how did you handle) past volatile markets?** Look at the past performance data for particular funds or particular types of portfolios and ask yourself how you would (or did) react to such scenarios.

12

Some Advice
on Financial Advice

When I was named president of Vanguard, I received a congratulatory phone call out of the blue from an older man whose daughters were childhood friends of mine. The man, whom I'll call Bob, said some nice things about Vanguard and mentioned that he had financed the college educations of his daughters (I will call them Kara and Allison) with investments in a single balanced fund, Vanguard Wellington Fund. Bob didn't have to invest so simply—he was a stockbroker with many investment options from which to assemble a balanced, diversified portfolio. But he was wise enough to understand the elegance and effectiveness of simplicity. I'll always remember his words, "Kara and Allison went to college on Wellington Fund." One fund and 20 years. Pretty simple. Tremendously effective.

When to Seek Help

The premise of this book is that with a bit of knowledge, confidence, and discipline, you can achieve investment success on your own. This is especially true, in my view, for investors who are accumulating assets for a long-term goal like retirement. But not everyone has a financial professional in the family to give them investment guidance and offer fund recommendations. And not everyone's situations are as simple and straightforward as Bob's—establishing a time-certain program to finance his daughters' educations. As such, there are plenty of instances when it makes sense to seek advice from a financial advisor or digital advice platform, commonly called a robo-advisor.

So, how do you know if you should engage an advisor to help you? It's a very personal decision, but here are a few reasons to enlist the help of an advisor:

- **To deal with a life event.** There are occurrences in life that may warrant consulting an advisor. Consider a scenario in which the spouse who is the primary financial decision maker and household investment manager, if you will, passes away. The surviving spouse, who may little experience to take on this task, may want to turn to professional help. From my experience in assisting several widows of close friends to establish a relationship with a trusted advisor, it was an important step in helping them transition to a new stage in life. And, frankly, as I check in with them now, I feel gratified that I could take one worry off their minds. Indeed, years later, not only are they in good financial shape but they have peace of mind as well.

  A similar situation may arise in a divorce or when a spouse loses cognitive ability to make sound financial decisions. An advisor's counsel can also be useful when you inherit a large sum of money from a deceased parent or receive a large windfall from the sale of a business.

- **To seek reassurance.** At some point during your investing journey, you might want to check in with an advisor to ensure you are on the right track. Say you're in your mid-30s and have about 12 years of investing under your belt. An advisor could analyze your portfolio and savings rate as they relate to your goals and then recommend any course corrections at a relatively early stage. "Lost time is never found again," as Benjamin Franklin said, and I'll demonstrate the power of time and compounding in a forthcoming chapter. Some advisors can consult with you on insurance and health savings options as well.

  The pre-retirement years are another life stage when you might be a candidate for advice. For example, suppose you are in your early 50s and thinking about when is the right time for you to retire. Obviously, your financial situation is a key part of that decision. An advisor can provide a "second opinion," offering you reassurance that you are well prepared for the next 25 to 35 years from a financial standpoint. Or, alternatively, they can provide guidance on increasing your saving rates, managing health care costs, or tweaking your portfolio to make your retirement dreams attainable.

- **To deal with complexity.** While I've professed simplicity as an investment strategy throughout this book, sometimes life, and related investing, can get complex. Let's return to the example above when you're in your mid-30s. You and your spouse are saving for retirement, and you have three kids to put through college in the next 12 to 18 years. At the same time, you'd like to move to the suburbs and a better school district, but you will face higher mortgage payments and real estate taxes. And, you still have student loan debt from earning your MBA. Since your oldest child is 12 years away from attending college, do you prioritize saving for college over your maxing out in your employer-sponsored retirement plan? What is the best vehicle for college savings, and how much do you need to save? What about getting out from under your student loan debt? Do you miss the opportunity to buy your dream house and send your kids to better schools if you wait to pay off that debt? An advisor can help you answer these questions and develop and oversee sound strategies to put your financial house in order.

- **To manage your retirement years.** I strongly believe most people should engage an advisor—to one degree or another—when they are in retirement. That opinion is shaped by personal experiences as I, my family, my friends, and longtime colleagues arrive at this phase of life. It's a complicated and often intimidating time, and an emotional one as well. There are so many decisions to make. You now likely need to rely on your lifetime savings, which may be sizable at this point, to sustain you for decades. There are also myriad questions:
  - Which accounts do I tap first—401(k), IRA, or taxable?
  - When should I take Social Security?
  - How long can I expect my money to last?
  - Should I take a lump sum from my pension?
  - Will my taxes decline?
  - What should I do if a bear market hits?
  - Should I supplement my portfolio with an income annuity?
  - How do I pay for medical coverage?

An advisor will develop an optimal plan to manage these complexities and, importantly, bring you some level of comfort and confidence. Of those in my own sample of 55- to 75-year-olds who have asked for my perspective on advice, most were comfortable investing on their own in the accumulation phase. But after we've discussed the pros and cons of hiring an advisor for the de-accumulation phase, the vast majority opted to do so.

Assessing Your Needs for Advice

An entire book could be devoted to assessing advice options and finding the right advice solution for you. I'll seek to highlight the key aspects of selecting the right advisor for you. It starts with you. Here's what I mean:

- **Your needs.** Are your needs relatively straightforward and simple? To get a recommendation on a tax-smart portfolio, a one-time engagement with a fee-only financial planner might be the ticket. (More on advisor compensation structures later.) Or, if you need help selecting investments, managing your portfolio, minimizing taxes, obtaining proper insurance coverage, and addressing multiple goals, an ongoing relationship with a financial advisor might make sense.
- **Your situation.** How large is your portfolio? What stage are you in your financial journey? If you are just starting out and have a modest amount, you might not need advice at this point; a target-date fund might be more suitable. Also, if your portfolio is on the small side, you might not qualify for the advisor's minimum. If you have considerable assets, but not the time or willingness to manage your financial affairs, you may choose to hire a financial professional.
- **Your preferences.** Are you comfortable as a DIYer, or do you prefer to delegate certain things? For example, do you prepare you own taxes, use a software program, or have an accountant do it for you? The impetus for the question is to determine if you are comfortable with, and confident in, an online tool or a digital solution, such as a robo-advisor. By contrast, when it comes to money, many people in my generation prefer a face-to-face meeting with a live human being—whether it is buying insurance, depositing a check, or getting financial guidance.

Finding the Right Financial Help

One of the great news stories of the past decade has been an explosion in options for individuals and families to access investment professionals to help them invest successfully. The result has been more choice and better pricing to consumers. Large firms like Vanguard, Fidelity, Schwab, and others that were not seen as mainstream providers of advice services are now very prominent, with a variety of options at very attractive prices. Thousands of registered investment advisor firms and independent advisors offer additional choice. Technology-based robo-advisory services have grown and evolved over the past decade. As a result, if you choose to seek financial advice, your options have expanded and, importantly, the costs have come down.

As noted above, there are countless individuals and institutions who would like nothing better than to give you financial advice and manage your money at a price—accountants, insurance agents, brokers, financial planners, investment advisors, and wealth coaches, to name a few. Advisors can be affiliated with a brokerage firm, a bank, or a mutual fund provider. Or, an advisor can be independent, working as a sole proprietor or with a team of advisors and support staff. The same holds true for robo-advisors, many of which were first offered by independent start-ups, and more recently, rolled out by the aforementioned established financial services providers.

As you do your research, you'll come across a variety of designations (e.g., CFP, CFA, RIA, CRP, RFP, CPA). Some of these certifications are earned by meeting qualifications and passing examinations of national professional organizations. Others are required by regulatory agencies, while still others denote membership in an organization. The Financial Industry Regulatory Authority (FINRA) has a great online resource that lists professional and accredited designations, which I advise you to consult (https://www.finra.org/#/) in your research.

You'll want to check the advisor's education, experience, licensing, employment history, regulatory record, and fiduciary status. (A fiduciary is obligated to act in the best interests of their clients.) For a robo-advisor, do your due diligence on the underlying firm—its history, track record, size, reputation, and so forth. You can do a background check on both the Securities & Exchange Commission and state-registered investment advisors by using FINRA's BrokerCheck, which enables you to ascertain if an advisor is registered to sell securities, offer investment advice, or both.

It is also important to understand if an advisor has *discretionary* control over your account, meaning he or she makes buying and selling decisions, as well as executes transactions on your behalf. Such authority enables the advisor to make trades without consulting or asking permission as long as such trades are in accord with the client's stated investments objectives. A *non-discretionary* account is one in which you make the trading decisions.

Assessing the Cost/Value Trade-Off of Advice

To determine the value of an advisor's services, it is important to understand what you are getting and how much it is going to cost. Are you receiving a one-time asset allocation plan and fund recommendations, or more comprehensive, personalized, and ongoing services that include portfolio monitoring, tax loss harvesting, and rebalancing? Also, check the advisor's investment philosophy, the types of products recommended, and performance and how it is reported to you. Ask for the advisor's Client Relationship Summary (known as Form CRS), which offers plain-English descriptions of the nature and costs of the services you'll receive from a financial professional.

The price you pay for advice services will vary in both level and structure. Equally important is to understand how the advisor is compensated. In terms of cost, I encourage you to think about how much you are paying for the advice and how much you are paying for the underlying investment products making up your portfolio. As noted in Chapter 10, I call this the *all-in costs*. Here is a summary of the arrangements that you might encounter as you evaluate advice providers:

- **Fee-only.** Fee-only advisors are compensated directly by their clients for advice, plan implementation, and ongoing management. Typically, fee-only advisors charge on an hourly basis, a flat fee per plan, or a retainer. Fee-only advisors do not accept fees or compensation based on product sales, although you will pay the expense ratio of the funds recommended to you. For comparative purposes, it might help to translate a fee-only advisor's fees into a percentage. For example, if you have a $100,000 portfolio and an advisor charges an annual fee of $1,000, that's 1%.
- **Asset-based fee.** In one of the most common arrangements, an advisor charges a fee based on the percentage of assets that he or she is managing on behalf of the client. These fees generally range from 0.25% of assets (i.e., $250 on a $100,000 investment) to 1.5% or more (i.e., $1,500 on a $100,000 investment). Many advisors use a sliding scale that reduces the fee based on the level of assets. For example, it might cost you 1% for a portfolio of $100,000 to $500,000; 0.75% for portfolio of between $500,001 and $1 million; and 0.50% on a portfolio of more than $1 million. Fund costs would be additional. Advisor compensation will vary from firm to firm; some advisors are salaried, and others may be compensated as a percentage of their personal "book of business."

- **Asset-based fee plus commissions.** Some financial professionals are registered to provide both advice and brokerage services. As such, you may be charged both an asset-based fee, as well as commissions and expense ratios on the funds recommended to you. These commissions may be explicit (e.g., front-end sales charge) or imbedded in the expense ratio of the fund in the form of a 12b-1 fee. This fee is part of the expense ratio and is used to compensate advisors for selling fund shares. It is worth knowing if an advisor is receiving payment to sell you specific funds.
- **Subscription-based.** Some firms or financial advisors offer subscription payment models, in which you pay an annual or monthly fee, or a combination of the two. Again, you'll also have the underlying fund or exchange-traded fund (ETF) costs of the products comprising the recommended portfolio.
- **"Free."** Some of the larger investment providers offer free online advisory services that develop and monitor a diversified portfolio of funds or ETFs. Recognize that nothing is truly free. While you won't pay an ongoing fee or commissions, you will pay the expense ratio of the investment products recommended to you—just as you would if you built a portfolio on your own. Be wary. Some providers may use low-cost index products but augment the portfolio with higher cost, in-house actively managed products. Some of these funds charge more than ten times a traditional index fund or ETF; for example, 0.03% versus 0.39%. Some firms also recommend holding a sizable amount of cash in a low-yielding, in-house money market product, which is a hidden opportunity cost. One additional warning: The advice provider may continually barrage you with "upsell" or "cross-sell" offers in an effort for you to sign on to more expensive wealth management services or convince you to buy other products and services.

When you evaluate an advisor, make sure you understand all the fees you'll pay and the associated compensation arrangements. A reputable advisor will be completely open and forthright when disclosing fees and discussing compensation.

Let's turn to the value part of the equation for a moment. In particular, it evokes Oscar Wilde's definition of a cynic: "A man who knows the price of everything, and the value of nothing." You'll definitely pay something for professional advice and, at the same time, receive value. Some of that value may be obvious—a prudent plan, a thoughtful savings analysis, and low-cost, broadly diversified fund recommendations. If this is the right type of relationship, you should also derive value from the relationship, with an advisor serving as a sounding board and coach who helps you navigate tough markets and prevents you from making big mistakes. The emotional benefits of feeling safe and secure with a trusted advisor should not be overlooked.

Making a Choice

Selecting the right advisory solution for you will take some due diligence, as it should, because you are turning over some responsibility for your financial future to another person or entity. You can rely on referrals from family members or friends, or a recommendation from your accountant or lawyer. Some professional organizations, such as Certified Financial Planner Board of Standards, Inc., the Financial Planning Association, or the National Association of Personal Financial Advisors, have online search tools that may prove useful.

Narrow down your candidate list based on some of the factors discussed here, and then screen potential advisors. Conduct an interview. Ask questions. Probe further if something is unclear or you don't understand it. Get a feel whether you can put your trust in the individual (or firm, in the case of a robo-advisor). At the end of the day, you are looking for a solution that provides comprehensive and quality services at a reasonable cost.

In a Nutshell

Some of us do not have the time, willingness, or ability to manage our financial affairs. If you find yourself in need of delegating this responsibility, be judicious in your selection.

- **Make a deliberate decision as you approach retirement.** Before leaving the workforce, give consideration to engaging an advisor. The financial complexities of this life stage alone are a compelling reason to get professional help.
- **Consider your needs.** What are your objectives? Do you need a checkup or ongoing advice? Are you comfortable with a digital solution or a human professional?
- **Choose with care.** The choices are many and confusing. Avail yourself of the many resources to find and vet an advisor.
- **Weigh the cost/value trade-off.** The cost of advice ranges from "free" to steep. The value in an optimal financial plan that improves chances for success, along with the accompanying peace of mind may be "priceless."

PART III
MANAGE YOUR
INVESTMENTS WITH FOCUS
AND DISCIPLINE

13

Buy-and-Hold Really Works

I was attending a Vanguard client conference in Pittsburgh one night in 1997 when a gentleman introduced himself and shared a terrific story. Back in 1958, when the man was in his teens, he had earned $1,200 and had asked his father what he should do with the money. The father and son consulted a financial advisor, who recommended that they invest in a new mutual fund called the Wellington Equity Fund. There the money sat untouched for the next 39 years, growing and accumulating reinvested distributions at an average rate of 13% a year. By 1997, this man's account in Vanguard Windsor™ Fund (as it is known today) had grown to $145,000— more than 100 times his original investment. He just wanted to say thanks! I returned that gratitude, telling him he's just provided one more real example of why getting in the investing game early and being patient can have tremendous results.

If you're determined to succeed at investing, make it your first priority to become a buy-and-hold investor. As the anecdote about the investor from Pittsburgh demonstrates, picking sound investments and keeping them for the long term really works. Not only will this simple strategy put you on the path to accumulating wealth, it will enable you to live your life without devoting a lot of time and energy to managing your investments.

In this chapter, I'll discuss why a buy-and-hold approach succeeds and how to implement it with your own portfolio. I'll then turn to being very blunt about two short-term strategies that don't work: frequent trading and market timing.

Developing the Buy-and-Hold Habit

You can establish the buy-and-hold habit through a strategy known as *dollar-cost averaging*—putting a fixed dollar amount into a designated investment on a set schedule. Dollar-cost averaging creates a discipline of investing and, at the same time, helps you avoid the temptations of market-timing and frequent trading.

And there's something even better about dollar-cost averaging: Over a given period, it can buy you more shares than you would have received by investing at the average share price during the period. That seems illogical, so let me explain. The key is that, whether the markets are up or down, you're investing the same amount of money in the same fund or funds at regular intervals. That fixed sum buys more shares when the price is lower and fewer when the price is high. For example, say you invest $250 every month in a mutual fund. If your fund has a net asset value of $10 a share in the first month, your $250 investment buys 25 shares. If the net asset value declines to $8.50 per share in the second month, the same $250 investment buys 29.4 shares.

As a result, the average cost of your shares is lower than the average market price per share during the time you were investing. In our two-month example, the share price averaged $9.25 on the market, but the price you paid for your 54.4 shares averaged $9.19 apiece. Figures 13.1 and 13.2 show two different dollar-cost-averaging scenarios.

Dollar-cost averaging need not mean you have to remember to write a check every month. In fact, you may already be using the strategy without knowing it, for example, if you are participating in an employer-sponsored retirement plan with a regular payroll deduction. You can also set up dollar-cost averaging in your other accounts by arranging for regular electronic transfers from your bank into your funds or setting up a program that moves money from your money market fund to your stock and bond funds. This way you'll make investing easy and automatic.

Month	Investment	Share Price	Shares Acquired
1	$400	$5	80
2	$400	$8	50
3	$400	$10	40
4	$400	$10	40
5	$400	$16	25

Total shares purchased		235
Total investment		$2,000
Average price per share*		$9.80
Average cost per share**		$8.51

* Average share price = $9.80 ($5 + $8 + $10 + $10 + $16 = $49; $49 ÷ 5 months = $9.80).

** Average share cost = $8.51 ($2,000 ÷ 235).

Figure 13.1 How Dollar-Cost Averaging Works When the Market Rises

Source: Vanguard

Month	Investment	Share Price	Shares Acquired
1	$400	$16	25
2	$400	$10	40
3	$400	$8	50
4	$400	$8	50
5	$400	$5	80

Total shares purchased		245
Total investment		$2,000
Average price per share*		$9.40
Average cost per share**		$8.16

* Average share price = $9.40 ($16 + $10 + $8 + $8 + $5 = $47; $479 ÷ 5 months = $9.40).

** Average share cost = $8.16 ($2,000 ÷ 245).

Figure 13.2 How Dollar-Cost Averaging Works When the Market Drops

Source: Vanguard

There are two things you need to remember to make dollar-cost averaging effective.

1. You must continue to make regular purchases through thick and thin—even through periods of market decline. Psychologically, this can be very difficult, so it's vital to remind yourself why you began dollar-cost averaging: to take a disciplined investment approach.
2. You must stick to the same investment allocation. Putting a fixed sum into the same investment month after month is dollar-cost averaging; putting a fixed sum into bonds one month and into stocks the next isn't dollar-cost averaging.

Of course, dollar-cost averaging cannot eliminate the risks of investing in financial markets. It doesn't guarantee you a profit, nor does it ensure that you'll be protected from loss in falling markets. But it sure has worked for many investors, including my family and me, over the years.

You Will Be Tempted to Abandon Your Buy-and-Hold Strategy

There will be times when you become dissatisfied with one or more of the funds in your portfolio. It's a reality that sometimes an investment will quit working for you and you'll need to move out of it. But it's also true that every good fund hits a bad patch now and then. When that occurs, you may question your judgment in picking the fund. If you are like many other investors who wrote me letters when I was CEO at Vanguard, you will also question the competence of the portfolio manager, not to mention the CEO!

As a buy-and-hold investor, you should be reluctant to abandon an investment unless you have very good reason to assume it is no longer sound. Here are three valid reasons to consider selling a fund:

1. The fund has dramatically changed its strategy, holdings, or investment approach.
2. The portfolio manager responsible for a fund's past performance has been removed from the fund or has left the firm.
3. The fund suffers a prolonged period of underperformance relative to its benchmark and peers. Short-term underperformance is no reason

to sell, as all funds will go through a period in which it fails to beat the market or like funds. Remember the story of the man from Pittsburgh—patience pays off.

Why Frequent Trading Doesn't Work

According to the tired adage, the way to make money in the markets is to "buy low, sell high." Obviously, that's a great idea. You just figure out what's going to go up and then buy it, and you sell it when it reaches its peak. Simply repeat that process again and again as you trade your way to immense wealth. And the faster the better, right?

Unfortunately, it's so much easier said than done. But the theory is so simple, and the prospective rewards so great, that it's not surprising plenty of people say to themselves, "I'm an intelligent person; I can see when stocks are going up and when they're going down. This isn't rocket science!" And pretty soon they're using their online brokerage accounts to buy and sell stocks every day. Or maybe they're not quite that aggressive, but they feel very cool about jumping in and out of stock funds or exchange-traded funds (ETFs) several times a month based on what they hear watching TV gabfests, reading blogs, or heeding tips from online communities.

We've witnessed a renaissance of online trading in 2020, as some brokerage platforms have "gamified" investing, making it fun and entertaining to trade individual securities. Don't try it. The odds are stacked against you.

In stock trading, even the professionals have a hard time coming out ahead, and they have all kinds of specialized knowledge, resources, and research to help them. Without those advantages, you would almost have to be psychic to win at trading. Need proof? Two professors from the University of California at Davis, Brad Barber and Terrance Odean, studied the impact of frequent trading on the investment returns of 60,000 households that were clients of a discount broker from 1991 through 1996. Their finding: The most frequent traders earned average annual net returns of 11.4%, while those who traded infrequently earned 18.5%. And that was during a bull market—stocks were up 17.9% during the period! In tougher market environments, the returns for traders would be much lower, or even negative.

Frequent fund traders also have little chance of success—the difficulty is in identifying the outperforming fund in advance, and the one

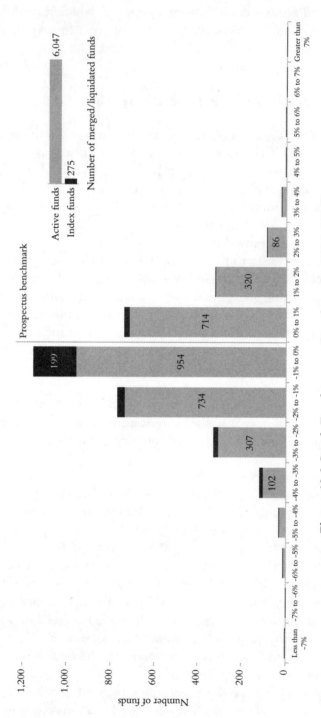

Figure 13.3 Stock Funds versus Benchmarks (2005–2019)

Source: Vanguard calculations, using Morningstar data.

fund in a large universe that outperforms by a meaningful margin. To analyze why, we examined how stock mutual funds fared in comparison to their prospectus benchmarks over the 15-year period ending December 31, 2019. Figure 13.3 shows the distribution of excess returns of domestic equity funds. Note that a significant number of funds' returns lie to the left of the prospectus benchmark, which represents zero excess returns. Once merged and liquidated funds are considered, a clear majority of funds fail to outperform their benchmarks, meaning that negative excess returns tend to be more common than positive excess returns. And meaningful excess returns (i.e., 1% or more) were less common than marginal excess returns (i.e., less than 1%).

There are two reasons that most frequent traders don't succeed: One is the unpredictability of the markets; the other is the drag of costs and taxes.

The Unpredictability of the Financial Markets

Some people claim to have a system for picking hot-performing securities or sectors. The fact, however, is that no one has yet proven to have the gift of seeing what lies ahead for the markets or individual funds or stocks. Even legendary investors make mistakes. Just look at all the professionals who got burned when the technology stock craze ended. And who could possibly have predicted the COVID-19 pandemic that roiled the world's financial markets in early 2020? Not I; probably not you.

The Cost Penalty

Whether you are trading funds or individual securities, the cost issues can be significant. If you trade funds frequently, you may incur short-term trading or transaction fees, and if you're dealing through an intermediary, you may incur other fees. If you trade individual securities frequently, you may incur brokerage commissions, and you'll also absorb the *bid–asked spread*—the difference between "bid" prices offered by potential buyers of a security and the higher "asked" price at which potential sellers are willing to part with it. These costs seem negligible, perhaps, but I assure you that they add up rapidly, and their impact is magnified over time because the money lost to costs is not there to grow via compounding.

An even bigger hit is likely to come from capital gains taxes. You will owe a capital gains tax if you make a profit by selling shares in a taxable account (but not if you trade in a tax-advantaged account, such as an IRA or a 401(k) plan). The active traders who make profits tend to realize short-term gains, which are taxed at rates ranging from 10% to 37%. By contrast, long-term gains, on securities held for more than a year, have a tax ceiling of 20%. On a short-term gain of $5,000, an investor in the top bracket would owe $1,850 in taxes—nearly twice the tax bill on a long-term gain.

Why Market-Timing Doesn't Work

Many market timers try to guess when to jump into the market and when to be out of it entirely. They wait to invest until the stock market or bond market seems attractive, and they switch out of the market when they foresee rough seas ahead. Essentially, you need to be right twice.

The "system" that a market timer uses to trigger such moves may be a sophisticated computer program that crunches all sorts of financial ratios or that looks for signals based on past patterns. Or, a timer may simply jump in or out of the market based on comments from some Wall Street expert or a newsletter. Or, a timer may base his or her moves simply on instinct.

However beautiful the theory or however logical the premise, the fact is that market-timing systems don't seem to consistently enrich anyone, with the possible exception of the broker handling a market timer's transactions. If market timing did work for long periods, the timers themselves would top the lists of the world's richest individuals. You'd certainly never see a buy-and-hold investor like Warren Buffett among the wealth leaders.

The world is simply too unpredictable a place to depend on patterns, or momentum, or logical assumptions that have worked in the past to prevail in the future. Some very smart and very well-heeled people running sophisticated hedge funds have gone belly-up simply because the markets behaved in unexpected—perhaps irrational—ways that were not anticipated by their sophisticated computer models.

Besides, in spite of the analytical approach that many market timers employ, most of them are subject to emotional decisions like everybody else. All too often, they either panic and sell at a loss when prices fall, as happened in both the bond and stock markets in 2020, or they jump on the proverbial bandwagon too late, which we saw with tech stocks in the late 1990s.

	Ending Value	10-Year Annualized Return
Total period	$353	13.4%
Minus best performing month	$316	12.2%
Minus best two months	$289	11.2%
Minus best three months	$266	10.3%
Minus best four months	$247	9.4%
Minus best five months	$230	8.7%
Minus best six months	$215	8.0%

Figure 13.4 The Perils of Being Out of Stocks (2010–2019)

Source: Vanguard. Stocks represented by the MSCI U.S. Broad Market Index through June 2, 2013, and the CRSP U.S. Total Market Index thereafter.

	Ending Value	10-Year Annualized Return
Total period	$145	3.8%
Minus best performing month	$141	3.5%
Minus best two months	$138	3.3%
Minus best three months	$135	3.1%
Minus best four months	$133	2.9%
Minus best five months	$130	2.7%
Minus best six months	$128	2.5%

Figure 13.5 Sitting on the Sidelines Hurts Bond Investors (2010–2019)

Source: Vanguard. U.S. Bonds represented by the Bloomberg Barclays U.S. Aggregate Float Adjusted Bond Index.

Another problem for timers is that market rallies often occur suddenly and over very short periods. If you happen to be out of the market during those times, you could miss most or all of the gains for that year. The accompanying figures demonstrate how risky it is to be absent from the markets at the wrong time. As shown in Figure 13.4, missing the six best months of the broad stock market's performance over the 2010–2019 period would have reduced your average annual investment gain by nearly 40%—8% instead of 13.4%. (The figure shows a $100 investment at the beginning of the period.)

And being out of the bond markets is equally risky. As shown in Figure 13.5, missing the six best months of the broad bond market's performance during that 10-year period would have reduced your average annual return from 3.8% to 2.5%. (The figure shows a $100 investment at the beginning of the period.)

I am reminded of a friend who panicked and sold during the market crash of 1987. He was in the investment banking profession, and you would have thought he would have known better. He compounded his error by not getting back into the market. He sat on cash waiting for the "right" time to invest and suffered tremendous opportunity cost when the market rebounded strongly. He finally called, looking for reassurance that stocks were in a good place to be—in 1994, when the stock market was up in value by more than 100% over the interim period. My response: "I have no idea what will happen this month or this year, but since we are both 40 years old, I would say this is a great time to invest for the next 40 years."

Both frequent traders and market timers are more like speculators than investors. You might think the chances are good that you'll be one of the few who succeed. But ask yourself whether you really want to play the odds with the money you are earmarking for retirement or your other important financial objectives. My advice is to forget timing and let time, and compounding, do their magic.

In a Nutshell

Once you've constructed a sensible, long-term portfolio, let a buy-and-hold strategy dictate how you manage your investment program. Holding onto what you've bought may not always be an easy strategy to stick with, but it is a proven way to build wealth.

- **Buy regularly.** Use dollar-cost averaging to make regular purchases of fund shares in fixed dollar amounts on a set schedule. Do this in up markets and down markets. Resist the temptation to think you can pick and choose when to invest and when to sit on the sidelines. The odds are against you.
- **Hold for the long term.** Hold your investments for years or even decades—don't try to be a frequent trader. Frequent trading is speculating, not investing, and it's a game that's far easier to lose than win.

14

Time Is Everything

After nearly 40 years in the investment profession, I continue to be amazed by the miracle of compounding. My first lesson in compounding came when my father, a banker, helped me open a savings account. Years later, I encountered it again as an economics student in college when I read Paul Samuelson's classic textbook, *Economics*. I rediscovered the wonders of compounding once more when I joined Vanguard in 1982.

Test your own knowledge of compounding with this exercise: If an 18-year-old made a single IRA investment of $6,000 and allowed that money to sit untouched, compounding at 8% a year, how much money would she have after 50 years? Venture a guess and then turn to the end of this chapter to see the answer. I think you will be astonished. I still am.

Most people underestimate the value of time in an investment program and might not realize that it picks up its greatest momentum toward the end. At the halfway point in the example above—after 25 years in the growth of our $6,000 investment—the value is only $41,091. The account gains half of its ending value in the last 9 years.

In this chapter, I'll discuss how you can make time work for you. And if you're one of the those folks who did not get as early a start on investing as you may have wished, I'll offer some tips on how to make the most of the time that's available to you.

Make Time Your Ally

If you start saving when you are young, time will be your greatest ally. Year after year, your investments will earn interest and dividends, and those earnings in turn will generate additional earnings. If you wait until later in life to begin saving, time will be your greatest enemy. You won't be able to accomplish nearly as much in your investment program.

Suppose it's your goal to accumulate $100,000 by age 65. As shown in Figure 14.1, if you wait until age 60 to start saving and count on an 8% annual return, you will need to save $1,361 a month to reach your goal. Conversely, if you start saving much earlier, at age 35, you need to save only $67 a month at the same rate of return. When you begin your investment program earlier, more of your wealth comes from compounding and less from your out-of-pocket contributions.

An early start is a huge advantage. Here's another hypothetical case study to demonstrate the point:

- Will starts saving for retirement at age 30. He invests $10,000 a year for 10 years, earning an 8% annual return, and then stops making contributions.

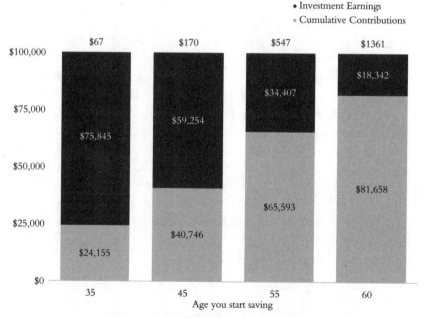

Figure 14.1 Monthly Savings Needed to Accumulate $100,000 by Age 65

Source: Vanguard

- Conor, who is Will's age, waits until age 40 to begin saving for retirement. He then contributes $10,000 each year for 25 years, earning the same 8% annual return.

Who has more money at age 65 when they are ready to retire? Believe it or not, the answer is Will. As shown in Figure 14.2, his $100,000 in aggregate contributions, with many more years to compound, grew to $1,071,477. Conor's $250,000 in contributions reached $789,544. Will contributed $150,000 less over the 25 years, but accumulated more than $280,000 more!

Time Is Your Ally

If you're a stock investor, having time on your side also provides an interesting fringe benefit in risk reduction. As we have explained throughout this book, stocks are a very risky investment in any single year, but you might not realize that the relative risk collapses over longer periods (assuming that your stock investments are diversified). By choosing sound investment vehicles and staying with them for the long haul, you're almost certain to make money, thanks to the accumulation of reinvested earnings along with whatever stock appreciation occurs.

Suppose you'd held a broad market index fund for the years 1995 through 2019. Your returns over a 1-year holding period would have ranged from a gain of 36% in 1995 to a loss of more than −37%. That's

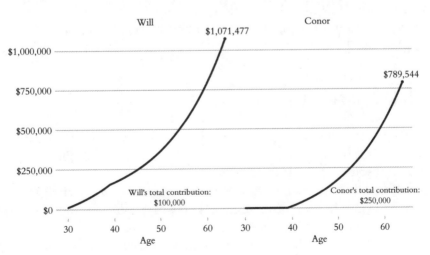

Figure 14.2 Who Has More at 65?

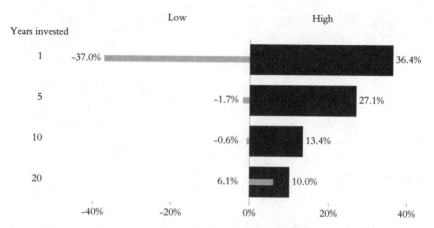

Figure 14.3 Range of U.S. Stock Market Returns (1995–2019)

Source: Vanguard. U.S. stocks represented by the Dow Jones U.S. Total Market Index from 1995 through April 22, 2005, the MSCI Broad Market Index through June 2, 2013, and the CRSP U.S. Total Market Index through 2019. Rolling calendar year periods are shown.

a huge span! However, if you instead look at the returns over rolling 5-year, 10-year, and 20-year periods as shown in Figure 14.3, the gaps between highs and lows are much narrower. The lesson is that letting the markets and time work for you is a terrific way to minimize the risk in your portfolio.

Let's look at another example that shows how differences in return and time period affect the growth of an investment. As shown in Figure 14.4, if you are making annual investments of $5,000 and you have 25 years to invest, you need to earn just 5% a year to accomplish your goal of $250,000. If your time horizon is only a little shorter, say 20 years, you need an annual return of better than 8% to reach roughly the same goal.

How to Make Up for Lost Time

What if you didn't start investing until relatively late in your working career? Is it too late to accumulate a retirement nest egg? The answer is no. Absolutely not. It is never too late.

If you are 52, reading this book and regretting the fact that you haven't begun to save for retirement, know that you're in the minority, but not alone. According to 2018 by the Federal Reserve, some 64% of Americans do not believe that their retirement savings are on track, and

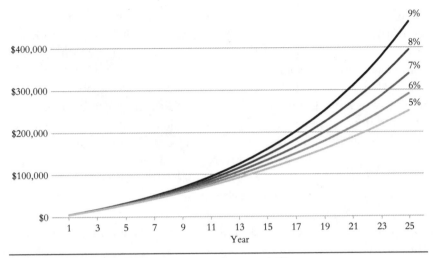

Years	Annual Growth Rate				
	5%	6%	7%	8%	9%
1	$5,250	$5,300	$5,350	$5,400	$5,450
5	$29,010	$29,877	$30,766	$31,680	$32,617
10	$66,034	$69,858	$73,918	$78,227	$82,801
15	$113,287	$123,363	$134,440	$146,621	$160,017
20	$173,596	$194,964	$219,326	$247,115	$278,823
25	$250,567	$290,782	$338,382	$394,772	$461,620

Figure 14.4 Growth of $5,000 in Annual Investments at Different Rates and Different Time Periods

Source: Vanguard

nearly one in four Americans do not have any retirement savings at all. If you are in this latter group, I encourage you to start now.

Actually, you really have no choice. A century ago, the biggest financial risk that ordinary people faced was that they might die too soon to provide for their families. The life insurance industry grew to meet that need. These days, longer lifespans mean that, for most of us, the biggest financial risk is that we'll outlive our savings. It sounds hard-boiled, but starting an investment program late in life comes down to this choice: Save more now or risk not having sufficient assets to cover your living needs.

You are likely to be living in retirement for 20 or 30 years, so it's not just a matter of accumulating as much as you can by age 65. According to government actuarial tables, today a 65-year-old woman is expected, on average, to live to age 86, while a 65-year-old man is expected to live to nearly age 83. To make your savings last for such a long period, you need to be very thoughtful in how you allocate your investments and plan your retirement spending.

A 24-year-old and a 52-year-old who are just starting out as investors need to pursue different strategies. Their different time horizons will dictate different asset mixes. The 24-year-old should consider investing entirely in stocks. The 52-year-old should consider a balanced portfolio made up of funds with relatively conservative risk/return profiles. There are some things they should do alike, however. For instance, each should invest in a Roth IRA because of its very attractive provisions. Withdrawals from a Roth IRA are tax-free after you reach age 59½, provided you've had the account for at least 5 years and meet other basic conditions.

Working in the 52-year-old's favor are "catch-up" contributions. If you are 50 or older and you meet certain income limits, you can sock away $7,000, which is $1,000 more than investors under age 50.

There are also catch-up provisions for contributions to employer retirement plans. If you are over age 50, check with your employer to learn how much of your salary you can put into a 401(k) or 403(b) plan. Plan rules vary, but if you can take advantage of the catch-up provisions, you might be able to sock away a considerable amount more for retirement.

If you're starting late, you won't have the advantages of decades of compounding, but less time and smaller compounded returns shouldn't dissuade you from saving for retirement. I've spent a lot of time coaching kids' lacrosse games, and I always emphasize to my players that it's just as important to be able to scoop up loose ground balls as it is to make good passes. In lacrosse, the team that's best at the apparently unglamorous work of getting ground balls always wins the game. In a similar way, in investing, even unglamorous returns will make a big difference over time. If you earn 6% a year, you will still double your money in roughly 12 years.

Whatever your situation, don't overlook the chance to get your children, or the children of your friends and relatives, started early on their investment programs. Dazzle them with this simple but powerful data. Table 14.5 shows the monthly savings required to reach the lofty goal of having $1 million at age 65. I've assumed the money is invested at an annual gain of 8%, and for purposes of this illustration, I've omitted the effects of taxes.

Age Savings Begins	Monthly Payment Needed to ReachGoal
Birth	$38
5	$56
10	$84
15	$126
20	$190
25	$286
30	$436
35	$671
40	$1,051
45	$1,698
50	$2,890
55	$5,466
60	$13,610

Figure 14.5 Investment Goal: $1 Million at Age 65

Source: Vanguard

Answer to the question in the chapter opening: A one-time investment of $6,000 in a tax-free account, left untouched to compound at 8% a year, would be worth $281,410 after 50 years.

In a Nutshell

You can accomplish impressive things if you start investing early and keep investing.

- **Compounding adds up.** Your investments will earn interest and dividends, and those reinvested earnings in turn will generate additional earnings.
- **Time is your ally.** While stocks are a very risky investment in any single year and have underperformed other asset classes in some periods, they have outperformed over the long run.
- **It's never too late.** Don't be deterred if you're getting a late start on a retirement savings program. You can still put time to work on your behalf.

15

Routine Maintenance for Your Portfolio

I f you own a car, you understand the importance of maintaining it properly—or you should. A car that's well maintained will run more smoothly, get better mileage, and be less likely to break down. To keep a car in good working order, you take it to the shop periodically for routine service, and, when necessary, a tune-up.

Your investment portfolio will also benefit from periodic checkups and maintenance. And the good news is that with your portfolio—unlike your engine—you should be familiar with what's under the hood.

There are two reasons to make adjustments in your portfolio:

1. Your personal financial situation changes.
2. Market fluctuations alter—sometimes substantially—the mix of your assets.

The focus of this chapter is rebalancing and portfolio maintenance, and I'll also discuss how to go about making changes when appropriate.

Your Personal Situation

No successful investor I know puts everything on autopilot. Why? Personal financial situations change. Your income will drop if you lose a job or retire. Your wealth could increase if you inherit money or sell a business. Other life events, such as marriage, the death of a spouse, or a child's departure from home, can cause fundamental changes in your financial situation. Whenever you experience such a change, it's a good idea to reassess your financial affairs, including your insurance coverage, your will, and your investment portfolio.

You may need to adjust your portfolio's risk level or take steps to increase its liquidity. For example, if you lose your job, you will likely need to draw on your emergency savings and temporarily stop contributing to other accounts. But if you switch jobs and move to a position that pays more but offers less job security, you may decide to increase your savings rate and put more into your emergency fund in the event things don't work out as planned.

You'll also likely want to make some changes in your portfolio as you get closer in time to your investment objective. For example, most investors shift to a more conservative asset mix as they approach retirement. And, if you're saving for a child's education, it's best not to be dependent on the stock market's benevolence when those first tuition payments get near. In other words, it's a good idea to shift some money to bond and money market funds to preserve capital to pay for tuition, room-and-board, and incidentals.

Life events don't always dictate massive changes in your investment program. There are plenty of smart, successful investors who stick to the same program, month after month, year after year, making steady progress toward their goals. But even if you want to be one of them, you'll need to do periodic checkups to make sure you're leaving things alone for good, solid reasons and not just because of inattentiveness or inertia.

Rebalancing a Portfolio

Even though most people don't need to change their investment programs very often, every long-term investor should rebalance his or her portfolio from time to time.

Rebalancing—the equivalent of an engine tune-up—means getting your investments back in line with your target asset mix. If you initially decided to split your assets evenly between stocks and bonds, you'll discover sooner or later that they aren't evenly split any longer; the different returns on the two asset classes will have changed the proportions. For example, if you started 2014 with a $100,000 retirement account divided evenly between stocks and bonds, you ended 2016 with a portfolio that was 54% stocks and 46% bonds. That's not a huge shift, but let's look at what the markets would have done to your allocation over the subsequent four years if you didn't do any rebalancing.

As shown in Figure 15.1, your half-and-half portfolio would have become a 61%/39% portfolio by the end of 2019. "Who cares?" you may be thinking. "Look how much money I made!" Yes, the value of the account would have a nice gain over the six years, growing nearly $157,333. But there's a risk lurking in this portfolio, and it came home to roost in early 2020. A monster of a risk, if you will.

The COVID-19 pandemic-induced stock market decline during the first quarter of 2020 would have shaved off $18,037 from your balance. If you had rebalanced your target asset allocation at the end of 2019 to its initial target of 50% stocks/50% bonds, your portfolio would have lost a less severe $13,926.

Of course, with the benefit of hindsight, we witnessed the stock market's subsequent rebound, and those paper losses, at least temporarily,

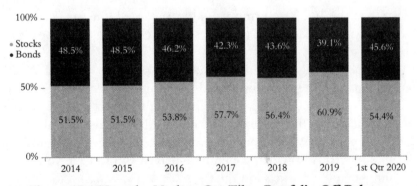

Figure 15.1 How the Markets Can Tilt a Portfolio Off-Balance

Source: Vanguard. U.S. stocks represented by the CRSP U.S. Total Market Index. U.S. bonds represented by the Bloomberg Barclays U.S. Aggregate Float Adjusted Bond Index.

erased and then some. That said, if you just retired or had a tuition payment due, you likely would not have felt very good about your portfolio during those dark days in the market.

We'll explore the risk/return trade-off of rebalancing in the next section. The risk being a considerable loss in your portfolio, perhaps inducing counterproductive, emotion-driven actions on your part; the return being a smoother ride and peace of mind.

Why Rebalance? To Tame the Risk Monster

Frequently, people tend to think about investing only in terms of making money. Making money is why we invest, but the reality is that if you don't remember to manage risk along the way, you won't do well at making money. **The point of rebalancing is to manage your risk, not to maximize your returns.** But if you don't manage risk, you may end up minimizing your long-term returns if you are overexposed to an asset class that suffers a severe reversal and you abandon your plan.

Let's think about the impact of rebalancing on a portfolio held for a long time. Consider another hypothetical portfolio, evenly divided between stocks and bonds, and rebalanced every six months from January 1980 through December 2019. That long span included some great periods and some bad periods in terms of performance. A portfolio that was rebalanced twice a year would have generated an average annualized return of 9.9% over the period, which is marginally lower than the 10.3% return it would have earned if never rebalanced. Does that mean that rebalancing "lost the race"? Not unless you have nerves of steel.

The rebalancing substantially reduced the portfolio's volatility. Without rebalancing, the portfolio would have suffered declines of −5% or more during more than approximately 8% of those six-month periods. With rebalancing, the portfolio declined to that degree in only about 3% of the periods. Which portfolio would have produced more anxious, sleepless nights? And which would have helped you to keep your equilibrium when the markets lost theirs?

Portfolio Pitfall: Don't Forget Those Buckets When You Tune-Up Your Portfolio

Remember our discussion in Chapter 3 about the buckets that represent your financial objectives? You'll want to keep those separate buckets in mind when you are giving your portfolio its checkup. Suppose your portfolio includes retirement investments and savings earmarked for your children's college costs. If you are using the bucket approach, you've probably designated different asset mixes for each of those investment programs, so you should review them separately rather than as parts of an overall portfolio.

And when you're looking at asset weightings, take a holistic view of everything that belongs in your retirement savings bucket. I've noticed that investors often mentally segregate their retirement savings by account type. For example, they think of their IRA and 401(k) accounts as two separate stashes, instead of as parts of the same nest egg. (It's especially easy to compartmentalize like that if you're dealing with different providers on the accounts.) And don't overlook your pension assets if you are fortunate enough to have them—even a small monthly pension is equivalent to earnings on a substantial lump sum of savings. For example, a $10,000 a year pension is equivalent to a $250,000 investment portfolio from which you draw 4% of the assets each year. That's a considerable amount of "hidden assets."

While we are on the subject of retirement income, Social Security should also be considered a bucket. While clearly beyond the scope of this book, Social Security provides guaranteed income (with inflation adjustments) and a "balance" that doesn't fluctuate with the financial markets. It can serve as a great foundation for retirement income. The average retired worker receives about $1,500 a month, according to the Social Security Administration. As with pension assets, this is the equivalent of having $450,000 of assets from which you draw 4% per year. Again, a meaningful sum to consider when reviewing your balance sheet.

(continued)

> **Portfolio Pitfall: Don't Forget Those Buckets When You Tune-Up Your Portfolio** (*Continued*)
>
> To make sure you are seeing things clearly, it's not a bad idea to take inventory of all your financial resources when you give your portfolio its periodic checkup. Put everything down on paper, as I suggested doing in Chapter 7 with your investment policy statement. Add up all of your assets bucket by bucket. Laying it all out in front of you will provide a scorecard, so that over time you can easily see whether you are progressing toward your objectives as you intended.

When to Rebalance

When you rebalance and how you go about it will depend on your personal circumstances—your age, your net worth, and your tax bracket. You may even want to discuss some of the decisions with your financial advisor or accountant. Here are some general rules of thumb:

- **Rebalance on a regular schedule (quarterly, semiannually, or annually).** Vanguard research shows that the frequency of rebalancing is not a big deal; in other words, results do not vary considerably to whether you're rebalancing quarterly, semiannually, or annually. What's important is that you do it. For most people, annual rebalancing is adequate. Choose your birthday, anniversary, or some other fixed date, such as April 15, the tax-filing deadline. This will impose some discipline on the process. Otherwise, you might permit external events, short-term market swings, or emotions to sway your decision about when to rebalance.
- **Rebalance only if your asset mix has strayed from its target by more than 5 percentage points.** If the variation is less, the benefit of rebalancing probably isn't worth the bother.
- **Don't get too carried away with micro issues.** Some investors try to establish precise weightings for specific market segments in their portfolios. For example, they try to maintain certain proportions of U.S. and international stocks, growth and value stocks,

large-cap and small-cap stocks, or bonds of particular types and maturities. These micro matters aren't the most pressing rebalancing issues. Worry about them only after you have made sure you are on target with your overall asset mix. The 5-percentage-point trigger for rebalancing makes sense here, too.

The Tax Monster Joins the Risk Monster

If all your assets were in tax-advantaged retirement accounts, rebalancing would be relatively simple. You can move money around within your IRA and your 401(k) plan without triggering any capital gains and tax liabilities. But sooner or later, you will probably have to rebalance your taxable accounts, and that could lead to a tax consequence. Let's say you need to adjust the stock component of your $100,000 portfolio from 80% to 75%. You decide the best way to do that is to move $5,000 from a stock fund into a bond fund, but you'll likely have a capital gain on the sale, which will mean taxes. In such a case, it's generally best to just bite the bullet, exchange the shares, and pay the tax. It is better not to let the tail wag the dog here, so I advise against allowing tax considerations drive your overall investment strategy.

One way to minimize tax liabilities when rebalancing is to change your investment pattern instead of moving existing assets from one fund to another. You can redirect new investments to the part of your portfolio that you want to beef up. Or, since your dividend and capital gains distributions are already being taxed anyway, you could redirect those distributions from the asset that has performed well and have them invested in the one that has fallen below your target weighting.

Rebalancing Takes Discipline

The biggest challenge of rebalancing is finding the discipline to do it. To some, rebalancing feels unreasonable. If stocks are booming and bonds are hurting, you're apt to ask yourself why you would want to move money from stocks to the bond portion of your portfolio. It's hard to see the wisdom in shuffling the cards when it looks like you're holding a winning hand.

Remember the importance of your asset mix in determining your investment returns. You originally decided on your asset allocation plan for specific reasons, one of which was managing risk. Trust your own good judgment and force yourself to rebalance periodically. If you don't, you could very well wind up with a portfolio that's far riskier than you intended.

You can always learn lessons as an investor, and the value of rebalancing is one of the key things that I've learned by seeing it firsthand over 40 years. What drove it home was watching fund managers pursue their own rebalancing chores. I've talked about the challenge of this discipline for an individual investor; fund managers face the same thing on a much larger scale.

One event early in my career, in particular, underscored for me the value of disciplined rebalancing. It occurred on October 20, 1987, the day following the largest one-day percentage drop in stock market history—the market fell more than 22% on October 19. Professionals and non-professionals alike felt very panicky about stocks that day. But the managers of Vanguard Wellington Fund bought millions of dollars' worth of stocks to restore its targeted 65%/35% stock/bond mix. The plunging stock market had taken their stock allocation well below their prospectus-dictated targets, so they had to sell bonds and add stocks to rebalance. Had they let emotions rather than discipline dictate their actions, they might easily have missed the sharp rally that began the next day. It was a wonderful learning experience for a young person like me.

The value of that no-emotions-allowed discipline was demonstrated again during the week of September 17, 2001, when the stock exchanges reopened after a hiatus due to the September 11 terrorist attacks. The market immediately plunged, and over the next few days, Wellington Fund again had to buy stocks to maintain its target allocation. Although the move was a simple rebalancing, not an attempt to time the markets, it appeared prescient when the stock market began rising the very next week.

As we discussed in Chapter 6, Wellington Fund is the paragon of balance and diversification. Since its inception in 1929, the fund has produced an average annual return of 8.3% compared to 9.5% for the broad stock market, while taking roughly 35% less risk. Rebalancing served as an important source of that outstanding risk-adjusted return.

Keep Things Simple

Your periodic portfolio inspection should also include a review of your fund holdings. The old notion that if X is good, more of X is better does not apply. If you have more than ten funds, it's probably too many. The ultimate in simplicity is to own just two or three broadly diversified total market index funds and call it a day.

Investing in a large number of funds can be problematic. First, a big collection of funds can be difficult to track, making it more complicated to monitor your portfolio and rebalance it effectively and efficiently. Second, a big collection of funds can provide a false sense of security about the level of diversification of your portfolio. Third, a portfolio with many components may mimic the performance of a market index, but with far higher costs and lower tax efficiency than an index fund or ETF doing the same thing.

And yet, lots of investors make this mistake. In a recent check of Vanguard's defined contribution plan data from 2019, we learned that more than 9,000 Vanguard plan participants were invested in 20 funds or more. While that's a relatively small group of people within a base of many millions, it is concerning. Even more mindboggling were the more than 300 investors who held more than 45 funds each. One investor was listed as holding 116 funds. I can't imagine how this person even attempts to keep track of it all.

Investors who accumulate lots of funds may be collecting investments like butterflies, according to longtime Morningstar research director John Rekenthaler: "Something pretty and bright flaps its wings and catches their eye—an article in a magazine or an advertisement with a great total return number—and they get excited and buy some of that fund. That's not an investment strategy; that's investment opportunism."[1]

How to Clean Up a Messy Portfolio

When investors end up with a jumble of similar funds, it is usually a result of chasing performance. It's easy to understand how this happens. Funds that performed well during a given period are apt to have followed similar investment styles and objectives. They're the funds near the top of the rankings for some financial websites and magazines, and they're the funds whose managers are being profiled or interviewed. Those funds might as well be festooned with neon lights that flash "Buy me. Buy me now." You'll avoid the risk of accumulating a hodgepodge portfolio if you resist the temptation to chase performance.

If you have built a portfolio and are wondering whether it needs some pruning, here are some questions to ask yourself:

- Do you know why you own each of your funds? Each one should play a defined role in your portfolio.
- Do two or more of your funds share the same investment objective or investment style? If so, you may want to consider paring one fund.
- If you were starting fresh today, would you invest in the funds you now own? In a sense, each day that you continue to hold a fund is like buying it all over again.

If your answers to those questions persuaded you to eliminate a fund or two, fine. But don't act before considering the potential tax issues discussed earlier. An alternative to selling a fund is to use it for a charitable gift. That way, you can avoid incurring capital gains taxes and do some good in the world at the same time.

Of course, the best reason to clean up a messy portfolio is to keep things simple. Trying to keep up with the transactional mechanics of ten stock funds and four or five bond funds can be a recordkeeping chore. Multiple quarterly statements aren't the only headache—you also have the tax burden of reporting distributions from all of those funds. You probably have better things to do than spending an inordinate amount of time on your portfolio. Investing with simplicity is liberating because it lets you live your life.

In a Nutshell

Your investment portfolio needs a periodic checkup to make sure it's still serving your needs. Here are some considerations:

- **Life events may dictate some changes.** You may need to adjust your portfolio if your financial situation has changed or if you are getting closer in time to your investment objective.
- **Market fluctuations can knock your portfolio's asset mix off-kilter over time.** It's a good idea to check your portfolio once a year or so and rebalance it if it has drifted by 5 percentage points or more from the target asset allocation.
- **Keep it simple.** You can assemble a balanced, well-diversified portfolio with two or three total market index funds.
- **Make sure each fund serves a distinct purpose in your portfolio.** If you have more than 10 funds in your portfolio, consider eliminating a few.

Note

1. "An Interview with Morningstar Research Director John Rekenthaler," In The Vanguard shareholder newsletter, Autumn 2000, page 1.

16

Stupid Math Tricks for Smart Investors

I f you are a fan of late-night talk shows, you may remember one of the staples of one program was "Stupid Pet Tricks," in which pet owners would show off the antics of their animals. Believe it or not, there are quite a few "stupid math tricks" in investing. They're not really stupid at all, of course—just fun and useful to know, and to me, more interesting than a jump-roping dog. I'll devote this chapter to covering a handful of the math tricks of investing, which will help you to become a sharp-eyed buyer of financial products and services.

1. **Dollars, not percent signs, are what you carry in your wallet.** The investment management industry measures costs and performance in percentage terms. However, for practical decision-making, it can help to translate those percentages into dollars. For example, suppose you have a portfolio worth $100,000 with an average expense ratio of 1.00%. You may not mind paying 1%, but how do you feel about paying $1,000 per year? It's a more real-world way to assess the value you're receiving.
2. **Make estimates in a flash with the Rule of 72.** Want to know how fast your money will double? You don't need a calculator. Estimate your yearly rate of return and divide it into the number 72.

The result is the number of years it will take for your investment to roughly double in value. The rule works with any amount of money.

The Rule of 72 is a nifty trick, but it can do more for you than impress your friends. Suppose you're mulling what to do with a long-term investment of $100,000. If you put the sum in a bond fund and earn an average of 3% a year, you will double your money in about 24 years (72 ÷ 3 = 24). But if you invest the same sum in a stock fund that earns the long-term average market return of 9% a year on average, you'll get to $200,000 after about 8 years (72 ÷ 9 = 8). (For simplicity, I'm ignoring taxes in these examples.)

The Rule of 72 also gives a powerful demonstration of the impact of small differences in return over time. Consider two mutual funds that have the same *gross returns*—that is, performance before costs are subtracted—but different expense ratios, which result in average net returns of 8% and 7%, respectively. The Rule of 72 tells us that an investment in the 8% fund will double after nine years, while money in the 7% fund will take more than a decade to double. Keeping costs low can help you boost your returns and double your money more quickly.

3. **Even in the bargain basement, something can be worthless.** Back in the days when internet stocks were all the rage, someone gave me a T-shirt bearing the name of a prominent dot-com company. The company's stock then fell from around $180 a share to less than 50 cents, and I calculated that my T-shirt was worth ten shares of stock. When I made this observation to a friend outside the financial industry, he said earnestly: "Maybe I should buy that stock. At 50 cents a share, how much money could I lose?"

The answer is "all of it." (That's another one of my favorite investing aphorisms.) If an investment is risky, it doesn't matter whether you pay 50 cents a share or $50 a share, you are still at risk of losing all of it.

Investors sometimes get suckered into thinking that a stock whose price has fallen a long way must therefore offer good value. They forget that maybe it hasn't yet fallen far enough. This attitude

Annual Return	3%	6%	9%	12%
Years until investment doubles	24	12	8	6

Figure 16.1 Growth of an Investment at Varying Rates of Return (Pre-Tax)

Source: Vanguard

was especially noticeable after the collapse of the dot-com bubble in 2000. Although the prices of many stocks fell at that point, market prices overall were still quite high in relation to traditional yardsticks. Few investors seemed to realize how much risk was still embedded in those prices.

4. **Up 100% and down 50% puts you right back where you started.** Suppose you invest in a fund whose share price falls from $50 to $25, a decline of 50%. If you hope to get back to your starting point, you need a 50% gain, right? Wrong! You need a 100% gain. Here's the same math, but starting from the other end. A stock that goes from $25 to $50 a share is up 100%. If it falls by 50%, you're back where you started.

This is important to keep in mind, especially during periods of stock market euphoria. Percentages seem particularly perplexing for investors at such times, as perhaps the market's rapid rise goes to people's heads. Stupid Math Trick #4 will stand you in good stead if anyone tries to sell you a volatile investment by emphasizing its upward moves more than its downward moves. Remember a stock that soars by 100% in a short time may be capable of falling 50% just as fast, putting you right back to your starting point.

5. **The bigger the fall, the longer the recovery.** When the price of a stock or a fund declines by a considerable amount, it generally takes a very long time to recover. (The dramatic recovery in stock prices in 2020 is one exception to this rule.) This stupid math trick is something that conservative investors understand intuitively. Suppose a stock falls by 60%—declining from $100 a share to $40. That's a large decline. And if it's your money, you might even call it cataclysmic. As Figure 16.2 shows, even at a hearty recovery rate of 10% a year the stock would need a decade to regain its value

An understanding of the mathematics of downturns and recoveries will give you a new perspective on the financial news. For example, at the turn of this century, after the Nasdaq Composite Index plunged from its high of 5,048.62 on March 10, 2000, to a low of 1,423.19 on September 21, 2001, the pundits were all wondering whether the Nasdaq would get back to 5,000 again anytime soon. That would be mathematically challenging, to say the least. Although it took the Nasdaq Composite just under 4 years to zoom from 1,423 to 5,048, the index would have needed 13 years to regain that peak at a more reasonable growth rate of 10% a year. The fall took just a bit more than six months.

Year	Value at Beginning	Change	Value at End
0	$100	−60%	$40
1	$40	10%	$44
2	$44	10%	$48
3	$48	10%	$53
4	$53	10%	$59
5	$59	10%	$64
6	$64	10%	$71
7	$71	10%	$78
8	$78	10%	$86
9	$86	10%	$94
10	$94	10%	$104

Figure 16.2 Recoveries Can Take a Long Time

Source: Vanguard

The math of market drops and recoveries also demonstrates the folly in waiting to "get back to even." Just like gamblers on losing streaks, some investors feel that they absolutely have to stick with a volatile investment until they get back to their breakeven point—what they paid for it. But it's extremely difficult to get back to even on an investment that has lost a significant chunk of its value. Some investors never get there. I'll talk more about dealing with losses in a future chapter, but I want to make the point here that optimism is emotion, and you should never let emotion override mathematics.

6. **Cumulative returns can be misleading.** When a fund reports cumulative returns, it is giving only starting and ending values, with no indication about what happened along the way. Would you be attracted to a stock fund that had earned a cumulative return of 250% over 20 years? Sounds great, doesn't it? But if you do the math, you'll find out that the fund was earning an average of 6% a year—nothing spectacular. When you're evaluating a fund's performance, focus on average annual returns, not cumulative returns. An investment that averages about 11% annually over 20 years produces a cumulative return of 706%.

7. **If you're a long-term bond investor, a falling share price could be a good thing.** Over the years in hundreds of one-on-one conversations with investors, this is one of the tricks that I have had

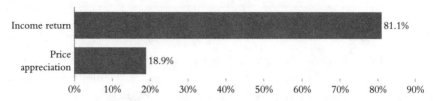

**Figure 16.3 Components of Total Return on a
Broad Bond Market Index Fund (2010–2019)**

Source: Vanguard, using data for the Bloomberg Barclays U.S. Aggregate Float Adjusted Bond Index.

the hardest time convincing people is true. When interest rates rise, a bond fund's share price falls. This can look like bad news when you view your accounts online or receive an account statement in the mail. But if you're a long-term investor, it's actually something to cheer about.

As Figure 16.3 illustrates, over long periods, most of the return on a bond fund comes from interest payments reinvested in additional shares of the fund, not from increases in bond prices. Let's assume that your bond fund's share price falls from $10 to $9 as interest rates rise from 3.5% to 5%. Since you're there for the long term, the share price shouldn't matter to you. In fact, you should be very pleased. In this example, one dollar of reinvested dividends buys 11% more shares in the fund. The bottom line: If you are a long-term investor in a bond fund, don't worry about losses in your fund's share price caused by a rise in interest rates. In fact, too many investors have fallen into a buy high/sell low trap by not understanding this math, and panicked when rates rise and bond fund values fall.

The converse of this stupid math trick: When a decline in interest rates drives up the share prices of bond funds, don't join in the stampede of investors who suddenly want to own bonds. The decline in interest rates means that the fund's yield, and thus the income you earn on your reinvested dividends, is about to decline.

In a Nutshell

You don't need to keep a calculator at your side whenever you are thinking about investing, but as a consumer of investments, you do need to be aware of some math tricks of the trade:

- **Use the Rule of 72 to make quick projections.** Divide your rate of return into 72 and the result is roughly the number of years that it will take an investment to double.
- **Don't get flummoxed by percentages.** Paying a 1% fee for your investments of a $100,000 portfolio may not sound like much, but that's $1,000 of your hard-earned money.
- **Look past the cumulative return.** When you are evaluating a fund's performance, focus on average annual returns, not cumulative returns.

PART IV
STAY ON COURSE

17

"It's a Mad, Mad, Mad, Mad World"

At the outset of this book, I asserted that the key to success-ful investing is to get a few important things right and avoid making big, costly mistakes. I've already discussed the good habits that you need to develop—saving money, investing regularly, adhering to a buy-and-hold approach, and minimizing costs, among others. Now, we'll turn our attention to circumstances and tempta-tions that can undermine your investment program.

As we've witnessed during the first two decades of this century, the financial markets have presented challenges to investors, including severe stock market declines and subsequent run-ups, as well as historically low interest rates. It may seem paradoxical, but we'll see why run-ups can be a challenge in a moment.

The tests from the markets aren't the only ones that you will face as an investor. You'll encounter advice that can lead you astray. You'll be buffeted at times by your own emotions or behavioral biases that can hamper your decision-making and cloud your judgment. You'll be tempted by opportunities that appear alluring. In Part 4 of this book, I'll aim to examine these enticements and urges in an effort to provide you with some defensive tools as you embark on your journey as an investor.

In the hope that a little knowledge will help to inoculate you against temptations and the potential for self-inflicted mistakes, this chapter will be devoted to reviewing a few past manias and bubbles. There's no question that it is a "mad, mad, mad, mad world" out there, to borrow a title from a classic movie. As an investor, you're sure to encounter hot stock tips, multiply-your-money promises, invitations to seminars on "secrets even the pros don't know," and maybe even solicitations for illegal pyramid schemes. I hope you're equipped by now to resist these siren songs. And, from time to time, you'll be tempted by something much more seductive—a speculative fever over a stock, a sector of the market, or some other "can't miss" chance for quick profit. You'll try to stay level-headed about it, but before long you might feel out of touch because it seems that everybody else appears to be getting rich while you cling to your seemingly outmoded investment precepts. Maybe they're right and you're wrong, you'll think. And maybe you should alter your investment plan and get on the bandwagon with everyone else. But, to quote Kipling, "If you can keep your head when all about you are losing theirs . . ."

Speculative Bubbles

A speculative bubble is a kind of social epidemic. Euphoria over stocks or some other asset seems to spread rapidly through the population. In a bubble, it is the enthusiasm itself and not the fundamental value of the investment that drives prices higher and higher. Afterward, the reality becomes abundantly clear. Once a speculative bubble bursts and prices collapse, it suddenly seems absolutely incredible that people could have been so foolish.

There have been many epidemics of speculation throughout the course of history, and one that I'll cite here dates back centuries. Bubbles have swelled around many different things, including stocks, real estate, gold, oil, and silver, and believe it or not, even Beanie Babies, baseball cards, and tulip bulbs! It's important for every investor to know something about bubbles. If you're familiar with some of the crazy things that led individuals to part with their money in the past, you may be better able to hold out against manias that you're likely to encounter in the future. I'll share the brief stories of several bubbles so you can develop a sense for when the mania about a topic—whether it is tulip bulbs, precious metals, or stocks—sends signals to be wary.

Tulipmania

In Holland during the early 17th century, investors went bonkers over tulip bulbs. The frenzy erupted after it was discovered that some bulbs produced flowers with special colorations. (Nobody knew at the time, but the bulbs were infected with a non-fatal virus called mosaic.) People bid up the prices of the diseased bulbs to unbelievable levels; some sold for more than houses at the time. People from all walks of life were trading in tulip bulbs at the peak of the mania. My longtime colleague Burt Malkiel provides this account of the end of "Tulipmania" in his investment classic, *A Random Walk Down Wall Street*:

> Apparently, as happens in all speculative crazes, prices eventually got so high that some people decided they would be prudent and sell their bulbs. Soon others followed suit. Like a snowball rolling downhill, bulb deflation grew at an increasingly rapid pace and in no time at all panic reigned. [Despite government attempts to halt the panic] prices continued to decline. Down and down they went until most bulbs became almost worthless—selling for no more than the price of a common onion.

A Modern Gold Rush

Precious metals have also seen their share of speculative bubbles over the years. In times of crisis—when the stock market tumbles, or inflation climbs, or the dollar weakens—gold and other precious metals are seen by some as a safe haven. One of the biggest gold booms in recent history occurred in the late 1970s, when inflation was high and the dollar was declining. Gold prices shot up to $850 an ounce on the London market in January 1980 from $208 an ounce a year earlier. (A personal aside: I was getting married later that year and as a grad student with lots of debt, I couldn't afford a gold wedding ring for my wife at those prices. I settled up a few years later when I had a somewhat better balance sheet and gold was 60% cheaper!) As Peter L. Bernstein says in his book, *The Power of Gold*:

> Few people who bought at $35, or even under $100, held on to sell at $850. Most of the early buyers undoubtedly took their profits and bailed out long before the peak, for the path to $850 was volatile all the way. The likelihood is that many more people were sucked into the gold market as it approached $850—and shortly afterward—than those who were farsighted enough to go in when the price was fussing around $40.

Except for a brief spike after the 1987 stock market crash, 1980 was as good as it got for gold bugs for decades as gold didn't break the $800 level again until 2008. Today, it is trading at near-record levels and perhaps is another bubble in the making. Like oil and other commodities, gold prices are subject to booms and busts. Unlike oil, however, gold has limited economic value and, if it isn't clear to you, I am not a big fan of holding it as an investment.

The Dot-com Bubble

One of my favorite films is called *King of Hearts*, which is about a Scottish soldier in World War I sent to a French village to defuse explosives that the Germans have set to detonate at midnight. The village has been abandoned by its residents and now is populated by the patients of a nearby asylum who were set free after their caretakers fled. The soldier, played by Alan Bates, doesn't understand why the shopkeepers and other residents are behaving so oddly. (For example, the proprietor of the crowded barbershop explains that he has many customers because he pays them. The zookeeper leaves the door of the lion's cage open, saying that the beast is too accustomed to captivity to want to escape.) Surrounded by such bizarre behavior in the face of danger, the soldier wonders whether he has lost his mind.

Some of us felt like the Bates character in *King of Hearts* during the late 1990s frenzy over the internet and just about any newly issued stock that was called a *dot-com*. No matter how deeply we believed in our stalwart investment principles, such as diversification and discipline, and our allegiance to stock fundamentals, like earnings and cash flow, we began to think we had lost our senses. In fact, it was the people around us who had abandoned rational thinking. Companies with no profits or revenues were suddenly seen as smart investments just because they were involved in e-business. CEOs would say with straight faces that their companies' revenues and profits would grow at 25% a year more for the foreseeable future—a highly implausible prognosis, if you do the math, because as a company gets larger, each percentage point of growth requires ever-larger amounts of revenue. Both sophisticated and unsophisticated investors seemed to have abandoned all skepticism, blinded to risk by the prospect of riches. The generous returns of dot-com stocks (and stocks at large) compelled many to *panic buy*—loading up on stocks with hopes of continued extraordinary gains.

Trillions of dollars of wealth evaporated in less than a year when the dot-com bubble burst, earning it a spot in the record books as one of history's worst speculative manias. Fortunately, although the collapse affected just about all investors, it appears that most ordinary people had not sunk all of their retirement savings into internet stocks. And now, having experienced a bubble firsthand, they are much better equipped to weather future ones.

One last point on manias: Sometimes the investment recovers, and sometimes it doesn't. Many sound tech companies remained in business after 2000 and subsequently prospered. Gold prices, as noted, re-inflated at some point after bursting. Tulip bulbs did not. But the underlying point is beware of bubbles.

Some Commonalities among Manias

When you read about something like Tulipmania, it's tempting to think of this as a quaint tale of long ago when people were much more gullible and foolish than they are now. But as the recent past has demonstrated, the progress of civilization hasn't changed some aspects of human nature. Here are things common to all bubbles.

A valid reason for investor optimism. There's typically some real basis for the excitement that starts a bubble—whether it's the strong demand for rare and beautiful tulip bulbs, the glitter of rising gold prices, or the potential of leveraging a technological breakthrough like the internet. But as buyers pour in, prices begin rising on their own momentum, not because of business fundamentals. Another well-worn, but important to remember investment aphorism: "Trees don't grow to the sky."

Manias feed on greed. Once a bubble starts growing, many people jump in purely as speculators. They're not interested in the underlying investment; they just believe they can make a killing by buying something and then selling it to someone else at a higher price. This is called the *greater fool theory*—the notion that although prices may seem high, a buyer can always find some bigger fool who is willing to pay an even higher price. It's a prime inflator for a bubble. We saw this phenomenon more recently with house flipping.

"It's different this time." In a bubble, the believers dismiss naysayers as hopelessly out of step with the times. At the height of the dot-com bubble, we heard endless talk about the "new economy" in which old notions about stock price valuations no longer applied. Things certainly were changing—15 years earlier, would most of us have imagined anything like the internet? More prosaically, who would have predicted the peaceful collapse of the Soviet Union, or the rise of global commerce, or a crippling global pandemic? But changing circumstances don't imply changes to the core principles of prudent investing. That's why "it's different this time" are said to be the four most dangerous words in investing.

What risk? Though the old adage is that Wall Street knows only two emotions—fear and greed—people lose their fear of risk in a speculative bubble. All they see is that caution does not make you rich. One young investor, quoted in *The Wall Street Journal* near the peak of tech stocks at the turn of the century, said, "What's scarier is not to be in the market now than to worry about a downturn." This emotion is also known today as *FOMO*—fear of missing out. Reacting to it is far more likely to cost you money than make you rich.

Here's an example that has stuck in my mind for years. One evening in the late 1990s, after running the Boston Marathon, I stopped into a fast-food restaurant in Connecticut while returning to my home in Philadelphia. Though I was still in my running clothes, I was recognized by two retired couples who were sipping coffee at a table as they watched the financial news on the restaurant's television, and we struck up a conversation. They told us that they met there every night at this time to catch the financial programming on CNBC since they didn't have cable at home. It was astonishing to me—and more than a little frightening—that these senior citizens were so actively engaged in following the daily movements of the stock market even though they apparently couldn't afford cable television at home.

Some people who join in a mania are confident that they will be able to get out before it bursts. That's a dangerous delusion. In the 1990s, some very smart people who had studied the markets for many years were sure they were seeing a bubble, but none of them could predict how or when it would end, which it did in stunning fashion in 2000. Booms can go bust because of broad economic factors or unexpected bad news from one of the companies at the center of the boom. But neither the bubble nor the pin that pops it is apparent until afterward.

Fast-forward several years to 2008, and we saw the bursting of the hedge fund bubble. The onset of the global financial crisis was a death knell for many funds. In August 2007, there were more than 8,400 listed hedge funds, based on the number of funds reporting to the Lipper TASS Hedge Fund Database. A short two years later, 6,100 funds existed. I'll examine hedge funds and other sophisticated investments in Chapter 21.

How to Protect Yourself from Speculative Manias

You'll know there's a speculative bubble in the making when the friends and acquaintances who usually talk to you about family, sports, hobbies, or other interests start chatting instead about how much they have made in oil futures, aerospace stocks, silver, beach-front real estate, cryptocurrency, or whatever. There is a great anec-dote, perhaps apocryphal, about Joseph Kennedy in the late 1920s. One morning, Kennedy, father of the future president and a wealthy Bostonian, stopped to get his shoes shined and, reportedly, the shoe shine boy leaned in conspiratorially and gave a recommendation on a stock. As the story goes, Kennedy thought to himself, "When you start hearing stock tips from shoe shine boys, it is time to get out of the market."

If someone tells you about a sure-fire technology that's certain to produce great wealth, don't believe it. Just because a new technol-ogy offers great promise doesn't mean every company will profit from it. Railroads and commercial aviation revolutionized transportation, but they have never produced huge profits for the everyday investor. Exciting new technologies often attract considerable competition, and many of the companies that supposedly have "first-mover" advantages don't survive.

Yes, some people will make money in a speculative bubble. But most won't. Most people who try either get there too late to profit in a big way or stay too long at the party and get caught in the stampede out. For example, for most instant-wealth seeking who trekked West during the California Gold Rush of 1849, it just didn't pan out. One of the most famous success stories of the period was Levi Strauss, who made his money selling clothing to "forty-niners" instead of mining gold himself. Carrying that forward to today, it is the Wall Street investment banks, not you, who are most likely to profit from the next mania and the next one after that.

Be wary, too, of chasing the trend. Here's some concrete data to help you fend off people who say there's money to be made on a hot sector of the market. In the stock market, it's a reality that some sectors will outperform the others at any given moment. But history shows that the top performer in a given year rarely stays at the top of the heap. As shown in Figure 17.1, there has been only one time since 2000 when a sector managed to stay on top two years running. And in no instance has one sector led the market for three years in a row.

Earlier in this book, I made it pretty plain that I think most investors would be wise to use broad market index funds as the core of their portfolio. So now you may be wondering: If you're invested in a broad index fund, how can you escape short-term, collateral damage from fads and bubbles? After all, your fund will be exposed, by definition, to whatever sector of the market is exciting so many investors.

Year	Top Ranked Sector for Performance	Rank in Subsequent Year (among 11 sectors)
2000	Utilities	10
2001	Materials	2
2002	Consumer staples	10
2003	Information technology	10
2004	Energy	1
2005	Energy	3
2006	Real estate	10
2007	Energy	6
2008	Consumer staples	8
2009	Information technology	9
2010	Real estate	4
2011	Utilities	11
2012	Financials	4
2013	Consumer discretionary	8
2014	Real estate	5
2015	Consumer discretionary	8
2016	Energy	10
2017	Information technology	4
2018	Health care	10
2019	Information technology	Time will tell. . .

Figure 17.1 Top-Performing Stock Market Sectors, 2000–2019

Source: Vanguard calculations using S&P data.

I'll be frank: If you are broadly invested in the markets when a major speculative bubble occurs, it's impossible to escape the effects entirely. But here again, diversification proves its benefits. If your portfolio is broadly diversified, you're likely to suffer less damage than someone with a portfolio concentrated in the hot investment. And if you are a long-term investor, you will have time to recover from the bubble's collateral effects. In any case, don't be deterred from participating in the markets because prices look, well, "bubblicious." If you sit on the sidelines debating when to get in, you're making little progress toward your financial goals.

What can you do if you have lost a lot of money by allowing yourself to become swept up in a bubble? That's a tough situation, particularly if your investment time horizon is limited. Don't roll the dice again by betting on another hot trend. The only thing you can reasonably do is to dust yourself off, make an honest assessment of your investment program, and decide upon a sensible course of action going forward. If you conclude that you are uncomfortable overweighting small-cap growth or emerging-market stocks, for example, because you now realize they are too risky, pare your holdings. You must be able to say, "I made a mistake, but that's in the past. Now I'll go forward based on my best assessment of what I need to do for the future." But recognize that, once you make such a decision, a time is sure to come when small-cap growth or emerging-markets stocks have a great two-year run. You can't let yourself say, "If only I hadn't sold those stocks!" and buy them all over again.

In a Nutshell

Don't let seductions like speculative bubbles derail your investment program. You can protect yourself if you:

- **Don't follow the crowd.** Speculative fevers grip investors periodically throughout history, and we haven't seen the last of them. Refrain from joining the herd.
- **Remain grateful, not greedy, when the markets are bountiful.** During periods of euphoria about the markets, greed blinds investors to the dangers in investing. Never forget that risk is always present.

(continued)

In a Nutshell   (*Continued*)

- **Tune out anyone who claims that a particular company, industry sector, or new technology is a sure-fire, risk-free way to achieve great wealth.** If it sounds too good to be true, remain skeptical.
- **Stay broadly invested and don't be tempted to jump into top-performing market sectors.** Hot-performing sectors eventually cool. And chances are high that you'll be joining the party just as it is ending.

18

Why You May Be Your Own Worst Enemy

E conomist Benjamin Graham once said, "The investor's chief problem—and even his worst enemy—is likely to be himself." The quote captures perfectly that tendency for investors to act irrationally and in ways that are contrary to their own interests.

Over the past few decades, an entire academic discipline has sprung up on this topic—*behavioral finance*, which is the study of the influence of psychology on investor behavior. Scholars have written dissertations on how people make investment choices, and several universities have established endowed professorships in the field. Researchers in behavioral finance apply scientific methods to analyze behavior that has been observed anecdotally for a long time.

While we investors would like to think we always carefully weigh our options and sensibly choose the ones that offer the most benefits, the fact is that we often don't. It turns out that real people aren't very good at even identifying options, let alone choosing the right one. We tend to misinterpret information and miscalculate simple statistical probabilities. And we react to events in emotional and often counterproductive ways.

Although I haven't formally studied investor psychology, I have had the opportunity over the years to observe many investors, both successful and not-so-successful ones. My experience bears out some of what the behavioral finance experts have been telling us. On the basis of how real people react to real events in the markets, here's a list of some of the miscues to avoid.

Being Overconfident About Your Own Abilities

Remember humorist Garrison Keillor's mythical town of Lake Wobegon, where "all the women are strong, all the men are good-looking, and all the children are above-average"? I have no data about strength and looks, but it turns out to be pretty common for people to think they are above-average in many ways. Numerous surveys have found that a large majority of people believe they are better drivers than most other people, or are less likely to lose their jobs than their co-workers, or have a better chance than their friends at avoiding a heart attack.

If you are overconfident about your abilities as an investor, you are likely to underestimate risk. Such thinking could lead you to dismiss time-tested principles of investing—balance and diversification, for example—in the belief that you can win big by picking one or two superbly performing funds or stocks.

One last point about confidence. Over my career of hiring people and firms to manage clients' assets, I have always kept a checklist of character traits that tilted the odds of making a good hire in our favor. Humility—not at the expense of strongmindedness—is always at the top of the list.

Allowing the Current Environment to Blind You to the Larger Context

People have a tendency to assume that present conditions will continue—whatever those conditions may be. As a result, when markets are very good, investors tend to be overly optimistic, and when markets are bad, investors tend to be overly pessimistic. It is called *recency bias*.

I observed this tendency again and again at the conferences we held for Vanguard clients all over the country. We customarily opened these sessions by asking the attendees to jot down a forecast for stock market and bond market returns for the next 12 months. At the end of the meeting, we announce the results of our informal poll. Almost invariably, the returns that the clients predict are very, very close to the actual returns that the markets produced in the most recent past.

It's uncanny how this tendency repeats itself, even though the market conditions change. During the roaring bull market of the 1990s, when stocks were compounding at 18% or 20% a year, the attendees at our client meetings would project stock market returns of 18% to 20% for the next 12 months. Once the markets headed downward in 2000, our clients grew much more pessimistic in their forecasts.

There's a real danger in the tendency to base expectations on recent market conditions. Investors who lose sight of the big picture can end up constantly revising their strategies. In essence, they're always buying firewood just in time for the heat wave, or throwing away their umbrellas just as the heavy rains move in.

Thinking You See a Pattern Where None Exists

Human beings like patterns and tend to believe they exist even when events are totally random. People also think they can use those patterns to their advantage. Indeed, one of the first things every baby learns is a kind of cause-and-effect pattern. My youngest granddaughter throws her spoon on the floor and I bend down and pick it up. And she then throws it down again!

Statisticians explain the mirage of patterns in terms of coin tosses. If you toss a coin five times, the probability of getting heads (or tails) remains 50/50 each time, no matter what the sequence of previous tosses. Each toss of the coin is what statisticians call an *independent event*. That's a difficult concept for many people to internalize. They expect a sequence of coin tosses to result in heads-tails-heads-tails-heads-tails more often than in some other mix of results.

Given this general human tendency, it's no surprise that investors also expect to find patterns in the financial markets whether they're there or not. During the 1990s, investors noticed that each sharp drop in the stock market was followed by a sharp recovery. They concluded that quick rebounds were the rule these days and started telling each other to "buy on the dips." In fact, the markets don't always rebound quickly, as investors were reminded by the prolonged decline that began in 2000, and a few years later in 2008–2009. (The rebound in 2020 is one of the exceptions to this rule.)

Focusing Too Much on Short-Term Losses

People tend to feel losses more acutely than gains. Suppose I invite you to bet on a coin toss in which you'll lose $100 if tails comes up or win $100 if heads comes up. Would you make that bet? Probably not, even for the chance of taking some of my money out of my wallet. Well, how about if I offer to ante up more on my end—how much would I have to agree to pay in order for you to feel it's worth the risk of losing $100? If you think like most people, you'd insist on receiving at least $200, according to experiments conducted by two leading academic experts on investor psychology, Daniel Kahneman and Amos Tversky. In other words, it takes the potential pleasure of winning $200 to balance out the potential pain of losing $100.

Since investors perceive losses to be more painful, they sometimes do peculiar things to avoid incurring even a short-term loss. They may hold onto losing funds or securities far longer than they should, waiting to get back to even before they sell. Or, they may sell investments that are rising because they're fearful of future losses. If you are a long-term investor, you shouldn't permit this instinctive aversion to loss to cloud your judgment. In investing, realize that you'll win some days and lose some days, but if you stick to the prudent principles I've been discussing in this book, you'll win in the long run.

Portfolio Pitfall: Smart People Can Do Dumb Things

Everybody is subject to tendencies and biases that can play havoc with their investment program. In addition to the ones covered in more detail in this chapter, here is a summary of a half-dozen additional behavioral issues.

- **Inertia.** Some people have difficulty taking action—whether it is starting an exercise program, renewing a driver's license, or making investment decisions. Inertia can cause investors to delay starting a portfolio and making necessary changes to their portfolios, such as rebalancing. The retirement industry is helping to fight the problem by recommending auto-enrollment and automatic default options to sponsors of employer 401(k) plans. Employers have considerably improved investment outcomes by automatically putting new employees into a retirement plan upon hire and directing their contributions to a balanced investment portfolio, such as a target-date fund. If you are not part of such a plan, be sure to sign up. And make sure you save and invest outside your plan, too.

- **Paralysis by analysis.** When faced with a decision, some individuals tend to overthink the choices and become "paralyzed"—delaying the decision or forgoing making one altogether. We saw that at Vanguard in the early days of 401(k) plans. Believing that offering more choice was better, sponsors loaded up their plan menus with a dizzying array of investment choices. Plan participants were confused and made suboptimal choices or no choice at all. Sometimes, less is more.
- **Home bias.** Many investors tend to invest predominantly in markets of their home country. In other words, investing in what is familiar to them. U.S. investors, for example, overweight U.S. stocks and bonds. You are losing out on potential return and diversification benefits by not investing a portion of your assets in foreign markets.
- **Herding.** Humans tend to do what other humans are doing, especially peers. We see herding in all facets of our lives—whether it is drinking boutique coffee, buying the latest fashionable clothing, or driving a luxury SUV. In investing, you may follow the crowd and they may lead you right over the cliff.
- **Representativeness bias.** Some investors make decisions based on superficial characteristics rather than comprehensive evaluation. For example, investors might assume the stock of a prominent, well-managed company is automatically a good investment. The thought process is reasonable on the fact of it, but fails to consider that the share price already reflects the company's quality and future prospects.
- **Confirmation bias.** Once we make a choice, we tend to seek or value information more highly that confirms that the choice we made was a good one. For instance, if you chose to earmark a portion of your portfolio to a top-performing health-care fund, you are more apt to overemphasize positive news about the sector and discount negative news.

Feeling Compelled to Do Something—Anything

Even investors who understand the wisdom of the buy-and-hold philosophy sometimes feel uncomfortable doing nothing, especially when so many environmental forces are enticing us to trade, switch providers, try new investment strategies, and so on and on. Thanks to the internet and smartphones, it's easier than ever to give into that impulse to tinker.

First, you are constantly bombarded by market and business news. As you toggle through news and social media feeds on your phone or tablet, you'll see myriad headlines that might compel you to act. For fun, I used a popular newsfeed and found the following six headlines after just a few minutes. Note, in particular, the last two headlines that provide contradictory messages.

- "Monster Rally: U.S. and Japan Pumping $10 Trillion into Asset Bubbles"
- "Is Gold's Rally Over? Here Are Five Key Charts to Watch"
- "Top Ten ETFs for September"
- "Market Forecast: Stormy Weather Ahead?"
- "Today's Stock Market Is a Mirror Image of 1999"
- "The rally in U.S. tech stocks is 'nothing close' to the dot-com bubble"

Second, online account management offered through your financial provider's app or website is a great convenience, but it has the drawback of providing increased opportunity to meddle with your investment program. Some people check on their account balances obsessively. Let's call it the *app mentality*. You can check the weather, your text messages, your Instagram or LinkedIn page, and your account balance with a few taps and in a few minutes. And by spending just a few minutes looking at your portfolio, you could be tempted to switch from one fund to another or cash out of an investment that seems to be underperforming. And you can do it all over again later in the day or tomorrow. There was some benefit back in the day when investors heard about the day's market events on the car radio on the way home from work.

In most cases, you won't be doing yourself any favors by continually checking your accounts and doing the mental math on your gains or losses. Research has shown repeatedly that active traders underperform buy-and-holders. I'll repeat my advice: Resist the temptation to look at your account balance more than once a quarter, if at all possible. One of the best things Vanguard did for me as an investor, besides offering terrific low-cost funds for my investment program, was to discontinue its online bill-pay service a couple years ago. While mildly annoyed about losing this convenience, I found a huge benefit, too. That is, I no longer log on frequently to Vanguard.com to pay my bills. As a result, I am no longer forced to see my account balance (essentially my net worth), which popped front and center on the screen after I inputted my user name and password. That was a distraction that I didn't need and I'm grateful it's gone. As they say, "out of sight, out of mind." To me, it is "out of sight, peace of mind."

Letting False Reference Points Distort Your View of Value

Ever wonder why car dealers like to quote you such high prices initially, when you and they are fully aware that they're going to permit you to negotiate a lower one? It's because of *anchoring*— the tendency of buyers to relate their estimates of value to some previously established benchmark. Without always realizing it, people tend to form opinions based on a reference point that may or may not be meaningful. Once a car's sticker price is lodged in your mind, you are likely to think that anything that's a little lower is a good deal.

In investing, anchoring can cause you to judge the performance of a particular investment in light of factors that aren't truly relevant— the price you paid for it long ago, its all-time high or low price, or an analyst's estimate of its future price. It is difficult to shake an anchor once it's in your consciousness. For example, if you learn that a prominent financial analyst predicts a stock's price will rise from $100 to $250 a share, you are likely to conclude that it's a good value at $150 a share, even if the company's fundamentals don't support that valuation.

Another dynamic of anchoring relates to a topic discussed earlier in this chapter— looking at the value of your portfolio too frequently. After a big market run-up, you might feel pretty good about your now higher balance. You might say to yourself: "I just made $25,000 last month." Then, when the market takes a sudden plunge, you'll anchor to your higher balance and likely feel pretty badly about your considerable loss. This exercise is not only counterproductive, but is likely to cause you undue stress and angst.

Remembering Things Selectively

Unfortunately, people's memories are very uneven. We tend to remember our triumphs and forget our failures. You've probably noticed that people who regularly go to casinos tend to talk about the times they won, not the trips when they lost. Similarly, lottery players remember the stories about winners of multi-million-dollar jackpots, not the stories that mention the multi-million-to-one odds against winning. We also tend to remember the tales we've heard about people who made a pile in the financial markets by following some scheme or other. We forget about those who swung for the fences and struck out.

How to Foil Your Own Worst Enemy

Have I depressed you enough? At this stage, you may be wondering why you should even bother to try to invest successfully, given that we are all so likely to sabotage ourselves. But don't let these examples of investor foibles leave you in despair. The reason the study of behavioral finance is so useful is that it can help us to recognize self-thwarting behavior. Then we have a chance to take preventive measures.

By now, you know which ones I recommend:

- Make conscious, deliberate decisions about risk and reward when you construct your portfolio.
- Be a buy-and-hold investor.
- Keep an eye on costs.
- Invest with a trusted provider.
- Let time be your ally.
- Stick to your program in good times and bad.

If you do all of these things, emotion and irrationality won't have free rein.

Portfolio Pitfall: Not a Seller, But a Buyer

Investors in commercial real estate have discovered how easy it is to get tripped up by emotional thinking. Commercial real estate is an asset class notorious for its fickle cyclicality. Many fortunes have been made there and lost over the years as the following anecdote underscores.

A friend of mine who owned an office park complex found out that a similar property in his community had just sold for $195 per square foot—a big increase over its previous sale price of $145 per foot. Shortly thereafter, some foreign investors offered my friend $220 per foot for his property. In the belief that the market would drive prices still higher, my friend turned them down.

Not long afterward, the real estate market collapsed. My friend was forced to sell his property to pay off loans, and he realized only about $130 per foot. Years later, he said to me: "You know, something that I learned in this whole episode was that when I didn't *sell* it at $220 a foot, I *bought* it at $220 a foot."

My friend's experience was a great lesson in the pain of a missed opportunity. By not being a seller, he was, in a very real sense, a buyer. His mistake was in thinking that he knew where the market was headed. Had someone offered him $190 a foot for that property a year earlier, he probably would have accepted it gladly. But he thought he recognized a pattern—the market was clearly headed higher, or so it seemed. He assumed that the momentum would keep going. I've never forgotten that line, "When I wasn't a seller, I was a buyer."

What's the Lesson?

Understanding our human tendency toward illogical and unwise behavior won't protect any of us from doing dumb things sometimes. But if you can develop a bit of awareness about your own motivations, you'll have a better chance of maintaining a focused and disciplined approach to investing. Feelings and biases are intangible things, but they can have very tangible effects on your investment program.

In a Nutshell

It's human nature to do some pretty irrational things. Self-awareness cannot prevent all of these mistakes, but you may be able to keep yourself in check if you:

- **Remain humble about your ability to pick winning investments.** Instead of trying to trade your way to wealth, design a sound portfolio and then follow a buy-and-hold strategy.

In a Nutshell   (*Continued*)

- **Recognize in both good markets and bad ones that "this too shall pass."** Don't pay attention to short-term fluctuations that are meaningless to your long-term plan.
- **Don't believe investment gurus who claim to have spotted patterns in the market that can be turned to financial advantage.** If they exist at all, those patterns probably are short-lived. In the long run, balance and diversification are the only reliable investment strategies.

19

Bear Markets Will Test Your Resolve

Can you advise me of the action to take regarding this fund?
I have lost $50,000 in this fund (I want to throw up as I write
this) and am curious about the reason for the losses and, more
importantly, the prediction for the future performance.
I usually stay the course but am now questioning that course of
non-action and seek your advice.
                                    —Letter from a Vanguard client

B ear markets are a regular part of investing in stocks and bonds.
But that's small consolation when you're stuck in the middle
of one. Even the most seasoned investors, such as the Vanguard
client above, find bear markets difficult to endure.

As I was putting the finishing touches on the first edition of this
book in July 2002, we were mired in a deep and prolonged bear market.
It would turn out to be the longest bear market in U.S. stocks since
World War II; stock prices declined more than −49% over two-plus
agonizing years.

Stocks rebounded strongly in 2003, but it was trying times for stock
investors who rode out the slump. The bear market began unofficially in
March 2000 with the bursting of the speculative bubble in technology
and internet stocks. Though the tech stocks in the Nasdaq Composite
Index were hit hardest, they pulled many other stocks down with them.

As measured by the price change in the S&P 500, the U.S. stock market fell −10.1% in 2000, −13.0% in 2001, and another −23.4% in 2002. U.S. stocks have since experienced two additional bear markets: 2008–2009 (−57%) and February–March 2020 (−34%).

Obviously, market slumps are no fun, but they offer some lessons that can help you to be a better investor. In this chapter, I'll discuss these lessons and offer some advice on how to get through the emotional and financial challenges posed by a bear market.

Some Background on Bear Markets

Since the terminology can be confusing, let's begin with some definitions. A *bear market* in stocks is loosely defined as a price decline of 20% or more. A less severe downturn is a *market correction*, usually defined as a decline of more than 10%, but less than 20%.

Don't get too hung up on these definitions. The news media typically note with great fanfare when the S&P 500, the Dow, or the Nasdaq suffers a correction or passes into bull or bear market territory. But if you're a long-term investor, it's irrelevant to you whether the market is officially a bear or just down 19%. In neither case should you necessarily make changes in your investment program. Worrying about whether we're in a bear market or "only" a correction is like worrying about whether a spell of hot weather is technically a heat wave as you sweat in 95 degree temperatures.

Most corrections and mild bear markets result from normal business-cycle fluctuations. But stock market declines don't always predict economic recessions, nor are they always caused by recessions. The severe bear markets in the U.S. markets have typically been related to wars, the bursting of speculative bubbles, or exogenous economic factors.

No one can predict the length or magnitude of a bear market, but history reveals some interesting facts. Over the last 65 years, bear markets in stocks have occurred once every five years on average (Figure 19.1). They have lasted a bit more than a year, again on average. Prior to 2020, the shortest bear market was three months in duration; the pandemic-triggered bear market in 2020, though severe, lasted only one month. The worst bear market in the nation's history was the one that lasted from September 1929 through May 1932, when stock prices fell 83%. Regulatory changes and economic policy changes in response to the Great Depression make it unlikely that we'll experience another decline

Start Date	End Date	Length (months)	Price Return
8/2/1956	10/22/1957	15	−21.6%
12/12/1961	6/26/1962	7	−28.0%
2/9/1966	10/7/1966	8	−22.2%
11/29/1968	5/26/1970	18	−36.1%
1/11/1973	10/3/1974	21	−48.2%
9/21/1976	3/6/1978	18	−19.4%
11/28/1980	8/12/1982	21	−27.1%
8/25/1987	12/4/1987	3	−33.5%
7/16/1990	10/11/1990	3	−19.9%
3/24/2000	10/9/2002	31	−49.1%
10/9/2007	3/9/2009	17	−56.8%
2/19/2020	3/23/2020	1	−33.9%

Bear markets calculated using the price change in the S&P 500 Index

Figure 19.1 Bear Markets in Stocks (1956–2020)

Source: Vanguard calculations using the price change of the S&P 500 Index.

of such magnitude, but I'm of the school that says you should always keep in mind that anything is possible in the financial markets.

Bear markets strike bonds as well as stocks. For bonds, the most recent one started in June 2016 and continued into October 2018, a period when rising interest rates sent bond prices tumbling 16% (as measured by the price of 10-year U.S. Treasury bonds), as shown in Figure 19.2.

How Does a Bear Market Feel? Very Scary

You should expect bear markets to occur periodically during your investing lifetime and prepare for them by being prudent in the ways I've already discussed throughout this book—holding a balanced and diversified portfolio that is appropriate for your investment time horizon. But even if you are doing the right things financially, I assure you that you will feel some anguish. You may experience emotional and physical symptoms; for instance, you may have trouble sleeping or walk around all day with a pit in your stomach. The impulse to do something might be strong.

Start Date	End Date	Length (months)	Price Return
2/28/1967	5/29/1970	39	−20.0%
3/31/1971	9/30/1975	54	−16.1%
11/30/1976	2/29/1980	39	−27.0%
6/30/1980	9/30/1981	15	−20.8%
3/31/1983	6/29/1984	15	−13.2%
12/31/1986	9/30/1987	9	−11.0%
8/31/1993	11/30/1994	15	−14.3%
8/31/1998	1/31/2000	17	−14.0%
4/30/2003	6/30/2004	14	−9.8%
11/30/2008	3/31/2010	16	−14.4%
6/30/2012	12/31/2013	18	−15.5%
6/30/2016	10/31/2018	28	−15.9%

Figure 19.2 Bear Markets in Bonds (1967–2020)

Source: Vanguard calculations based on price data for 10-year U.S Treasury bonds.

Imagine what it was like to be an investor caught in the bear market that lasted from January 1973 until October 1974. The U.S. stock market declined a stunning 48% over a 21-month period. In dollar terms, an investor who had $100,000 invested in the broad stock market lost $48,000—nearly half the value of his or her portfolio. In addition, because inflation jumped significantly at the same time, the loss in terms of purchasing power was even worse. An investor at that time had no way of knowing how long the bear market would last or how bad it would get. I was in my late teens, and my recollection is that the evening newspaper was always full of bad news about the markets and the economy. There was plenty of other unsettling news to go with it. The period saw the resignations of both the Vice President and the President of the United States, the drawn-out ending of an unsuccessful war in Vietnam, and continuing conflict in the Middle East.

Some of today's investors have been at it only a relatively short time and, until the 2020 correction, they had known only a bull market. Now here comes a statement that may surprise you: I think anyone who has been investing for just the past 20 years ought to count herself fortunate to have experienced several bear markets. Believe me, these things were going to happen to you at some point. Living through the 2000–2002 bear market, for example, provided valuable lessons to investors and prepared them to weather a future bear market in 2008–2009. And it is far better to experience a severe market downturn at the beginning of your investing career than near the end, when your portfolio is likely to be much larger and you won't have as much time to recover. Moreover, you'll likely be using your investment assets to meet your living expenses at that point as well.

The Lesson of Balance and Diversification (Again)

Bear markets are the times when well-designed portfolios show their strength. For example, a balanced portfolio of stocks and bonds fared much better during the 1973–1974 bear market than one invested entirely in stocks. The investor with 60% in stocks and 40% in bonds lost "only" $29,000 of a $100,000 portfolio, compared with the $48,000 loss of an investor with a 100% stock portfolio.

Recognize, however, holding a balanced, diversified portfolio will reduce the pain of a bear market, but it won't protect you completely. Moreover, your specific holdings will determine how severely your portfolio is affected. Generally, growth funds are likely to see sharper declines than more conservative, value-oriented funds. During the 2020 correction, large-cap tech stocks, energy stocks, and small-cap suffered greater losses than the overall market. If interest rates are rising and you hold bond funds, you should be prepared to see prices fall farthest for the funds with longer durations.

Bear markets can both demonstrate the benefits of diversification and offer the opportunity to gain valuable perspective. Here's an e-mail we received from a shareholder who was very concerned during the 2000–2002 bear market but had learned to take the long view and adhere to his investment program.

> How much further can the market drop? At one period in my investing life, I would really worry about any market decline. All my waking hours were dominated by the same dismal thoughts—I was losing money and I was sorry I ever invested. But since I changed my investments I don't give the market much thought. Oh, I keep abreast, but I know everything that can be done has been done properly. With proper diversification, low expenses, looking at the long term, and expecting inevitable losses and downturns, I know my final returns (in ten years) will be very pleasing.

The market has always recovered from its declines—eventually. But here again there is no reliable pattern. The recovery can take quite a while, as with the eight years that the stock market spent getting back to its pre-collapse peak after the 1973–1974 slump. Or, the recovery can occur quickly, as with the 2020 bear market that took one month.

Bearing a Bear Market?

The correct response to a bear market is to take an objective look at the situation and reassess your circumstances. What's your time horizon? What are your objectives? If your time horizon is long and your financial standing hasn't changed, you should probably sit tight.

It may sound counterintuitive, but for people who are investing regularly for a long-term goal—not those who are drawing on their investments—bear markets are good things. If you are investing for retirement, and retirement is decades away, a decline in your account value is not a "real" loss. What matters is what your account will be worth in 30 years, not 30 days or even 30 weeks. If prices are depressed, your contributions are now buying more shares at a cheaper price, so that's more wealth for you in the future when the market has recovered.

In bond investing particularly, what seems like bad news can actually be good news. Yes, the prices of your bond investments fall when interest rates rise—but does that mean you should get out? On the contrary, if you're a long-term investor, you should congratulate yourself. That's because if you are reinvesting the dividends in your funds, those dividends buy more shares at the lower net asset value of the fund. (I realize that I've covered this point about bonds already, but it's so important and so widely misunderstood that it bears repeating.)

However, if you are in retirement and not appropriately allocated, a bear market may prove to be a menace to your investment goals. You might not have the luxury of waiting for the markets to rebound as you draw upon your assets, and you can't take comfort in the thought of making regular investments at lower prices. Perhaps you amassed a sizable nest egg by investing regularly and sensibly for more than 30 years, only to watch the bear market ravage your portfolio.

What do you do? Again, if your portfolio has an appropriate asset mix for your objectives, time horizon, and risk tolerance, your best move may be to sit tight—provided you have some level of short-term reserves on hand to meet living expenses during the downdraft. You can compound the damage if you react emotionally and make sweeping changes in your investment strategy. If you must change your mix of assets, make small changes and implement them gradually. It's possible that you may have to revise your expectations for retirement. In the aftermath of the dot-com meltdown, some investors who had been dreaming of early retirement, and got caught in the downturn, said they were resigning themselves to saving more, spending less, and working longer.

It's to avert such situations that financial advisors recommend gradually moving your portfolio to a more conservative balance as you near your retirement years. Target-date funds and model portfolios do the same. That can be hard to do on your own, especially if no bears are in sight. You'll never feel joyous about moving your money into bonds while the stock market is on a roll. On the other hand, it's a lot more pleasant to move some assets to bond funds than to need to keep working when you had planned to relax at last.

This point holds true for college savers, too. If you are not in an age-based option, you'll need to gradually move money from stock funds to bond and money market funds as your child approaches his or her freshman year. Your college portfolio should contain a weighting of no more than 20%–30% in stocks when you drop your daughter or son off at the dorm. (Scholarships and financial aid may give you reasons to be slightly more aggressive.)

Tips for Enduring Bear Markets

If you had a sound plan in place before the bear market started, the main task is to keep your head. That can be harder than it sounds, once the financial press gets going with dire analyses, the politicians start weighing in, and your account balance seems to have gone on a crash diet. During the 2008–2009 bear market, one pundit quipped that many 401(k)s had turned into "201(k)s" because they lost half their value. Clever, but disconcerting. The following practices can help you get through the slump and the accompanying noise around it.

- **Continue investing regularly.** If you invest through an automatic investment plan or a payroll deduction at work, continue making contributions. Remember that what you are doing is dollar-cost averaging, and it can achieve the most for you when the markets are down. I won't repeat all that was said about dollar-cost averaging in

Chapter 13, but I want to remind you about the two biggest benefits because they can help you endure a bear market. First, since prices are low, your regular investments will be buying you more shares. Second, the discipline involved will fortify you against emotional decisions. Another point that is worth repeating: You've got to stick with dollar-cost averaging in bad markets as well as good to reap the benefits.

- **Maintain perspective.** Your purpose as a long-term investor is to achieve your ultimate goals, not to avoid interim losses. When you originally set up your investment plan, you put your money where it offered the best prospects for long-term reward. That meant accepting some risk—and now you're seeing what the risk entails. But that doesn't mean your plan was a mistake. So your account is way down from where it was? "Where it was" may have been an unrealistic level. Remember that the bear market that started in 2000 wiped out a considerable amount of nominal wealth, but investors who had the fortitude to remain in the stock market for many years were still far wealthier than when they started.

- **Make gradual shifts (if necessary).** Resist the temptation to make major changes in your investment strategy simply because one part of it is in trouble. Moving your money from stocks and bonds to more conservative investments in hopes of avoiding a loss or finding a gain is seldom successful. If you absolutely must make a change, do so gradually, selling or exchanging shares in small increments to prevent yourself from careening from one impulse to another.

- **Have realistic expectations.** Over time, the direction of the stock market has been up. However, it is realistic to expect market pullbacks from time to time, and it is equally realistic to expect the market to recover in due course. Figure 19.3 shows the worst stock market performance over various periods, along with the best performance. At worst, stocks experienced a 1% decline over any ten-year period over the past century.

	10-Year	15-Year	20-Year
Best	20.0% 1949–1958	18.2% 1942–1956	17.2% 1979–1998
Worst	−0.9% 1929–1938	0.6% 1929–1943	3.1% 1929–1948

**Figure 19.3 A Look at the Worst and Best of
Stock Market Returns over Various Periods**

Source: Vanguard. U.S. stocks represented by the S&P 500 Index from 1926 through 1974, the Dow Jones U.S. Total Market Index through April 22, 2005, the MSCI US Broad Market Index through June 2, 2013, and the CRSP U.S. Total Market Index through 2019. Data based on calendar year returns.

Baseline Basics: The Advantages of Buying "Hamburger" in a Sideways Market

While at Vanguard, I had a regular routine of running at lunchtime with some colleagues who were 15 years younger, and, in the mid- to late 1990s, they would continually remind me how lucky I am to have been investing for retirement since the beginning of the bull market in 1982.

In my view, that's not something to envy. As a regular investor through payroll deductions, I was dollar-cost averaging into an upward market for 15 straight years. As the market climbed higher and higher, I was buying fund shares at steadily higher prices. In my view, these younger colleagues are on a much better footing. During their investing tenure, they've been investing through sideways and declining markets as they accumulate wealth, so they are buying fund shares at a much cheaper price than I was able to do at their age. After all, it's the value of your assets at the "goal line," not interim periods, that truly matters.

For a regular investor with a long time horizon, a market moving sideways or down is a good thing—even though it no doubt feels uncomfortable. Buying shares at a lower price improves your chances of making money over the course of your investing years.

Renowned investor Warren Buffett, the chairman of Berkshire Hathaway, talks about this investing trade-off in terms of buying hamburger. In a letter to his company's shareholders in 1997, he wrote:

> A short quiz: If you plan to eat hamburgers throughout your life and are not a cattle producer, should you wish for higher or lower prices for beef? Likewise, if you are going to buy a car from time to time but are not an auto manufacturer, should you prefer higher or lower car prices? These questions, of course, answer themselves.
>
> But now for the final exam: If you expect to be a net saver during the next five years, should you hope for a higher or lower stock market during that period? Many investors get this one wrong. Even though they are going to be net buyers of stocks for many years to come, they are elated when stock prices rise and depressed when they fall. In effect, they rejoice because prices have risen for the "hamburgers" they will soon be buying. This reaction makes no sense. Only those who will be sellers of

(continued)

> ### Baseline Basics: The Advantages of Buying "Hamburger" in a Sideways Market   (*Continued*)
>
> equities in the near future should be happy at seeing stocks rise. Prospective purchasers should much prefer sinking prices.
>
> As a retirement-oriented investor, I bought "hamburger" at continually more expensive prices from 1982 to 2000. Meanwhile, my younger colleagues have experienced more volatile markets and time is on their side.

What Not to Do in a Bear Market

There are two main risks when markets sour. The first risk is that you may panic and want to get out, particularly if the decline is severe. The second risk is that you may think a decline spells good value and want to "buy on the dip."

Neither of those responses is the correct one. If you panic, you may end up selling at or near the bottom of the downturn and missing the rebound. Many investors did just that in the market decline of 1973–1974. Those who fled stocks missed an extraordinary climb in stock values. After reaching a low point in October 1974, the stock market became extremely generous. The S&P 500 Index returned 37.1% in 1975. The market provided yearly returns that averaged 14.8% over the 10 years from 1975 to 1984, 16.6% over the 15 years from 1975 to 1989, 14.6% over the 20 years from 1975 to 1994, and 16.1% over the 25 years from 1975 to 2000.

As for buying on the dips, hindsight makes it obvious why that's not a good plan in a bear market. The problem is that you don't have hindsight in the beginning. There can be numerous interim rallies in a bear market, and if you are trying to dabble in market timing, you can get severely burned. The 1973–1974 slump featured several of these so-called *sucker's rallies*. People who bought on those dips merely deepened their losses. These facts prove the wisdom in a comment once made by economist John Maynard Keynes: "Markets can remain irrational longer than you can remain solvent."

In a Nutshell

Bear markets are a regular part of investing. You can endure the emotional and financial challenges if you:

- **Prepare for tough times by holding a balanced and diversified portfolio that is right for your needs.** Knowing that you have designed an appropriate portfolio can give you the confidence to ride out a bear market.
- **Continue investing regularly.** Dollar-cost averaging can give you the discipline to weather tough times.
- **Make gradual changes, if necessary.** If your long-term strategy is still sound, you will do best to avoid major changes during a bear market. Should a change be necessary, make it thoughtfully and gradually.
- **Maintain perspective.** Your ultimate objective is to achieve your financial goals. If you have a time horizon of 10 years or more, you shouldn't be concerned about your gains or losses in any single year.

20

Navigating Distractions to Reach Your Destination

I've used several car and driving analogies in the course of this book. Let me roll out another with the hope that you don't tire of them. When you get behind the wheel, there are a number of things that can prevent you from reaching your destination safely and on time. You could encounter traffic, experience car trouble, or, heaven forbid, have an accident. Accidents happen, but some are a result of distracted driving—talking on a cell phone, texting, fiddling with the radio, or eating a fast-food burger. Similarly, *distracted investing*—being swayed by experts, falling for fads, or chasing performance—can be more than just speed bumps to reaching your investment goals, or as I will relate to you in Chapter 23, "Getting to Boca."

One of the biggest distractions facing investors today is coping with the onslaught of financial information and news. We're all bombarded online, in print, on TV and radio, and on social media by information about investing and news coverage of the financial markets. Much of what's reported is either exaggerated, flat-out wrong, or simply not relevant to an ordinary individual investor. Even sophisticated investors can find it very tough to maintain perspective in the face of these distractions.

Every morning before I go on a run, I quickly catch up on the news and can't help but hear a report about what happened in overnight trading in S&P futures and on the Asian stock markets, along with the weather and sports scores. These reports may be useful to professional traders, but it's not information that most listeners need in order to manage their day. Indeed, it is about as relevant as forecasted thunderstorms in Boston and a Red Sox win for a person living in Kansas City (unless the Sox beat the Royals). If you're a long-term, buy-and-hold investor with a sensibly constructed portfolio, there's no good reason to pay attention to reports on the short-term movements of the financial markets. What the market did yesterday and what people think it will do tomorrow simply do not affect your investment strategy.

I acknowledge that news can be useful and entertaining. And most thoughtful people enjoy being well informed about current events. For these reasons, I'll focus in this chapter on how to manage the distractions of our mass-media culture, absorbing the useful stuff and tuning out the rest.

Over the past four decades, the news media have done a great deal of good by educating the public about investing. Ordinary people have become much more financially literate and investment savvy. While a long bull market in the 1980s and 1990s was a huge factor in attracting more individuals to investing, the growth of news about financial matters and investing also played a big role. Over the years, many of the personal finance columnists in the major newspapers, magazines, and wire services performed a valuable service by providing sensible information on investing that truly serves the needs of their readers. There remain today a few, high-quality columnists whose work I often circulate to colleagues or email to family members.

At the same time, there has been a tremendous increase in the number of self-proclaimed financial experts promoting their books, radio shows, and websites, as well as a rise in the number of online outlets for just about anybody with a computer to post their views on the markets and strategies for investing. There has also been a rise in "sponsored content," in which an investment company purchases space on an online outlet that resembles the site's editorial content but is paid for by an advertiser and promotes their products or services. Note, too, that some financial bloggers might get paid for recommending a particular fund or financial service. Bloggers should reveal such arrangements, but it isn't always easy to find the disclosure, if it appears at all.

As a result, you have to exercise extreme caution as a consumer of business and financial news. If you're new to investing, you may think you should subscribe to multiple financial podcasts, read financial content on a daily basis, and tune into radio and TV programs covering the financial markets. Don't do it. You won't know how to distinguish useful information from what's worthless or misleading or wrong, and you will feel quickly overwhelmed. To get started as an investor, what you need is an understanding of the fundamentals of investing, not a blizzard of data and commentary about the current state of affairs in the financial markets.

Once you've set up your investment program and developed some confidence about investing, it is wise to remain selective about the content you choose to consume. Information overload isn't just annoying—it can be downright dangerous for someone who intends to be a buy-and-hold investor. Even if you aren't normally inclined to fret over your portfolio, listening to the constant media chatter may make you think you need to check on your investments frequently to see how you are doing. And once you start doing that, you may be tempted to begin second-guessing your decisions. The insidious danger of the noise is that if you pay attention to it, it can tempt you to act and make investment moves that aren't in your best long-term interests. If you hear that the stock market is down 100 points for the third day in a row, you may begin to wonder, "Should I shift from stocks to bonds or cash?" Resist the urge. As Warren Buffett wryly noted in his 1990 letter to Berkshire Hathaway shareholders, "Lethargy bordering on sloth remains the cornerstone of our investment style."

Trust the Truths You Already Know

This may seem odd, but the most valuable information you'll encounter in the media, by this point, should be old news to you. Pay attention to stories that emphasize the value of holding a diversified portfolio, minimizing costs and taxes, and maintaining a long-term perspective. Those are the important and enduring principles in investing, and they are reaffirmed over and over again by events.

A former financial columnist who worked with me at Vanguard once shared a quote from the great American novelist Willa Cather. He carried it in his wallet, and here's what it said: "There are only two or three human stories, and they go on repeating themselves as fiercely as if they had never happened before." My colleague believed that something similar is true for financial writing and that there were only a handful of truly important themes for individual investors—save money for your future needs, invest in stocks for the long term, and so forth. And ever since he told me that, I've been struck by the wisdom in it.

The remainder of this chapter offers some tips to help you be an intelligent consumer of news about investing.

Recognize That Everyone Has an Agenda

It may sound cynical, but it's a fact of life. When politicians and government officials appear on TV to discuss the issues of the day, we're all aware that they are advocating a particular point of view. Whether we agree or not, we recognize that the arguments they make are part of a larger agenda. You should approach financial news with a similar awareness.

One of the major contributors to the dot-com bubble of the 1990s was that people failed to recognize the agendas of all those talking heads on TV financial news programs. News is supposed to be objective, but the information provided on the business news programs often was not objective at all. The journalists themselves tended to be overly bullish on the stock market. And no wonder, since enthusiasm about stocks would attract more viewers and garner better ratings for their programs. The CEOs who made guest appearances also had agendas—talking up their companies would entice investors and pump up stock prices. And, as investors learned later, yet another set of agendas was being pursued by the Wall Street analysts who made all those rosy stock recommendations. Many of their brokerage firms were hoping to get or keep lucrative investment banking deals with the very companies being evaluated.

I'm not saying that all commentators are self-interested or even that everyone with an agenda is nefarious and not to be trusted. But I am suggesting that you need to consider their biases before you buy what they're selling.

Be Wary of Market Predictions

Today's wired investment world is full of pundits ready to give sound bite predictions about what the markets will do next, which are amplified by social media and news aggregators. But despite all their computer models or impressive-sounding rationales and rhetorical flourish, these experts don't have any certain knowledge of what is coming. Sure, some of them will be right sometimes, but that could just as easily be luck as brains. Jane Bryant Quinn, a financial journalist covering the markets and investing during my tenure as Vanguard CEO, put it succinctly: "The chief function of stock-market forecasters is to make astrologers look respectable."

Why do the financial news programs keep airing market predictions? Consider their agenda. Predictions are entertaining and "infotainment" attracts audiences. The money managers and Wall Street analysts happily provide those predictions because it's the way they gain exposure. No one will call them to appear and make predictions if they're honest enough to say, "Beats me. I don't know what stocks are going to do next."

Or, as William Bernstein says in his book, *The Intelligent Asset Allocator*:

> There are two kinds of investors, be they large or small: those who don't know where the market is headed, and those who don't know that they don't know. Then again, there is actually a third type of investor—the investment professional, who indeed knows that he or she doesn't know, but whose livelihood depends on appearing to know.

Be Skeptical of Hype About Hot Performance

Some financial outlets claim to be champions of investment fundamentals, but then they splash headlines across their websites about fund rankings and the "five 'safe' stocks to buy now." We once had one of our index fund managers interviewed on TV and the anchor kept pressing him—to the point of exasperation—on "what stocks he was buying now." He demurred, and replied with a straight face: "All of them."

I suppose sound bites and headlines on hot stocks and top-performing ETFs help to attract eyeballs and clicks, but they don't really do readers any service. The problem with rankings is that they focus on yesterday's high performers, regardless of long-term merits. As discussed in Chapter 9, fund rankings are meaningless when based on past performance.

Other distortions occur when someone or something involved with investing is acclaimed or maligned. I've seen this happen many times with money managers, investment strategies and products, or even market sectors—they're acclaimed as infallible or condemned as worthless, when in fact the reality is usually somewhere in between.

Be Suspicious of "Experts"

It's human nature to put too much credence in the opinion of someone who's presented as an authority on a complex subject. Unfortunately, the fact that you read something on the internet or hear it on television doesn't mean it's true. As you develop your knowledge about investing, you will come to recognize that there can be many different points of view about the meaning of a given financial or economic trend. That someone has a lofty title and an air of authority does not make his or her interpretation correct. Sometimes the experts are dead wrong. Even if they are right, you should ask yourself whether the information is relevant to you. If it's not, tune it out.

Here's a great example. Newscasters often report that on a down day in the markets there were "more sellers than buyers." Feel free to laugh out loud when you hear that statement. For a trade to happen at all, there must be a buyer and a seller. Indeed, the simple fact that there is always someone else on the other side of any transaction should give us pause when we are tempted to speculate in the markets. Maybe that other person knows something we don't.

What Makes Headlines Is Not Always New

The news media are in the business of reporting what's new, and that's a difficult job to do well day in and day out. In reality, many significant developments that are reported as news are already known widely.

A case in point is the coverage of the collapse of Enron, the nation's seventh-largest company, in the fall of 2002. Though the media had written many glowing stories about the company over the years, reporters were slow to learn of its problems. Talk about the company's troubles was filtering through investment circles during the summer of 2002, when CEO Jeffrey Skilling stepped down, citing personal reasons. But the full story of Enron's problems didn't become public until after the company filed for bankruptcy that December. (To their credit, journalists themselves are often their most severe critics. The *American Journalism Review* called the profession's handling of the Enron story one of the biggest failures in financial journalism.)

There have been many other occasions when the news media were slow to report on positive trends, including the rise of the internet.

I mention this tendency to be late with the news as a warning to investors who think that the media are a good source of investment tips. If you are hearing about an investment with fabulous potential, recognize that lots of other people know about it, too. The chances are high that this information is already reflected in stock prices.

Beware the "New, New Thing"

The news media are very competitive with each other, and there is enormous, constant pressure to come up with fresh angles and new ideas. As a result, it's easy for journalists to become infatuated with fads.

Fads are part of our popular culture. New ones are surfacing all the time. Fortunately, most fads are pretty innocuous things. Many people enjoy getting swept up in the latest craze, whether it's the latest app among kids or the fitness regimens of adults. Sooner or later, every craze fizzles, but most of them do little damage. So what if you succumbed to the rage for skinny jeans, and then they go out of fashion? You're out $60—no big deal.

Investment fads are a different matter. Allowing yourself to be carried away by an investment fad can endanger your financial well-being. You can lose serious money, and there's an extra, hidden cost: When you detour from your investment program to indulge in a fad, you miss the opportunity to make money on worthwhile investments. And that means you have squandered not just money but also that very precious commodity, time.

In the 1980s, a decade when income taxes were very high, tax shelters became a big investment fad. Investors put billions of dollars into esoteric tax shelters based on investments in real estate and energy resources without a clear understanding of the underlying economics and without thinking about how future changes in tax laws could affect the shelters. Many were later very sorry.

Today, many people, especially young adults, seem enamored with online trading platforms. Lured by commission-free trading, engaging, game-like trading apps, and no minimum investment requirements, average folks are trying to play the market and trade their way to quick wealth. Worse, some are buying on borrowed money, commonly called buying on margin. While investing in stocks is not a fad, approaching it as a game to be played is dangerous. It is akin to gambling, and, as we know, the house usually wins.

In his book on investing, *Winning the Loser's Game*, my colleague Charley Ellis has a pithy bit of advice about investment novelties:

> Don't invest in new or "interesting" investments. They are all too often designed to be *sold to* investors, not to be *owned by* investors. (When the novice fisherman expressed wonderment that fish would actually go for the gaudily decorated lures offered at the bait shop, the proprietor's laconic reply was, "We don't sell them lures to fish.")

That's something that news people and news consumers would do well to remember. Beware of investment fads. Unless you're someone who equates success in life with joining in whatever is making headlines at the moment, fads are not worth the risk.

The bottom line for you as an investor in a mass-media environment is that the media are both your friend and your foe. Good information about investing will help you to become a better investor, but bad information can lead you to make big mistakes. You will need to assess which stuff to heed and which stuff to tune out.

In speeches and in casual conversations with investors, I often emphasize the importance of tuning out distractions by sharing a story about "the three best investors I know." People always expect me to name Wall Street legends or famous portfolio managers, but the three best investors I know are my children when in their younger years participated in the markets through the college accounts my wife and I set up for them at birth. Frankly, the kids had no idea that the accounts were set up for them until they reached adulthood.

As such, they were never subject to euphoria during bull runs, nor did they feel despair during bear markets. They did not get caught up in the financial news cycle. They didn't succumb to fads because they were unaware of fads. In the end, they reached their appointed destinations largely as a result of having minimal, if any, distractions.

In a Nutshell

With so much news and information about the financial markets surrounding us, trying to be an informed investor is, paradoxically, very challenging. You probably can't tune out all the noise, so apply a few caveats:

- **Be selective about the financial content you consume.** You'll drive yourself crazy, and perhaps do some real damage to your financial program, if you pay too much attention to financial news.
- **Trust the truths you already know.** Diversification and balance pay off in the long run. Cost matters. Buy-and-hold works.
- **Tune out information and advice that is irrelevant to you.** Never believe market predictions. Recognize that many experts have agendas, and they may not be in sync with your investment goals.
- **Beware of hype.** Whether the hoopla focuses on a money manager who seems to have a golden touch or on a "new, new thing" in investing, it always pays to be skeptical.

21

Is the "Smart Money" Smart? Yes, but. . .

One of the terms that you'll read or hear as you pay attention to investing is the "smart money." You'll see it in headlines and hear it on financial news programs. Frankly, it's a dumb term, applied randomly to groups of seemingly sophisticated investors who some may think have the secrets to success to which the rest of us aren't privy. Don't believe it. That said, there is a particular group among these investors who can teach us a thing or two. While this group invests billions of dollars, maintains professional staffs, and possesses long traditions of prudent, successful investing, their goals and objectives are very similar to yours. I am speaking of the endowment teams at America's premier universities.

I truly believe there is a considerable amount that individuals can learn about long-term investing and retirement planning by studying how these universities manage their endowment funds. Think of a mid-career professional, Vickie, pondering her retirement investment strategy and life after working. And then think of the manager of a large university endowment. Here are the parallels:

- Both are responsible for overseeing a critical pool of assets. For an endowment team, the pool is often the source of 30%–50% of the university's operating budget and its financial security for the future.

For Vickie, it is likely her 401(k) plan account, which is the most money she's likely to ever amass and it has to sustain her in her retirement years.

- Both need to maintain a long-term outlook. Vickie needs to build a nest egg for 30 to 40 years in retirement. For an endowment, the time frame is perpetual.
- Both have to beat inflation in order to maintain their real purchasing power over time. For the endowment team, they want the *real* value— that is, after accounting for inflation over time—of the university's assets to grow in perpetuity. For Vickie, in many ways, inflation is the biggest risk she faces in retirement since she won't be working and receiving inflation-beating compensation changes as she moves through a career.
- Both should have a balanced and broadly diversified asset mix to help smooth the inevitable ups-and-downs of the markets. Vickie, of course, will have to assess the risk/reward trade-offs, as I've discussed several times in the book, to determine how smooth of a ride she wants to and through retirement. An endowment team performs the same analysis and develops a strategy within the context of the institution's risk/reward policies.
- Both need to generate sufficient income to meet regular expenses and also cover some large, one-time purchases. Vickie will certainly have Social Security payments as part of her income (and any other pension-like payments), but supplementing those is an important reason for saving in the first place. Her investment portfolio will be the source of those supplements. Again, the endowment team performs the same analysis to ensure that the assets in their care can provide the current revenue needed for annual university operations, while, of course, meeting long-term growth objectives.

Hopefully, these parallels make sense to you. In the end, Vickie's goals are personal and relate to lifestyle and financial security. The primary mission of leading universities is to provide a first-rate education and conduct world-class research. Over the past decades, no one has been better than these schools at educating all of us on the basic principles of sound investing.

And with those basic principles, the best endowment managers have done a wonderful job for their institutions over the long-term— producing returns that are the envy of the institutional investment

Time Period	Large Endowments	60% Stocks/ 40% Bonds	Global Equity
15 years	7.6%	7.0%	7.6%
20 years	7.8%	6.0%	5.3%
30 years	9.8%	8.0%	7.4%

Notes: Data are as of June 30 for each year. Data through June 30, 2019. Large endowment performance is represented by endowments with greater than $400 million in assets through 1997 and endowments with greater than $1 billion in assets thereafter. 60% stock/40% bond portfolio: Domestic equity (42%) is Dow Jones Wilshire 5000 Index through April 22, 2005, and MSCI U.S. Broad Market Index thereafter. Non-U.S. equity (18%) is MSCI All Country World Index ex USA. Bonds (40%) are Barclays U.S. Aggregate Bond Index. Global Equity is represented by the MSCI All-Country World Index.

Figure 21.1 Large Endowment versus Benchmarks: Performance over Various Time Periods (ending June 30, 2019)

Sources: Vanguard and NACUBO Study of Endowments.

community and enhancing the financial positions of their universities. As shown in Figure 21.1, the largest endowments have produced returns equal to or greater than both a domestic 60% stock/40% bonds portfolio and a global stock portfolio (with significantly less volatility than global equities) over each listed period. You'll note that we include only truly long-term periods (15, 20, and 30 years) since these are the time frames that are important to universities, just as they are for individuals.

While we may be able to relate to the investment approach of endowments, it's important to recognize that these investors have had some advantages over most individuals. Mostly, they've had access to certain investments and investment classes that have not been generally available to the investing public. In addition to learning from these investors' strategies and habits, an important reason to highlight their success is because it's very likely that access to some of their categories of investment options will be coming to the readers of this book.

That's a good news/bad news story. The good news is that more sound investment vehicles offered at attractive prices by trusted partners are good for all of us. The bad news is that far too many of these products will come to market than is necessary and most won't be worth your time or, more importantly, your trust and your money. Indeed, you might gain access to alternative investments but not to the "best and brightest" managers. My hope here is to make you a smarter evaluator of, and potential investor in, these investments as they become more readily available to you.

An Introduction to Alternative Investments

The most important investment options that have served the best endowments so well for decades are generally called *alternative investments*, that is, alternatives to traditional stock, bond, and cash investments. There are many, many alternative categories, but I will mention just three that have been important to the success of the larger endowments:

- **Hedge Funds.** A good friend of mine (a longtime competitor, actually) has a favorite expression about this category of investment products. He says, "It's a compensation strategy, not an investment strategy." And, over time, he's been proven right. The term *hedge fund* gets used for all sorts of investment products with varying strategies, but I'll try to simplify it for you. Some traditional hedge funds will both buy stocks and sell stocks short to leverage their research expertise. Others are limited capacity, very highly concentrated long-only stock funds that look like mutual funds, but with far less diversification. Still others pursue strategies such as buying "distressed" bonds, or making bets on the global economy, or seeking to take advantage of merger activity, and so on. The common trait, as my friend highlights, is that each of these strategies is generally tied to an incentive fee structure that is a core part of why managers work in this realm rather than more traditional asset management. (More on that later.)
- **Private Equity (PE).** You can think of this category as having started in the "leveraged buyout" days in the 1980s. Managers would raise a pool of assets from investors to buy a company—on a friendly or hostile basis—or a division of a company, and do so with borrowed money (thus, the leverage). The industry has come a long way since then and there are many, many variations on the PE theme today. In fact, there are now more private companies in the hands of PE managers than there are publicly traded stocks in the United States today (Sources: Capital IQ and Burgiss).

- **Venture Capital.** The great Keith Jackson, a long-time sportscaster for ABC television, coined the phrase "the granddaddy of them all!" to describe the Rose Bowl football game between the champions of the Big 10 and Pac 12 conferences. That is how I think of venture capital. In many ways, it was the first category of alternative investments used by smart-money investors and it has been the biggest source of value-added results. The short description: Venture capitalists are the source of funding for new ventures and for the early stages of growth for ventures that make it to the market. It is very high risk—a rule of thumb for many VC professionals is that less than 20% of the companies that they fund will end up being profitable investments. But, the compensation for these long odds is that those that do become successful can be very profitable. That's the reward part of the risk/reward equation. Think Google, Amazon, and other Silicon Valley startups.

Now that you have a bit of a better understanding about each of these three categories of investments, you should also be aware of a few of the downsides:

- **Illiquidity.** These alternatives are generally *illiquid*, meaning that, unlike a mutual fund or an exchange-traded fund (ETF), you may not be able to access the investment immediately if you wanted to, or needed to, raise cash. Illiquidity is the core to the investment strategies, not something punitive, but investors need to recognize the trade-off.
- **High costs.** The three alternatives generally come with higher costs—far higher in many cases—than more traditional, high-quality options in the mutual fund and ETF market. There are also incentive fees tied to performance, which is a topic I address later in this chapter.
- **High risk.** These alternatives generally are thought of as higher risk/ higher reward investments, with the potential for generating market-beating returns, but with a greater risk of suffering significantly market-trailing returns as well.
- **Potentially complex strategies.** As I've mentioned, there are many sub-strategies within each of these categories and some can be very complex. One of the best investors in alternative assets that I know has a very simple test: If you can't easily explain how the strategy intends to invest and make money, then it isn't worth investing in. Keep that in mind at all times.

- **Highly variable results.** The inside baseball term for this topic is
  dispersion and it relates to the difference in results between, say, the
  top 25% of investors and the bottom 25% in any alternative asset
  category. As in many endeavors, the top performers are really (and
  often consistently) very good and bottom performers are consistently,
  well, at the bottom. This issue places a premium on access to the best
  managers in alternatives and having a very trusted sponsor if such a
  product is presented to you.

The best of the smart money investors have used these three alternative investment classes to enhance returns and minimize volatility
in their portfolios. However, those results have not been a free lunch,
which brings me to the "but" in this chapter title. It relates to the fact
that, like all of us, these exceptional investors continue to learn, and
one of the best "classrooms" was the Global Financial Crisis (GFC) of
2008–2009.

There's an aphorism that is relevant here: Experience is a hard
teacher because she gives the test first, the lesson afterward. The GFC
was a remarkably difficult test for even the best of investors. When
I reflect on that period of time and think about the various professional roles I held in the endowment arena, four lessons, in particular,
stand out. These lessons are very relevant for you if you choose to
complement your investment program with alternative investments.
Here they are:

- **Illiquidity can enhance your returns, but you have to be
  prepared for the cost that potential brings at all times.** Smart
  money investors understood that most of their alternative investments
  were illiquid. In fact, the *illiquidity premium* (i.e., the extra return one
  receives for investing in illiquid assets) became an accepted part of
  the investment equation. But a not-so-funny thing happened when
  the markets experienced a rapid and severe collapse during the GFC,
  while, at the same time, other stresses put pressure on normal university business operations. Several of the world's leading universities
  had major cash flow problems, resulting in the need to borrow substantial amounts of money to meet current expenses; sell assets from
  the endowment at fire-sale prices; and enter into intense negotia-
  tions to expunge obligations to fund additional illiquid investments,
  among other issues. Fortunately, the schools survived these challenges, but my advice to you is to stress test your ability to handle

illiquidity before you accept it so you never have to go through a similar situation.

- **While it's "what you keep" that matters with respect to cost in investing, sometimes too much is simply too much.** Another lesson learned by many of the smart-money investors is that alternative investments are expensive and unproductively so in some cases. For years, many endowments regularly contracted with hedge funds that charged 2% of assets plus 20% of profits. Some arrangements charged 3% or 4% of assets. Do the math: Let's assume your investment earns 10%, before costs. In a typical case, after the manager takes a 2% fee, your net return is 8%. But, as TV infomercials proclaim, "Wait, there's more!" The manager's incentive fee is 20% of profits, which lops off another 1.6% of your 8%. This leaves you with 6.4%, less than two-thirds of what the market returned for you. Well, when times are good, those costs seemed easy to swallow for many endowments. But, in lower return or negative return environments, these costs are very damaging. It's an instance where sophisticated investors may have been blinded by the glow of trailing results when forming future expectations. The silver lining is that most of these fee structures have been reworked in subsequent years to leave more of the returns in the hands of the investor, not the manager. My advice to you is to demand full disclosure and competitive assessments of any fees you are charged in these products, just as you get from your mutual fund sponsor.

- **Incentives matter immensely.** A corollary to the "cost matters" principle is equally as important to grasp: The "how" of incentives in alternative investments is as important to understand as the "how much." In short, check the structure of the incentive payments to ensure the manager's interests are aligned with yours. This is another instance—largely with hedge funds—in which the smart-money investors apparently got enamored by past returns and became complacent. Quite simply, too many manager incentives simply didn't match the client's goals. For instance, the long-term orientation of endowments is a mismatch with many hedge fund incentives, which were annual and not based on multiyear performance records, encouraging short-term behavior. Endowments can always select a low-cost index fund to match the market, yet they were paying high-cost managers additional incentive fees whether or not they beat the market. Market up 20%; fund up 10%? Many managers still collected an incentive. Crazy. The list of mismatches could go on and on, but you get the point. The pain suffered during the GFC shined a light on this issue, and today the alignment of incentives between client and manager is greatly improved. That is good for you, should you choose to invest in such funds, but my advice to you is to focus your attention on this issue and ask questions before ever investing. It's a great day for you and your investment program when the manager earns an incentive fee. But, diligence on the front-end will ensure he or she actually does earn it.

- **Defining "enough" is a helpful discipline for all of us.** Just before the stock market began its collapse in 2008, I attended a university conference of investment firm leaders to discuss issues affecting the markets and our businesses. At the close of the session, the moderator asked us to provide to one of our participants—the newly appointed Chief Investment Officer of the host university—our forecast for returns she should expect for the next 10 years. Our choices were: (a) between 0–5% per year; (b) between 5–10% per year; (c) between 10–15% per year; or (d) greater than15% per year. The choice of our group of quite experienced investment professionals was "c"—a very robust forecast, which of course turned out to be totally off base. (You might recall from a previous chapter that we conducted a similar fore-casting exercise with Vanguard clients and the results were largely the same.) I happened to be in the "b" camp, and, as the session closed, the Chairman of the University's board came over and asked what I'd guessed. He said he was in the same camp and his subsequent pro-nouncement has remained with me for the past 12 years. He made the following statement: "Jack, we are fortunate as a university to be very well endowed by any measure you choose. If we can merely earn 6% per year into infinity, we can accomplish all our dreams for this great place." Unfortunately, the endowment wasn't managed with that sense of "enough" and suffered devastating losses, for which it is still trying to make up ground. They were nowhere near alone in that regard. **My advice to you is to very clearly define "enough" for you and your family.** And it is a challenge to know when you have enough money to meet all of your goals, whatever they may be:

1. Possessing sufficient money to live a comfortable lifestyle for the rest of your life.
2. Passing assets onto heirs.
3. Accomplishing your philanthropic objectives.

However you think about your financial goals, you need to define enough. Be very explicit about it. Again, talk to your spouse. Talk to your advisor if you have one. Know that number. Then assess how you think about risk in the context of what's enough.

In a Nutshell

You may have the opportunity at some point in the future to invest in alternatives, and you can learn some valuable lessons from the approach taken by university endowments. If you do choose to add them to your investment program, consider carefully these points:

- **Alternatives should be a complementary holding, not a core one.** The core of your portfolio should comprise stocks, bonds, and cash investments. Alternatives should only be added judiciously to a balanced, well-diversified investment program.
- **The risk/return trade-off is high.** Alternatives have the potential for greater returns than the stock market and, at the same time, a greater risk of significantly trailing the market.
- **Dispersion is high.** There is a wide variability in returns among managers in the alternatives business, generally far higher than among traditional asset classes. This dispersion places an even greater premium on selecting your trusted investment partner in this area. Experience and access to top investors are the two key criteria.
- **Costs and incentives matter.** Recognize that alternatives feature costs much higher than funds and ETFs, along with incentives that you should ensure are aligned to your goals and time frame.

22

Regrets? I've Had a Few

One of the toughest challenges in investing is dealing with our own mistakes. To underscore the point that investors need to be able to acknowledge their own missteps, I'll share a couple of mine with you.

Many years ago, my wife and her friends started an investment club. They were interested in assembling a portfolio of individual stocks, not mutual funds, and they sought some advice from me and another friend who was a successful fund manager.

The two of us recommended a stock called Dome Petroleum, which was selling at $1 a share at the time. In our collective wisdom, we thought, how much can it lose? (If you don't remember that the answer to this question is "all of it," go back and read Chapter 16.) So the investment club bought Dome Petroleum as its pick for the month. And sure enough, the investment club members lost all of their investment. *Ugh!*

My second mistake occurred just recently. As I've mentioned more than once in this book, I am a confirmed believer in funds and exchange-traded funds for my family's investments. I have owned but a handful of individual stocks in my adult life, and there's almost always a story behind my owning them. Here's an anecdote about being wed to an investment's price and, sorry for being cute, paying a price for that emotion.

Some years back, I provided some advice and counsel to a friend and his leadership team. To be supportive, I purchased shares of the company at $10, and three years ago, its stock was doing fine and trading at about

$18 per share. As I concluded my work with them, I announced, partly in jest, that I wouldn't even consider donating the stock to charity until it hit $50 per share—a near tripling that would, I presumed, take years to attain. I was trying to be both supportive and motivational! Apparently, they had plenty of motivation. The company did really well and, by early 2020, the stock was selling for $49.80.

At that time, I was planning some charitable giving and thought the stock would make a good gift. I would avoid capital gains taxes by donating the shares to the charity, and if I wanted to continue owning the stock, I could always purchase shares on the open market. But, I said to myself, "I promised I wouldn't donate shares until they hit $50, so I'm going to be good to my word." And I did not donate the shares.

One month—one month!—later, the stock was selling for $19.50. Yes, less than half the price as I waited for it to increase $0.20 so I could reach my purely artificial target of $50. I fell prey to anchoring—one of the behavioral mistakes covered in Chapter 18. I anchored on a predetermined value and the opportunity cost for me was huge. The only redeeming part of this story is that I made my gift by other means and the company's stock has rebounded nicely, but as you may imagine as I write this, $50 is no longer a relevant target in my mind.

If you've read this book from front to back, you can easily identify my regrets in these two instances. Here are the lessons I overlooked:

- Just because something has a low price doesn't mean it's a good value.
- Never anchor to an artificial price or value of an investment. The market today—yes, today—tells you what it is worth and you can't wish it to be something else.

Investment mistakes can serve you well as long as you draw the right lessons from them. This concept may seem glaringly obvious, but believe it or not, many investors don't learn from their mistakes.

Ever since I was in high school, I have coached kids' sports as an avocation. One thing I've told the kids over and over through the years is: "That's why we practice." Somebody drops a pass—"That's why we practice." Somebody runs the wrong way on a play—"That's why we practice." Athletes practice to learn from their mistakes and to build a cumulative knowledge base. The hope is that they'll leave most of their mistakes on the practice field, reducing the errors that they make when it's time to keep score.

From an investment standpoint, mistakes and regrets serve the same purpose. You may find it hard to tune out that nagging little voice in the back of your head that calls you a fool for this investment decision or that one. In fact, there's little you can do about the mistakes from the past except take lessons from them. Learn to think of your investment mistakes as *sunk costs*—losses that cannot be altered by current or future actions. You can't change history.

Here's an example. When a security that you bought for $20 a share is selling for $10, the market is telling you that, as of today, the market's best assessment of the value of that asset is $10 a share. The fact that the price used to be $20 is irrelevant. There may be tax benefits in selling the stock and realizing a loss, but from an investment standpoint the $10 decline is a sunk cost. Your challenge is to decide whether you want to continue to own that asset at the new price of $10 a share. The answer may very well be yes if you believe that, relative to other opportunities, the stock is still a good investment. But don't hang onto it simply to "get back to even." And don't pick on yourself about it—call it "practice" and look to the future.

Always remember, too, that short-term losses—or gains, for that matter—are irrelevant if you are investing for the long term. Interim changes in your portfolio aren't real—they exist only on paper until you sell out. If you're not planning to tap into those assets soon, a decline isn't a loss. Neither is a gain on paper an actual gain.

Over the years, particularly during very difficult times in the stock market, I've talked with many, many investors about lessons they learned from the bear markets. Interestingly, investors in very similar circumstances sometimes have entirely different reactions.

In some instances, a few folks who were heavily invested in stocks say they've learned they couldn't tolerate downturns as well as they'd thought. I'd say that is a valuable lesson, which ought to serve them well during their investment journey. But others in the same situation say that their painful losses have taught them not to own stocks at all—that stocks are just too risky. In my opinion, these investors are likely to have a new set of regrets down the road in a few years.

Others who are ruing the damage to their account balances say they've learned to monitor the news so that "next time, I'll get out of stocks when the market starts to drop." I wish that they were right about market timing, and that it were possible to know when to get out of the markets and, subsequently, get back in again. But I'm afraid the markets are just not that easy to figure out.

Still other people say they've learned, or relearned, the value of balance and diversification—how these simple strategies make it easier to endure the tough times. That lesson is a "keeper," a lesson to hold on to for life.

My own belief is that you should accept your mistakes and learn from them, and then get over them. Move on with a sense of optimism and confidence. That's a habit that the best of professional investors learn early on and keep front and center for their whole career.

23

Getting to Boca

Y our exchange-traded fund returned 7% last year. Are you pleased or displeased?

It depends, doesn't it? It depends on the type of fund you own and how it performed compared with the markets. Without a comparative dimension, absolute performance tells you only part of the story. Given that we're always comparing performance in other aspects of life—the gas mileage of our cars, the likes on social media posts, the batting averages of baseball players, the developmental milestones of our offspring, and so on—it should come as no surprise that there is a measure in investing called *relative fund performance*. Relative performance tells you how a fund stacks up against similar funds or a relevant market benchmark.

Absolute performance and relative performance are the focus of this final chapter because they're at the heart of the question on every investor's mind: "How am I doing?" You'll want to use both of those measures to assess your interim progress toward your goals and determine whether you need to make any course corrections along the way.

However, paying too much attention to relative performance can actually hamper you in your investment program. So, let's frame the discussion by getting one thing straight up front: Despite all the news you hear about performance ratings and rankings, making money is ultimately what counts—not how you did last year relative to the Dow Jones Industrial Average or your brother-in-law, Glenn.

Destination Boca

Some investors become so obsessed about beating the market (or other investors) that they lose sight of the reason they're investing at all. They measure their funds against the S&P 500 Index or the Nasdaq Composite or the Dow from quarter to quarter as if everything depended on staying ahead of these market barometers all the time. But it's misleading to obsess over whether your fund is two-tenths of a point ahead of this index or half a point behind that one. **In fact, the only meaningful measure of your success is whether you eventually reach your investment objectives.**

One of my all-time favorite commentaries on the beat-the-market obsession was a column written some years ago by Jason Zweig, then a senior writer with *Money* magazine and now with *The Wall Street Journal*. In the column, he pointed out, among other things, that it's hard to beat indexes because they don't have any expenses, and that many investors who think they are ahead of the markets really aren't. Zweig ended the column with a great anecdote:

> I once interviewed dozens of residents in Boca Raton, one of Florida's richest retirement communities. Amid the elegant stucco homes, the manicured lawns, the swaying palm trees, the sun and the sea breezes, I asked these folks—mostly in their seventies—if they'd beaten the market over the course of their investing lifetimes. Some said yes, some said no. Then one man said, "Who cares? All I know is my investments earned enough for me to end up in Boca."

We all would do well to think like that investor. Whether your "Boca" is a comfortable retirement, or a college education for your kids, or an estate to bequeath to your heirs or to charity, the idea is to focus on getting there and worry as little as possible about how your portfolio is performing relative to something else.

You Can't Eat Relative Performance

I'll admit to feeling a little conflicted on the subject of relative performance. When I was the head of Vanguard, I was very interested in how our funds performed against the competition and the indexes. Those results were critical to the success of our business, that is, generating wealth for our clients. I was also chairman of Vanguard's board of directors, and as such, had a fiduciary obligation to our shareholders to see that our investment products served them well. Simply put, shareholders are not well served by funds that do not provide good long-term performance relative to their peers and to their benchmarks.

But as a personal investor, I take a different point of view because, like any other investor, I like to make money. If I invest in a fund and it performs well, I tend to feel good about the gain and not to care much if the fund lagged its benchmark by, say, two percentage points over a 12-month period. By the same token, I can be disappointed about a fund that beats its peers but still loses money. Though the professional investor in me may see things differently, it's small consolation to me as an individual that I would have lost even more if I had invested my money elsewhere.

I was always gratified when I received letters from investors who seemed to understand that making money is what counts. Actually, though, most people tend to reveal this knowledge indirectly. For example, I rarely received letters of complaint from Vanguard clients when one of our funds gained 24% during a year in which its benchmark gained 27%. However, I did receive letters and emails if a fund posted a loss, even if the benchmark had a worse one. Sensible investors don't put too much stock in a fund's relative performance. As the old investment saying goes, "You can't eat relative performance." It means that you should care about the absolute growth of your money over the long term—the money that puts food on the table and feeds your family.

How to Make Sense of Relative Performance Information

Of course, comparisons can be useful, as long as you employ the information judiciously and appropriately. You'll find relative performance data on your fund sponsor's app or website, as well as in a fund's prospectus and shareholder reports. As noted previously, the Securities & Exchange Commission requires that all fund materials that discuss performance report one-, five-, and ten-year total returns—both on a pre-tax and post-tax basis.

When presenting performance in shareholder reports, funds are encouraged to provide at least two comparative measures. One is a broad market index and the other is the average return of a more narrowly based index that reflects the market sectors in which the fund invests. For a large-cap value fund, for example, you might find it compared to the S&P 500 Index (the broad stock market) and the S&P Value Index (a discrete market segment). You can use these measures to obtain a little perspective on your fund's performance. If the fund is way ahead of the broad index, ask yourself if that is because the portfolio manager is brilliant or is the peer group also ahead? If similar funds are having a great year as well, that's a clue that the fund's strategy is in favor (e.g., it's a "value" market) and not attributable to the manager's brilliance and individual stock selection,

Pay attention to which indexes are being cited. Some of the most widely known benchmarks may have very little relevance to your own fund. For example, the Dow Jones Industrial Average is probably the most-often-quoted benchmark for the stock market, but it is rarely (if ever) a meaningful benchmark for a stock fund. The Dow consists of only 30 large U.S. companies. Much better broad market barometers are the S&P 500 Index, which tracks 500 large U.S. companies, and the Wilshire 5000 Total Market Index, which is based on more than 3,400 stocks and is representative of the entire U.S. stock market. (I provide a list of market benchmarks in Chapter 9.)

Here are a few other words of wisdom to heed when assessing fund performance:

- **Look at short-term and long-term performance.** Extended performance is always more meaningful than quarterly or even annual performance. A fund that trounces its peers or the index during a short period may simply have been lucky enough to benefit from a surge in several stocks or one sector. It's the 5-year and 10-year numbers that will tell you the trend. Don't be tempted to shift money around because of a single year's results—or, worse yet, a single quarter's results. One of my favorite conversations with a new Vanguard portfolio manager ended this way as I left his office after telling him of his new assignment. "See you in three years." He seemed quite flustered by that send-off, but I explained, "I don't believe we'll have any sense of how you're really doing until at least that point. So, please, keep your eyes on the long term." (He is still at the fund's helm and doing a great job 14 years later.)

- **Don't count on a hot track record continuing.** There is an overwhelming tendency for the performance of funds to *regress to the mean*, which means that they tend to move closer to the average with time. The farther a fund diverges from the performance of similar funds in a given period, the more likely it is to fall back toward the average, which means that a turbocharged fund is particularly likely to hit a rough patch at some point. I'm always amused when I see fund managers lionized (or vilified) in the press for a year's performance. One of our fund managers was philosophical when he went from hero to zero and back again to hero over the course of a few bumpy years in the stock market. Looking back on a year when he was most out of favor in the eyes of the media, he mused: "I didn't get dumber last year than I was the year before, and I didn't get smarter this year than I was last year."

- **Always compare apples-to-apples.** Fund companies are prohibited from comparing a fund's performance with results from a dissimilar peer group or a dissimilar index. But sometimes investors make that error. A comparison is not fair unless the risk and return characteristics of the underlying investments are alike. Keep this issue in mind when you make performance comparisons. Suppose you're investing in a bond fund to reduce the risk in your portfolio. It would be silly to compare that fund's performance with results of a stock bogey like the S&P 500 Index. On the other hand, if your fund is a large-cap blend stock fund, it would make perfect sense to measure its performance against the S&P 500 Index.

- **Remember that indexes start with an advantage.** When you compare your fund's performance to the returns of an index, keep in mind that the index has no expenses to pay; it exists only on paper, so to speak. Funds do have operating expenses, plus the costs of buying and selling securities, and that money has to come out of their returns. So, your fund would actually have to perform better than the index in order to come out even with it after costs. (This is why even index funds typically trail their benchmarks by a small margin.)

Your Fund's Performance Isn't the Same as Your Investment Performance

In discussing performance comparisons, I've left the most important caveat for last: the uniqueness of your investment program. What's a benchmark for your fund is not a benchmark for you.

Obviously, if you own several funds, your overall investment performance is based on a combination of the behavior of each holding and its weighting within your portfolio. If you have a balanced investment plan, as I have so heartily recommended, then you'll expect to see some of your holdings doing better than others.

In addition, your buying and selling activity will make a difference in your actual performance. For example, if you are employing a dollar-cost averaging strategy and contributing to a fund gradually over the course of a year, you won't receive the reported 12-month return on every dollar of your investment. The same will be true if you sell some shares during the year. A number of fund companies and financial advisors provide personal performance information (called *dollar-weighted performance*) based on your actual transaction activity and performance of your holdings. That's a great way to answer the question, "How am I doing?"

My Dad's in Boca

I often think of my father as the consummate Boca resident (although he wouldn't leave his home in Boston to even visit a retirement community in Florida). He needed some investment advice when he retired in the early 1990s upon receiving pension assets in a lump sum. I set him up with a balanced, well-diversified portfolio based on an appropriate asset mix for his situation, and from that day forward he got on with his life and paid very little attention to investment performance. In fact, I can only remember him opening his statements a few times in the 20 years after we set his investment strategy. While my father has since passed away, his investment program succeeded wonderfully. He was able to live in the manner in which he wanted and was also able to gift generously to family members and support many charities, without spending much time or energy on monitoring his portfolio. In fact, I can assure you that this very satisfied, balanced, and diversified investor—who during his retirement experienced both a long bull market and some dramatic bear incursions—wouldn't have been able to tell you how he'd done compared with the Dow or the S&P 500. He really didn't care. Figuratively speaking, he got to Boca.

I hope that this book has helped you to build a sense of trust in your ability to invest wisely and fruitfully. I wish you the very best success with your investment program, and I hope you, too, get to your own Boca.

In a Nutshell

Your best measure of success as an investor is whether you reach *your* eventual financial goals, not whether your portfolio beat the Dow or the S&P 500 in any given year. To stay focused, remember these things about investment performance data:

- **Short-term performance doesn't matter.** Quarterly (and even annual!) returns are largely meaningless if you are a long-term investor. Look at average annual figures, not cumulative.
- **A fund's reported return is not necessarily what you earned.** The return you earn on an investment will be affected by your buying and selling patterns, so it probably will be something different than the fund's reported return for a given period.
- **Be careful about the comparisons you draw.** Make sure you're comparing like to like when you look at performance data on prospective investments.

Afterword

I covered a substantial amount of ground in this book about saving, investments, and developing a portfolio to meet your needs. Hopefully, it has helped build your knowledge base and your confidence to invest successfully. You'll need to supply the discipline necessary to ensure ultimate success. To help keep you on track, I've boiled down the book's most important principles into this 12-point list.

1. **Develop a financial game plan.** Identify your financial objectives and design an investment program that will enable you to reach those objectives. Be conservative in your projections about how fast your money will grow.
2. **Become a disciplined saver.** The four most important words for building a secure financial future are "live below your means." Make a habit of putting money away. If you aren't naturally disposed toward saving money, find ways to trick yourself into doing it.
3. **Start investing early and keep it up.** Make time your ally, and start setting aside money for your goals as soon as possible. Keep plugging away toward your objectives, contributing fixed amounts on a regular schedule in good markets and in bad.
4. **Invest with balance and diversification.** For balance, invest across at least two of the three major asset classes: stocks, bonds, and cash investments. For diversification, make sure you are not overly concentrated in any single company, industry, or category of issuer. For an individual, mutual funds and exchange-traded funds are the simplest, most effective vehicles for accomplishing both of these strategies.
5. **Control your costs.** Avoid funds with high expense ratios. The average mutual fund expense ratio was 0.63% in 2019, but there are funds that charge much, much less. While you watch your costs, don't forget to minimize the tax bite.

6. **Manage risk prudently.** Create a portfolio that will enable you to sleep at night. If you design it to suit your objectives, time horizon, risk tolerance, and financial situation, you should be able to endure volatile times in the markets without feeling that you have to make drastic changes in your investments.

7. **Be a buy-and-hold investor.** Investors who frequently buy and sell securities or funds rarely succeed over the long term. A surer path to long-term success is to find a trusted partner, set up a sensible portfolio, and stick to it.

8. **Avoid fads and "can't-miss" opportunities.** You're sure to encounter people promoting alluring new investment opportunities in individual securities or narrow market sectors. Don't be tempted to abandon your diversified strategy—you can undo all the good things you've accomplished by making these mistakes.

9. **Tune out distractions.** Resist the barrage of news and information about the daily movements of the markets. Much of this information is irrelevant to your investment objectives as a long-term, buy-and-hold investor. The danger is that it can tempt you to make investment moves that aren't in your best long-term interests.

10. **Maintain a long-term perspective.** There will be good times and challenging times during your investing career. When times are good, be grateful, not greedy. When times are bad, be patient. Remaining focused on your long-term objectives is a winning strategy for all seasons.

11. **Give your portfolio an occasional tune-up.** No investor should put his or her portfolio on autopilot. Life changes may necessitate tweaking your portfolio and periodic rebalancing to keep your portfolio aligned with its targeted asset allocation.

12. **Define "enough."** Know when you have enough money to meet all of your goals. You'll be content and, importantly, far less likely to reach for more and take on greater risk.

These principles will serve you well as a DIY investor. Should you need additional guidance, there are resources and professionals readily available. Indeed, one of the wonderful developments for investors in the twenty-first century has been the expansion of accessible and attractively priced options to help you attain your goals—whether it's a bit of free advice from a reputable website or a relationship with a qualified financial advisor.

Postscript

Where Did My Income Go?

Throughout this book, I've sought to focus on long-term, enduring principles, backed by anecdotes of actual investor experience and meaningful data. For instance, in Chapter 5, we tell the anecdote of changing our definition of long term from 10 years to 15 years, leading investors to think that we were figuratively moving the goal posts on them. My point then, as it is now, was to encourage investors to ignore short-term events and think, frankly, in terms of decades. So, in a very real sense, this short postscript about what could be seen as merely a "current topic" feels a bit odd, but it is extremely important nonetheless.

What do I mean by *current topic*? If we look at the role of fixed income and money market investments in a portfolio, we see how important they have been to investors for many reasons. The first important reason is the role as diversifiers, helping to reduce the volatility of investors' portfolios. The second important reason is current income, providing regular payments to their owners. In my view, the first purpose remains firmly in place in this third decade of the twenty-first century. But, frankly, the second traditional role is challenged, at best. And, it looks as though that situation will remain for the foreseeable future, given the state of the economy and current interest rate policies. As a result, I feel compelled to address it, with the hope that it's a cyclical, not secular, phenomenon. I'll provide a bit of perspective for you on this critical topic and conclude with a list of "dos and don'ts" as you think about your own strategy and actions with respect to investment income.

For over a decade now, as I have participated in investment meetings in a variety of places, one of the phrases that I hear oft repeated: "Interest rates will eventually rise again." Frankly, it is a statement that has seemed to many, many investors as unchallengeable. It's a topic that is raised if an investor fears losing money in fixed income securities because values decline when interest rates rise. It's raised if someone is optimistic that their cash investments will again be a productive source of current income. It's brought up for innumerable other reasons. But the reality is that as I write this chapter in the late fourth quarter of 2020, rates have not risen, and have actually fallen, since the Global Financial Crisis (GFC) of 2008–2009. In fact, interest rates on short-, intermediate-, and long-term fixed income instruments—and, thus, the income produced by these assets—have fallen continuously for nearly four decades, with just a few interim periods of meaningful rate increases. On one hand, such a systematic decline in rates has produced strong total return performance. On the other hand, it has devastated the income that investors received.

A few charts tell the story better than I can. In Figure 1, you see the interest rate available on what is arguably the safest investment in the world—the 90-day U.S. Treasury bill. Let me make a few observations:

- Short-term interest rates at the end of 2020 are almost precisely where they were during the Great Depression in the 1930s—very close to 0%. None of us would have expected that to be the case if, at that

Figure 1 U.S. Treasury Bill Yields (1930–2020)

Source: Federal Reserve Bank of St. Louis. Data through June 30, 2020.

time, we forecasted the future for 90 years hence. But that's where we sit today.

- From when I began my career in the financial business in the mid-1970s until T-bill rates peaked in 1981, the rates investors earned on these investments nearly tripled from 5.5% to more than 16%. While this certainly pleased buyers of these instruments as they saw their short-term income rise, those rates were indicative of the severe economic challenges facing the United States and, a very key point, inflation rates that were raging in this country.
- For the next nearly 30 years, rates moved up and down in an inverse relationship to the strength of the economy, but over that period, the trend was consistently down. While the nominal earnings an investor received on T-bills declined, since inflation was consistently under control, the real return didn't change all that much.
- The final point relates to the latest peak in rates, which was right around 5% in late 2006, during a period of great economic strength in the U.S. economy and two years before the GFC. What followed, of course, is the dramatic decline in rates to near-zero levels today.

Let's put this in dollar terms. If you invested $100,000 in 90-day T-bills in November 2006, you would have earned interest of $1,250 during the 3-month life of that investment. If you make the same investment today—and for most of the past 10 years—your income is not $1,250, it is closer to $25. Yes, that's right, $25! That's a 98% decline in the productivity from an investment in the safest instruments in the world. The implications for average investors and, especially people living off the income generated by their investment portfolio, are incredible.

We'll discuss the ramifications later, but I want to extend this discussion to longer-term investments first.

The second chart (Figure 2) is similar to the first, except it focuses on the yield, and thus income, available on 10-year U.S. Treasury bonds—again, among the most creditworthy instruments available. I need to note, though, that since these bonds have a maturity of 10 years, they are subject to interest rate risk since they will decline in value when interest rates rise. (That sentence came straight from the Department of Redundancy Department.) The picture is largely the same as we saw for short-term interest rates and the income available to investors. Over the past 12 years, the income generated from these 10-year maturity investments has fallen by nearly 80%, from just over $5,000 a year on

Figure 2 10-Year U.S. Treasury Bond Yields (1960–2020)

Source: Federal Reserve Bank of St. Louis. Data through June 30, 2020.

Figure 3 S&P 500 Yields (1960–2020)

Source: Standard & Poor's. Data through June 30, 2020.

a $100,000 investment to less than $1,000. Again, a staggering loss of income return for investing in safe, intermediate-term assets.

Let's turn now to stocks. Figure 3 shows the income yield from a diversified portfolio of stocks, in this case, the S&P 500 Index. The "big picture" is the same—declining yields for a considerable portion of the last four decades. In fact, when I began my career at Vanguard in 1982, the yield on this stock index was nearly 6%. Today, it is slightly less than 2%. There are a couple of messages here:

- You will see a sharp rise in 2008–2009; that's the result of the dramatic decline in the value of the stock market during that period. Income from stocks declined only about 23% in 2008–2009, while stock prices fell by 50%. Thus, you see a sharp rise in yield (dividends), although there was a slight decline in income.
- The last 12 years since the GFC are illuminating. While the yield on this basket of stocks has declined, that's mostly because the value of the index has increased by more than three times in this decade, while the income that investors received "merely" doubled. Yes, doubled, because the dividend available on a stock or a basket of stocks is tied to the underlying profitability of the company or the constituent companies in the benchmark.

As you'll see in Figure 4, we're now in an unusual period of time where the yield on the S&P 500 Index is now roughly equal to the yield on the 10-year Treasury bond. There are many explanations for that relationship, but it does raise the question on the role of stocks in generating current income in one's portfolio.

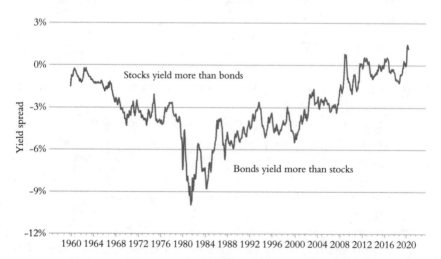

Figure 4 Stock and Bond Yield Spreads (1960–2020)

Source: Standard & Poor's and the Federal Reserve Bank of St. Louis. Data through June 30, 2020.

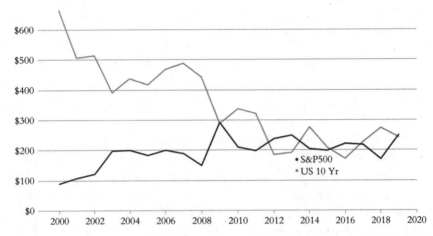

Figure 5 Annual Income Produced by a $10,000 Investment (2000–2019)

Source: Vanguard, based on Vanguard 500 Index Fund and Vanguard Intermediate-Term U.S. Treasury Bond Fund yields at the beginning of each year.

What's the message in these charts and my comments? Simply put, the environment described above is, and will likely remain, challenging for investors, and especially investors who depend on the income from their investment portfolios for living expenses. And, as with so much else we discuss in this book, this issue is another classic risk/reward trade-off. In some ways, it's even more apparent than in other parts of investing. Here are three trade-offs to consider:

- You can generate more income if you are willing to take more interest rate risk by investing in longer duration assets.
- You can generate more income if you are willing to invest in lower-quality investments.
- You can likely generate a growing stream of income if you are willing to take on the risks associated with owning more stocks than you might otherwise have planned. In Figure 5, the annual income produced by a discrete $10,000 investment in the S&P 500 index fund and an intermediate-term U.S. Treasury bond fund from 2000 to 2019 is shown. As you can see, the income generated by stocks has been generally reasonably steady (with occasional sharp movements driven by equally sharp movements in the stock market) over the two-decade period. The income produced by the bond fund has dwindled substantially.

The list of trade-offs could go on and on, but you get the gist. The most important point is to understand the risks you take in order to be rewarded with more investment income in this challenging environment. So, here's a short list of dos and don'ts as you confront this issue today.

- Do be thoughtful in assessing the how and how much of generating income you need from your investment portfolio for whatever purpose you identify. But, don't ever merely seek a higher yield or more income and select the investments that will get you that amount of income. You will inevitably take on far more risk than you are comfortable with and, at some point, regret that decision.

  One simple example of reaching for income from identical quality assets makes this point clearly. If interest rates increase by 1 percentage point, the price of 10-year Treasury bonds will fall roughly 9.5% in value—essentially wiping out the equivalent to 10 years of income advantage they hold over T-bills. This is why low real rates make the higher income available from long-term bonds more risky than historically has been the case.

- Do consider how much cash you need to sleep well at night and to meet near-term spending requirements. But, don't hold onto more cash than you need. Put your money to work. As we've discussed earlier, the productivity of cash has dropped to nearly nothing, so the penalty for maintaining excess cash has risen commensurately.

- Do consider all the options you have for the short-term portion of your portfolio. There are lots of great options from the T-bills to money market mutual funds. And don't dismiss the idea of certificates of deposit (CD) as attractive, "sleep at night" investments. I frequently hear from investors who somehow think a CD is old-fashioned. They are not.

- Do consider non-traditional ways of generating current income, and income that will grow to help you offset the effects of inflation. What I really mean is consider how, in the strategic asset allocation portion of your investment policy statement (see Chapter 7), stocks can be used as an important substitute for fixed income assets, which previously served as the prime engine of income generation but, for now at least, have lost much of their appeal. Don't immediately dismiss this idea as too risky for you. It may or may not be too risky for you, but it's worth a thorough analysis of whether stocks can serve an income purpose and not, importantly, result in disrupting your sleep habits!

- Do be leery of too-good-to-be-true investments that offer income returns that don't seem grounded in reality. Thus, don't fall for sales pitches for products that provide income that is far higher than you can get in liquid, regulated investments. There is no "free lunch," and these products, even if legal, are usually structured for the seller's, not the owner's, benefit.

There's a wonderful African proverb that says "Smooth seas do not make skillful sailors." There's much truth in that with respect to investing generally and this topic, in particular. Interest rates, and thus income available from fixed income assets, will rise again; we just don't know when. But, my hope is that we will all be more "skillful sailors" for having had to navigate this highly unusual and far longer than anticipated period of low interest rates. Challenging our preconceived ideas about the role of fixed income and equity assets, and being strategic about the risk/reward trade-offs in the search for investment income, will make us more successful investors in the long term, whatever the investment environment brings our way.

Appendix
Investment Terms

The financial markets and asset management industry, like baseball, have a language all of its own. In the following section, I'll define some "inside baseball" terms that will help you become better acquainted with the lingo and expand your knowledge about investing.

Active Management

An investment strategy that seeks to outperform the returns of a financial market. Active managers rely on research and analysis; market forecasts and trends; and their own judgment and experience to make decisions about what stocks to buy and sell, sectors to underweight or overweight, and how much cash to hold. You may choose to invest in an actively managed fund in the hopes of outpacing the market, but it's important to know that the odds are stacked against you.

After-tax Returns

Funds are required to report total returns on both a pre-tax and after-tax basis for various time periods. After-tax returns are disclosed in two ways. *Return After Taxes on Distributions* reflects payment of federal income taxes on the fund's dividend and capital gains distributions, assuming you continue to hold your shares and pay taxes. *Return After Taxes on Distributions and Sales of Shares* reflects the payment of federal income taxes on dividends and capital gains distributions, as well as on gains (or losses) realized on the sale of shares at the end of the stated period.

Aggressive Growth Fund

A fund that seeks to provide maximum long-term capital growth by investing primarily in the stocks of smaller companies or narrow market segments. Dividend income is incidental. In investing, "aggressive" is a code word for *risky*.

Asset Allocation

The process of deciding how your investment dollars will be split among various classes of financial assets—stocks, bonds, and cash investments. Spend a considerable amount of time on this decision as it's likely the most important one you will make.

Asset Classes

The major categories of financial assets or securities. The three primary classes are stocks, bonds, and cash investments. There are other, more exotic asset classes, but most investors can assemble a sound portfolio with a mix of these three.

Back-end Load

A sales commission paid when the investor sells mutual fund shares. This charge may also be called a redemption fee or a contingent deferred sales charge. Some funds gradually phase out back-end loads for investors who stay in a fund for several years. While less common today, avoid back-end loads when possible.

Balanced Fund

A mutual fund that invests in more than one type of financial asset (stocks, bonds, and, in some cases, cash). These funds may not be sexy, but they have demonstrated their value over time.

Blend Fund

A type of stock fund that features both growth and value stocks. See *growth fund* and *value fund*.

Bonds

One of the three major asset classes. A bond is an IOU issued by corporations, governments, or government agencies. The issuer makes regular interest payments on the bond and promises to pay back your "loan" at a specified point in the future, called the maturity date. The regular interest payments from bonds make them a key part of retirees' portfolios and can be comforting to any investor when the stock market is in a slump.

Capital Gains Distribution

A fund's payment to fund shareholders of gains (or profits) realized on the sale of securities. Capital gains are typically distributed annually and on a net basis, after the fund subtracts any capital losses for the year. When gains exceed losses, you—the fund investor—owe taxes on your share of the gain, unless those shares are held in a tax-sheltered account, such as an IRA or 401(k) plan. A fund may distribute gains even if it posts a negative total return for the year.

Cash Investments

One of the three major asset classes, cash investments include interest-bearing bank deposits, money market instruments, and U.S. Treasury bills or notes. These are conservative, short-term investments, typically with maturities of 90 days or less. They are suitable for near-term needs and emergency savings but won't do much to advance you toward your long-term goals, such as retirement.

Compounding

The growth that you get if you reinvest your investment income and gains instead of taking them in cash. You earn money on your investment, then you earn money on your original investment plus the amount you've earned. It might be the most powerful force in investing. Take advantage of it.

Credit Risk

The chance that the issuer of a bond fails to pay interest or to repay the original principal on time—or at all. Every bond is subject to credit risk, but some issuers are extremely safe (U.S. Treasury and government agencies), some are safe (large, financially sound companies and government entities with good track records), and some can be downright dangerous (small, young companies with shaky finances). The greater the credit risk, the higher the interest rate, or yield, a bond should pay.

Diversification

Spreading your money among the securities of many issuers. Along with balance, it's an investor's best friend. Diversifying your investments helps to smooth out volatility in your portfolio and eliminate single-stock risk so you can sleep better.

Dividend

A fund's payment of income to fund shareholders from interest or dividends generated by the fund's investments. Also, cash payments to owners of common stock, paid out of a company's profits.

Dollar-cost Averaging

A strategy in which equal amounts of money are invested at regular intervals on an ongoing basis. This technique reduces risk of loss from a sudden market downturn and reduces the average cost of shares over time, since you acquire more shares when prices are lower and fewer shares when prices are higher. It also requires a strong stomach because for dollar-cost averaging to work, you must continue to invest money when the markets are in a slump. The reward for your diligence, though, can be significant.

Donor-advised Fund

A type of fund employed by investors to support charitable organizations. An individual may contribute cash, appreciated securities, or other assets to a donor-advised fund and receive an immediate tax deduction. These contributions grow on a tax-free basis and the donor can, at any time, recommend grants to an IRS-qualified public charity.

Duration

A way to gauge how much the price of a bond or bond fund will go up or down when interest rates fluctuate. A fund with an average duration of ten years will see its price drop about 10% with every 1 percentage point increase in market interest rates; the price would rise 10% if interest rates rose 1 percentage point. A bond fund with a duration of two years would see a share price rise or fall of about 2% in response to a 1 percentage point decrease or increase in interest rates. In short, the longer the duration, the bigger the price change for a bond fund or bond when interest rates rise or fall.

Education Savings Account (ESA)

A tax-advantaged investment vehicle for education costs. Contributions are taxed but earnings are not, as long as they're used for qualified education expenses. Annual contributions to an ESA are capped at a fairly low level—a maximum of $2,000—but these accounts can complement a child's education savings program.

Environmental, Social, and Governance (ESG) Fund

ESG investing is an investment-related activity that accounts for some type of environmental, social, or governance consideration. Other terms to describe this type of investing include socially responsible investing (SRI), values-based investing, sustainable investing, and impact investing. Some ESG index funds and exchange-traded funds seek to follow a benchmark that excludes specific stocks (or bonds), such as alcohol distillers, tobacco companies, gun manufacturers, and fossil fuel producers.

Some active funds seek to outperform the market by integrating ESG-related risks and opportunities of companies into their selection process.

Exchange-traded Fund (ETF)

ETFs are a type of mutual fund that can be purchased and sold throughout the day like a stock at the then-current price. The most popular ETFs follow an index strategy and, hence, are low cost and broadly diversified.

Expense Ratio

The percentage of a fund's average net assets used to pay annual fund operating expenses. The expense ratio takes into account costs such as management fees, legal and administrative outlays, and any marketing and distribution expenses (such as a 12b-1 fee). You should care about expenses because they directly reduce the return you receive.

Factor Fund

A type of actively managed fund that seeks to achieve specific risk and return objectives by concentrating its portfolio in stocks exhibiting certain characteristics. Factors include quality, momentum, liquidity, and value. There are also multi-factor funds.

Financial Advisor

A broad term to describe a professional who offers financial advice and money management services. Advisors can be affiliated with a brokerage firm, a bank, or a mutual fund provider, or an advisor can be independent, working as a sole proprietor or with a team of advisors and support staff.

Front-end Load

A sales commission, or load, that you pay when you buy shares of a mutual fund. For example, if you invest $5,000 in a fund with a front-end load of 5%, you'll start off with an account balance of $4,750. Think hard before you pay a load to buy a fund. There are plenty of no-load funds from which to choose.

Growth Fund

A fund that emphasizes stocks of companies that are believed to offer above-average prospects for appreciation due to their strong potential for growth in earnings and sales. Growth stocks tend to offer relatively low dividend yields because these companies prefer to reinvest earnings in research and development rather than paying them out to investors. Growth is one of the two primary investing styles. The other is value. A well-diversified investor has exposure to both styles.

High-yield Bond

A bond issued by a company or a government with a low credit rating. Also known as *junk bonds*. High-yield bonds exemplify a key trade-off in investing: Higher-risk investments offer the potential for greater reward. Companies with iffy prospects must pay higher rates of interest in order to entice investors to lend them money.

Income

Interest and dividends earned on securities held by a fund. These earnings are paid to fund shareholders in the form of income dividends. The fund shareholders then owe taxes on this income unless the fund is held in a tax-sheltered account, such as an IRA or 401(k) plan.

Income Risk

The possibility that the income stream you're receiving from a fund or other investment will decline. This risk is most acute with money market funds and other short-term investments, such as an ultra-short-term bond fund. Here's how it works: Interest rates fall, short-term investments quickly reflect the new rates, and the income you subsequently receive from your money market fund drops.

Index

A statistical benchmark that's used to measure the performance of the stock or bond markets, or particular segments of these markets. They are standards against which investors can measure the performance of their investment portfolios. (Be sure to compare your fund's performance with a relevant index.)

Index Fund

A mutual fund that seeks to track the performance of a market benchmark or index. An index fund holds all, or a representative sample, of the securities in the index. Indexing is a very cost effective investment strategy that tends to outperform actively managed peers over time, so index funds should have a place in your investment program.

Individual Retirement Account (IRA)

A tax-advantaged way to save for retirement. If you have earned income from a job, you can put money in these accounts for yourself and for your spouse, if the spouse does not work outside the home. Investment earnings within a traditional IRA are not taxed until withdrawn from the account, and the money you put into the account can be deducted from taxes, subject to income limits. With a Roth IRA, you don't get an upfront tax deduction, but the earnings on the account may be withdrawn tax-free (under certain conditions, of course). Withdrawals from an IRA made before age 59-1/2 may be subject to a 10% federal penalty tax.

Inflation

A general rise in the prices of goods and services. This is a big concern for long-term investors because the amount you're investing and earning will lose purchasing power as inflation rises. The higher the rate of inflation, the more you'll have to invest or earn to stay ahead. Over decades, inflation can end up confiscating a significant chunk of lifestyle if you don't invest, and earn, enough to offset it.

Interest Rate Risk

The risk that a bond or bond fund will decline in price because of a rise in market interest rates. Prices move in the opposite direction from interest rates. If you own a bond that pays 3% in annual interest and new bonds coming onto the market pay 4%, the market value of your bond would fall to reflect the fact that higher-yielding bonds are available.

Investment Horizon

The length of time you expect to keep a sum of money invested. Many of your financial decisions will hinge on the answer to the question: When will you need the money?

Investment Objective

A mutual fund's stated goal. Stock funds tend to pursue long-term capital appreciation, bond funds typically seek high current income or tax-exempt income, and money market funds aim to preserve your principal while earning you some money along the way. Make sure that you know the objective of each fund that you own and that you've thought about how it can help you reach your goal.

Load Fund

A mutual fund that charges a sales commission or load. These commissions can be as high as 8-1/2% of the amount you invest.

Management Fee

The fee paid by a mutual fund to its investment advisory firm, which could be the fund sponsor or an external sub-advisor. The fee is based on a percentage of assets and is part of a fund's expense ratio (i.e., the expenses deducted from your fund's earnings).

Market Capitalization

What a company is worth in the stock market. Market capitalization equals a stock's share price multiplied by the number of shares outstanding. For a stock fund, market capitalization is determined by the market caps of the securities it owns. It's important to know whether a fund focuses on large-, mid-, or small-caps, or on companies of all sizes, so that you can build a diversified portfolio. This knowledge will also help you when comparing your fund's performance against a relevant benchmark or competitive group.

Market Risk

The possibility that an investment will fall in value as a result of a general decline in financial markets. This is one risk you can't avoid, no matter how much you diversify. When the broad stock market slumps, so will a well-diversified stock portfolio.

Money Market Fund

A mutual fund that seeks to maintain a stable share price and earn current income by investing in interest-bearing instruments with short-term (usually 90 days or less) maturities. Money funds are not insured by the federal government, but if you put $1 into the fund, you can reasonably expect to get $1 out, plus interest. Money funds are boring, but they're ideal for short-term investment goals and for the conservative portion of a long-term investment program.

Municipal Bonds

See tax-exempt bonds.

Mutual Fund

An investment company that pools money from individuals and uses it to buy securities such as stocks, bonds, and money market instruments.

Net Asset Value (NAV)

The market value of a fund's total assets, less its liabilities, divided by the number of shares outstanding. It's commonly known as a fund's share price.

No-load Fund

A mutual fund that does not charge a commission on purchases or sales. Even a no-load fund has expenses, but it doesn't charge you to buy or sell your shares.

Portfolio

For you, it's all the investments you own; for a fund, it's all the securities it holds. So, a fund's portfolio may be part of your portfolio. (But not the other way around.)

Portfolio Manager

An individual who manages a mutual fund portfolio and makes day-to-day decisions regarding what securities to buy or sell.

Principal

The amount of money you put into an investment. This term also refers to the face value of a bond and the amount still owed on a loan, like your home mortgage loan.

Prospectus

A legal document that provides detailed information about a mutual fund, including discussions of the fund's investment objectives and policies, risks, costs, performance, and other useful information. See Chapter 9 for suggestions on what to look for in a prospectus. It's important to read the prospectus.

Redemption Fee

A fee that you may be charged for selling shares in certain funds. Some redemption fees are actually good for long-term investors—they're paid to the fund, not the management company, to compensate all fund shareholders for the costs of buying and selling securities and to discourage short-term traders. Don't confuse these with loads. (See load fund.)

Robo-advisor

An online platform that delivers financial advice services, including portfolio allocation guidance and fund recommendations, through a digital interface. Robo-advisors employ market forecasting models and algorithms to develop an appropriate portfolio, based on inputs from the investor, such as age, time horizon, goals, and risk tolerance.

Stocks

Securities that represent part ownership in a company. Each share of stock is a claim on a proportion of the corporation's assets and profits, some of which may be paid out as dividends.

Target-date Fund

A type of balanced fund that starts off with a large percentage in stocks and gradually decreases that amount in favor of a greater weighting in bonds as the stated target date approaches. This is known as a glide path—the predetermined rate at which a fund changes its asset allocation over time, becoming more conservative as the investors come closer to retirement. Target-date funds are frequently used as automatic default options in 401(k) plans.

Target-risk Funds

Sometimes called life-cycle funds, these funds typically invest in stocks and bonds by holding other mutual funds, but unlike target-date funds, the allocation among asset classes remains static. Funds can feature a range of allocations, from aggressive (80% stocks/20% bonds), to moderate (60% stocks/40% bonds), to conservative (20% stocks/80% bonds).

Tax-exempt Bonds

Also known as municipal bonds. Typically, you won't pay federal income tax on interest you receive from an investment in bonds issued by municipal, county, and state governments and agencies. If you buy bonds issued by municipalities in the state where you live, you're generally off the hook on state and local income taxes, too.

Total Return

The percentage change, over a given period, in the value of an investment, including any income paid on it. For funds, the total return consists of changes in the fund's net asset value, plus income dividends and capital gains distributions. Total returns reported for a fund take into account the effect of fund expenses and assume that income dividends or capital gains distributions are reinvested. This is the best measure of fund performance over time.

Treasury Inflation-protected Securities

A special type of bonds by the U.S. Treasury whose principal value changes to reflect changes in the level of consumer prices. These bonds are not as complex as they sound. The key thing to know is that the principal value of the bonds goes up with inflation, so they can be a good addition to your investment program.

Turnover Rate

A measure of a mutual fund's trading activity, the turnover rate can affect a fund's tax efficiency. A turnover rate of 50% means that, during a year, a fund has sold and replaced securities with a value equal to 50% of its average net assets. Generally, the higher the turnover the more likely it is that a fund will have capital gains to be paid out in distributions. And if you hold the fund in a regular, taxable account, you pay the tax bill on those profits. A fund's prospectus and its annual and semi-annual reports will tell you its turnover rate, and you often can find out from the fund company's website as well.

Uniform Gifts to Minors Act (UGMA)/Uniform Transfers to Minors Act (UTMA)

UGMA and UTMA accounts are custodial accounts for children established under the Uniform Gifts to Minors Act or Uniform Transfers to Minors Act. These accounts enable an adult custodian (usually a parent or relative) to open an investment account on behalf of a minor. As far as taxes, the first $1,050 of the minor's unearned income is tax-free and the next $1,050 is taxed at the minor's tax rate. Anything exceeding $2,100 is taxed at the parents' rate.

Value Fund

A mutual fund that emphasizes stocks of companies from which the market does not expect rapid growth in profits. Although value, like beauty, is in the eye of the beholder, value stocks typically have below-average prices when compared with such factors as earnings, book value, revenue, and dividends. Value is one of two main investing styles. The other is growth. A well-diversified investor has exposure to both.

Variable Annuity

A tax-advantaged investment that is much like a mutual fund, but with insurance protection. Investors in variable annuities typically are guaranteed that they'll receive at least the amount they invested, thanks to a contract that insures their initial investment. Money you make on variable annuities is not taxed until you take it out. However, because of the added cost of the insurance feature, and the taxation of withdrawals as regular income, variable annuities aren't for everyone.

Volatility

The fluctuations in market value or returns of a fund or other security. The greater a fund's volatility, the wider the spread between its high and low prices. As an investor, you'll face volatility in stocks and bonds. As you develop your investment plan, consider your ability to ride it out without overreacting. Balance and diversification can help to mitigate volatility.

Yield

The rate at which an investment earns income, expressed as a percentage of the investment's current price. Yield is what you get paid for owning a fixed income investment, such as a money market fund, a bond fund, or a bank certificate of deposit. Stocks that pay dividends to investors also have yields—the annual amount of the dividend, divided by the stock's price.

12b-1 Fee

An annual fee that some mutual funds charge you to pay for their marketing and distribution activities. In other words, the fund company takes money from you to attract other investors. This is good for you only if the fund company reduces its expenses as it attracts greater assets. Not all funds charge 12b-1 fees; those that do must disclose them in the prospectus as a component of its expense ratio.

529 College Savings Plan

A state-sponsored, tax-free way to save for a child's education. These plans, which are typically administered by investment firms, enable people to invest money that can later be taken out to pay for tuition and other education expenses. As long as the investor follows certain rules, investments in a 529 Plan are free of federal taxes both while they are growing and when the money is withdrawn. Contributions, however, are generally not tax-deductible.

Index